117 HOUSE DESIGNS
OF THE TWENTIES

GORDON-VAN TINE CO.

A Joint Publication of
THE ATHENAEUM OF PHILADELPHIA
and
DOVER PUBLICATIONS, INC., NEW YORK

Published in Canada by General Publishing Company, Ltd., 30 Lesmill Road, Don Mills, Toronto, Ontario.
Published in the United Kingdom by Constable and Company, Ltd., 3 The Lanchesters, 162–164 Fulham Palace Road, London W6 9ER.

This Athenaeum of Philadelphia/Dover edition, first published in 1992, is an unabridged republication of *Gordon-Van Tine Homes*, originally published by the Gordon-Van Tine Co., Davenport, Iowa, in 1923. The color plates have been reproduced in black and white. A preface and a publisher's note have been added.
We are grateful to Mary Herr of the Davenport Public Library for her kind assistance.

Manufactured in the United States of America
Dover Publications, Inc., 31 East 2nd Street, Mineola, N.Y. 11501

Library of Congress Cataloging-in-Publication Data

117 house designs of the twenties / Gordon-Van Tine Co.
    p.   cm.
  ISBN 0-486-26959-0 (pbk.)
  1. Prefabricated houses—United States—Designs and plans—Catalogs. 2. Architecture, Modern—20th century—United States. I. Gordon-Van Tine Co. II. Title: One hundred seventeen house designs of the twenties.
NA7208.A12 1992
728′.37′0222—dc20
                                        91-40731
                                         CIP

PREFACE TO THE ATHENAEUM/DOVER EDITION

THIS REPRINT EDITION of the Gordon-Van Tine Co.'s 1923 catalog is one in a series of reprints of books and trade catalogs published by special agreement between The Athenaeum of Philadelphia and Dover Publications, Inc. The objective of this series is to make available to the greatest possible audience rare and often fragile documents from the extensive collections of The Athenaeum in sturdy and inexpensive editions.

The Athenaeum of Philadelphia is an independent research library with museum collections founded in 1814 to collect materials "connected with the history and antiquities of America, and the useful arts, and generally to disseminate useful knowledge." It is housed in a handsomely restored National Historic Landmark building near Independence Hall in the heart of the historic area of Philadelphia.

As the collections expanded over the past 175 years, The Athenaeum refined its objectives. Today the library concentrates on nineteenth- and early twentieth-century social and cultural history, particularly architecture and interior design where the collections are nationally significant. The library is freely open to serious investigators, and it annually attracts thousands of readers: graduate students and senior scholars, architects, interior designers, museum curators and private owners of historic houses.

In addition to 130,000 architectural drawings, 25,000 historic photographs and several million manuscripts, The Athenaeum's library is particularly rich in original works on architecture, interior design and domestic technology. In the latter area the publications of manufacturers and dealers in architectural elements and interior embellishments have been found to be particularly useful to design professionals and historic house owners who are concerned with the restoration or the recreation of period interiors. Consequently, many of the reprints in this series are drawn from this collection. The Athenaeum's holdings are particularly strong in areas such as paint colors, lighting fixtures, wallpaper, heating and kitchen equipment, plumbing and household furniture.

The modern Athenaeum also sponsors a diverse program of lectures, chamber music concerts and exhibitions. It publishes books that reflect the institution's collecting interests, and it administers several trusts that provide awards and research grants to recognize literary achievement and to encourage outstanding scholarship in architectural history throughout the United States. For further information, write The Athenaeum of Philadelphia, East Washington Square, Philadelphia, PA 19106-3794.

ROGER W. MOSS
Executive Director

PUBLISHER'S NOTE

IN THIS CATALOGUE from its most prosperous decade, the Gordon-Van Tine Co., the original purveyors of the prefabricated house, offered the American consumer a phenomenal range of dwellings reflecting the architectural landscape of the era.

In the Mississippi River town of Davenport, Iowa, in 1865, Uriah N. Roberts started a wholesale building-materials company, using capital amounting to $673. The site was advantageous. Forests of white and yellow pine lay close by to the north; the river offered ready transportation by raft; and the first railroad bridge ever to span the Mississippi had been erected at Davenport in 1856.

The U. N. Roberts Co. thrived on its excellent service and reputation, and at Roberts' death in 1890 a substantial corporation passed into the hands of his sons Edward and Horace and the company's senior retainers. The firm's continuing success into the new century led its officers to the idea of augmenting sales by offering its construction materials directly to builders and consumers. In September 1906 the parallel company of Gordon-Van Tine was incorporated, with the same stockholders and officers, for the purpose of handling the retail business. The huge initial sum of $50,000 was allocated for advertising, the Chicago advertising firm of Lord & Thomas was retained and ads appeared in newspapers and magazines all across the country trumpeting the savings to be achieved by avoiding the markups of the retailing middleman. In eight months, according to the firm, its advertisements had reached 40,000,000 households (at a time when the U.S. population was only 85,000,000). The first retail catalogue contained some 7,500 articles. Within a year the company was declaring itself the largest specialized mail-order house in existence.

The company's expanding ambitions and the slow depletion of the northern forests led to the opening of a branch operation consisting of a lumberyard, mill and factory in St. Louis in 1908. In 1915, seeking to exploit the Douglas-fir forests of the northwest, the company would open another plant in Chehalis, Washington. Four years later it would gain access to the yellow-pine forests of the south by means of a new mill in Hattiesburg, Mississippi. With each new plant, the corporation was also extending and facilitating the effective geographical reach of its service.

In 1910 Gordon-Van Tine offered to the public its first prefabricated houses— apparently the first ever offered by a commercial firm. Can Gordon-Van Tine rightly claim to have invented the prefabricated house? It was perhaps an idea that imaginative minds had been idly conceiving for many years, but certainly a venture that only a major and comprehensive building-materials supplier could ever have undertaken. In America, the most aggressively expanding industrial power, such ideas were stirring. Concrete room modules had recently been produced for industrial use. Henry Ford's assembly lines would be churning out complete "prefabricated" automobiles within three years. (The term itself, incidentally, would not be coined for another twenty years.) Most significantly, in 1909 Sears, Roebuck had begun to offer plans and complete materials for a selection of house designs, though not until 1916 would Sears actually provide precut lumber.

An impressive number of designs was soon available from Gordon-Van Tine. The present catalogue—no larger than several earlier ones—offers over 100 "homes," 6 "cottages," 9 "summer cottages" and 10 garages, as listed on the first page following page 132. (On the pages showing the houses throughout, this is referred to as the "first page.") At the bottom of the same page, the customer is invited to send for a separate circular of two-family homes. Thus, perhaps 150 houses were being offered in 1923. In addition, all the houses were available in reversed orientation, and with a choice of stucco or wood siding.

By 1914 the company had taken a final step and, working with local contractors, was starting to offer fully constructed houses for its customers within the tri-city area (including the Illinois cities of Moline and Rock Island). The construction option continued to be offered for the rest of the firm's existence, but apparently never beyond a narrow geographical radius. (Its rival Sears, Roebuck did not offer actual construction until 1929, the very eve of the stock-market crash, and the ill-timed nationwide experiment lasted only four years.)

The Gordon-Van Tine Co. weathered the Depression, though undoubtedly at considerable cost. When it celebrated its 75th anniversary in 1940 (really the anniversary of the U. N. Roberts Co.), still led by Horace G. Roberts, it sounded bullish, and all its plants and numerous branch offices were still in operation. But it dropped from the rolls of the Davenport Chamber of Commerce in 1945, right at the beginning of a postwar construction boom that would rival or surpass that of the 1920s.

Significant as the company itself was, it is the designs that will primarily interest most readers. Like almost all the goods offered by the great mail-order houses, these were intended to appeal to the broad middle class of the American population. Several are genuinely handsome and imposing, several are tiny and stripped-down, but the majority are modest, practical and quite attractive. Many are Colonial in style, some are of an unassuming boxy type, a very few are slightly exotic. Large farmhouses are numerous, perhaps because of Davenport's location. The standard is perhaps the "bungalow," though the basic features of the type—properly a simple rectangular one-story dwelling with broad eaves, a large and shaded veranda or porch and an interior designed for maximum ventilation—are often missing. (Curious readers should compare the similar line of houses in the Dover reprint of Sears, Roebuck's 1926 catalogue of houses.)

The prefabricated house has had an uneven history in the years since Gordon-Van Tine embarked on its grand venture. The Sears, Roebuck and Montgomery Ward lines enjoyed flush years in the teens and twenties, but both companies jettisoned their operations in hard times. Despite considerable enthusiasm for prefabrication in the 1950s, today the commercial market has all but vanished. This in no way reflects on the quality of the pioneer product. Present-day owners profess satisfaction with their Gordon-Van Tine houses, which do not betray their origins easily. Quintessentially American in its conception and ambition, the Gordon-Van Tine undertaking deserves to regain its proper place in the history of architecture.

117 HOUSE DESIGNS OF THE TWENTIES

THESE STRONG BANKS
Combined Assets $3,000,000.00
Vouch for Us!

American Commercial and Savings Bank

Capital $700,000
Surplus and Undivided Profits
$1,100,000

Davenport, Iowa

November 17th, 1922.

To Whom It May Concern:

It gives us pleasure to testify to the square methods and honesty of GORDON-VAN TINE COMPANY. Their financial responsibility is well over nine hundred thousand dollars ($900,000) and they enjoy the highest credit with Western Financial Institutions.

To prospective customers we can say that you are perfectly safe in sending money with your orders, for if the goods are not entirely satisfactory, they may be returned at the Company's expense and your money will be promptly refunded.

The officers of this Company are well and favorably known to us and may be relied upon to do exactly as they agree.

Very truly yours,
Ed. Kaufmann
President.

WE GUARANTEE
SATISFACTION or MONEY BACK

IF you are not perfectly satisfied with any article you buy of us—send it back and we will return your money, including all transportation charges.

UNION SAVINGS BANK
A STRONG BANK

CAPITAL
$400,000.00
SURPLUS & PROFITS
$500,000.00

WILLIAM HEUER PRESIDENT
H. O. WEIR VICE PRESIDENT
JOS. J. BRUS VICE PRESIDENT
ALBERT JANSEN ASST. VICE PRESIDENT
F. W. ZABEL CASHIER
C. W. SCHAEFER ASST. CASHIER

Davenport, Iowa.

November 17th, 1922.

To Whom it may concern:

We take pleasure in testifying to the honesty, reliability, and high business standing of the GORDON-VAN TINE COMPANY. We have known the officers of the company for many years, and they enjoy a reputation in this community as men of upright business methods. They can be depended upon to treat all persons with fairness, and no one need hesitate to send money with orders for goods, as the same will be perfectly safe, and will be returned in case the goods are not entirely satisfactory.

The officers of the GORDON-VAN TINE COMPANY have a well deserved reputation for fair dealing and conservatism, and from our acquaintance with them, we believe that absolute reliance may be placed in their statements.

Yours very truly
Wm. Heuer
President.

THE IOWA NATIONAL BANK

CAPITAL AND SURPLUS $300,000.00

CHAS. SHULER PRESIDENT
FRANK B. YETTER VICE PRES.   LOUIS G. BEIN CASHIER
FRED GETTMANN VICE PRES.   HERMAN STARR ASST. CASHIER

DAVENPORT IOWA

November 17th, 1922.

To whom it may concern:

We hold in very high esteem the men composing the management of the GORDON-VAN TINE COMPANY, and consider them among the best and strongest business men of this City. With the absolute reliability, honesty and integrity of these men, and the strong financial condition of their company, we do not hesitate to recommend them to the Public, and consider them entitled to every confidence.

To their patrons are pleased to say that you are perfectly safe in sending money with your orders, as the Company rightfully enjoys a reputation of reliability, and will return your money if its goods are not entirely satisfactory to you.

Yours truly
Chas. Shuler
President.

COME AND SEE US

WE realize that seeing is believing and we therefore would like you to come and see us, look things over and check up our statements so that you will realize that what we have said is the truth. So we want to make you this offer: Come to see us, investigate in any way you desire and if you find that we have misrepresented in any way the quality of our goods or the scope of our service, we will allow your railroad fare both ways.

We make this offer sincerely and hope that you can avail yourself of it. *But, remember, whether you can come or not the goods and the service are here for you.* The fact that we make this offer simply gives added proof and force to our guaranty. You can order from Gordon-Van Tine with absolute assurance of getting what you pay for.

Strategic Factory Locations Get Lowest Freight Rates—Wherever You Live

REMEMBER, it makes no difference of whom you buy, the lumber you get has to be shipped in and 'ie freight charges have to be paid. If you buy locally they are simply added to your purchase price. You pay the freight, no matter of whom you buy. When you buy of Gordon-Van Tine you are sure of securing the lowest possible freight rate, because Gordon-Van Tine will ship you from the nearest source of supply direct. You certainly pay no more and you may pay less.

Five Mills and Factories

Gordon-Van Tine own and operate five mills and factories. Two at Davenport, Iowa, where most of the millwork, frames, inside finish, etc., are made; one of the largest assembling yards and factories in the country at St. Louis, Missouri; a large mill and factory at Hattiesburg, Mississippi; and one of the finest mills and factories on the west coast at Chehalis, Washington. The lumber for your home will be shipped from whichever mill has the most advantageous freight rate into your community. If it comes from St. Louis or Hattiesburg it will be the best quality Southern Yellow Pine. From Chehalis, the best quality Fir.

Ask us our prices *freight paid to your station* before you let any one tell you that Gordon-Van Tine's price is high.

What Gordon-Van Tine Service
Saves For You

THE advantages Gordon-Van Tine offers the homebuilder can be classified under the four heads of Price—Quality—Plans—and Service, which are the four elements in any transaction.

As you consider these advantages in detail, we want you to keep in mind the fact that the Gordon-Van Tine Company has been in continuous operation here in Davenport since 1865. These fifty-five years have seen it progress steadily, from a little one story, one room, sash and door factory on the banks of the Mississippi, to the present mammoth organization with branch factories in the four quarters of the country.

Fifty-five years ago the resources of Gordon-Van Tine Company were those of its founder, Mr. U. N. Roberts—a cash capital of $700, a reputation for rugged honesty and sincerity and an indomitable energy. Today the paid up capital of the company is over $1,000,000.00—but the honesty, the integrity and the energy are the same, bequeathed by the founder through his sons, the present owners, to this business.

When a Business Merits
Your Confidence

We dwell at this length on the history of the Gordon-Van Tine Company not only because we are proud of it—but because of what it means to *you*. Any business which has operated continuously in the same place for fifty-five years, and has during that time grown from a very small start to be one of the greatest organizations of the nation—that business has proved its *responsibility* and its *reliability*. A concern with a record like that *makes good*. Without question it *merits your confidence*. So we tell you these facts about Gordon-Van Tine that you may know and realize the background of experience and record of performance that is behind every statement we make concerning the advantages Gordon-Van Tine offers home buyers in Price, Quality, Plans and Service.

Gordon-Van Tine
Savings in Price

The corner stone of the Gordon-Van Tine Company's business policy and the most important reason for the progress of this concern to its present dominant position in the industry has been—*better building material for less money.* We have made this not an empty slogan but an *actual fact.* We have accomplished it first, by more efficient manufacturing methods and, second, by selling the goods we make *direct to the user,* thus eliminating middlemen's profits.

We are first and primarily manufacturers of building material and our mills are among the largest and most modern in the country—our costs are as low or lower than anyone's. Years ago when we used to sell to dealers and wholesalers we competed successfully for their business on a strictly price basis. Today, selling direct to the consumer our prices are figured *on the same basis we used to sell dealers.* Gordon-Van Tine material, laid down at your station, therefore, represents an *actual wholesale price.*

You can prove these savings yourself by taking Gordon-Van Tine's prices on individual items such as doors, windows, paint, hardware, roofing, etc., and checking them against local retail prices on like quality goods. The fact that we now sell every year as much material to consumers on competitive bids (individual orders for lumber, sash, doors, trim, hardware, etc.), as our total volume of complete houses amounts to, shows conclusively that our prices are *right.*

"Be as Particular as if the Material Went Into Your Own Home"

Our assemblers, men of long experience in the building Material Business, have only one rule to guide them in shipping or rejecting materials. We tell them simply. "Be as particular as if the material went into your own home."

These men know lumber and millwork, hardware and paint, and all of the rest of the materials, thoroughly, through long years of working with them. They can detect hidden defects at a glance which the average man would not see. And if, in their judgment, whatever they are handling is not absolutely top quality, 100 per cent good, they throw it out. They are your inspectors, and they ship you the same quality material you would pick if you came to Davenport personally and loaded it yourself.

But the final proof rests not on what we say about ourselves, but on what our customers say about us. We have in our files thousands of letters from people who have bought from us, copies of some hundreds of which will be sent you in an early mail. This testimony will prove to you beyond all shadow of doubt that we do sell better material for less money. *These customers say their savings average from 30 to 50 per cent.* The primary reason for the success of the Gordon-Van Tine Company is this saving we made them and which we offer you.

What Gordon-Van Tine
Guarantees in Quality

Savings at the sacrifice of quality are not actual savings. What, then, of Gordon-Van Tine quality?

On the cover of this book and on the order blank you have seen our guarantee— briefly it reads "Satisfaction Guaranteed or Money Back.' Nothing could speak more eloquently of the quality of our materials than that we invite every customer to return every stick we sell to him and receive every cent of his money back if he is not satisfied with it. We *cannot afford* to ship out anything that is not top quality. If you could come to Davenport or visit any other of our four mills, you could see for yourself the absolute high quality of Gordon-Van Tine materials. No place in America are there such quantities of fine building material of all sorts as at the factories and warehouses of the Gordon-Van Tine Company.

Complete Specifications

But even though you cannot come, you can inspect the specifications of materials which are furnished for Gordon-Van Tine homes on pages 9 and 10 of this book. These are the most complete specifications published by any building material firm and list out in the greatest detail all the materials which go into your home. The kind of material, the grade, the size are all specifically given and any one who is familiar with building will testify to the high qualities shown. Our guarantee is based on these specifications. We *must* furnish these qualities of material or we would be open to lawsuit and would be out of business in three months.

Again we refer you to the testimony of our customers. Many letters are shown in this book—more will be sent you in an early mail. Look them over carefully and read what they say of the quality of the material Gordon-Van Tine furnished them.

Gordon-Van Tine Plans

Fine material alone does not insure a fine home, and savings in material costs are easily dissipated through mistakes in plans and construction. Because it takes just as much material and labor to build a poorly planned home as one which is well planned, Gordon-Van Tine's plan service is of the utmost importance to you.

The designs, shown on the following pages, speak for themselves. Nowhere else in America can you find such a collection of handsome, thoroughly practical, livable, moderate priced homes, with the utmost in convenience and comfort built into them as are shown in this book. In fact, until Gordon-Van Tine entered the field there was no plan service for the homebuilder who must consider cost, and even today there is no one else to whom the home builder can turn with complete insurance of satisfaction than to Gordon-Van Tine.

First of all Gordon-Van Tine assures you of a practical home—livable, sound in construction and engineering, in arrangement and ventilation. For the designs our architects have taken the best types in every part of the country, from New England Colonial mansions to cozy California bungalows.

The arrangement of the interior is not the work of one man—it represents the judgment of many people, all of them experts in home planning. Special attention is paid to the placing of doors and windows to secure the best light and ventilation and the freest communication from room to room as well as give ample wall space for furniture. Unusually careful thought is given the kitchen and pantry arrangement. Each kitchen is provided with a splendid big case with room for all utensils and the various fixtures are carefully located so that the work can be done with the greatest convenience and the least effort. Linen closets are provided in nearly all designs, and countless little thoughtful touches are given each individual design which are only appreciated after the home is built.

We recognize frankly the difference in living conditions in the city and on the farm and you will find homes designed to fulfill your needs no matter where you live.

Furthermore, and not least important, we are ever mindful to plan with an eye to eliminating waste in the use of material, keeping to stock designs and sizes, and thus keeping costs down.

The Meaning of "Guaranteed Against Extras"

But *planning* your home, important as it is, is but one step. Just as essential are the steps which make it possible for you to obtain the materials to build that house, from the special cabinet, and stair work down to the last nail and pint of paint, at a wholesale guaranteed price from one source at one lump sum.

After the plans are drawn and checked until they are absolutely correct, lists of material are made up from them by men skilled in construction and plan reading, with years of experience behind them. Every stick of lumber, every pound of nails, every piece of hardware from the front door lock down to the closet coat hooks must be listed—nothing overlooked and nothing over estimated for the price must include *everything* as specified, but your money must not be wasted for needless materials.

When you consider that every year millions of dollars are wasted for American home builders by inaccurate lists—you can readily see how vitally important this work is—and what a wonderful service Gordon-Van Tine's Guarantee against Extras is.

Gordon-Van Tine Service

Gordon-Van Tine service includes all the foregoing, of course, Guaranteeing against Extras is an important phase of our service. It includes too the Ready Cutting of material, described on the following pages. Physically, Gordon-Van Tine Service consists of all the materials as specified

to build your home according to perfected plans at one lump, wholesale price.

But our service consists of other things also—not so tangible but just as important. Careful attention to your letters, expert advise on any question regarding building are a part of it. A distinct department devoted to handling your order smoothly and anticipating your wants is another. The results of this type of service you will see reflected in the letters our customers write, which will reach you in an early mail.

Added Service Which Insures Your Final Cost

There are some items, of course, such as tile, brick, cement, or plaster, which we do not furnish. Because of the high freight rates it costs too much to ship this kind of material with lumber and we advise you to purchase it locally.

To make it easier for our customers to know the amounts they need and to make absolutely definite a final cost of the building, our service includes without extra charge a complete list of all the material you need to buy for foundations, footings, cement floors, plastered walls, chimneys, etc. These lists are accurately prepared and make it possible for you to buy intelligently. Moreover they are so complete that they tell you the amounts of material needed for different kinds of foundations, such as solid concrete, cement block, hollow tile, etc. Special list covering all this information is furnished along with our complete plans and building instructions to every purchaser.

Contract Forms Furnished Free

We also furnish you blank form for any kind of a contract which you may wish to draw up with your carpenter or general contractor. To insure your final cost you may want to make a contract for just the carpenter labor or you may want the contract to include all the labor and all of the material which we do not furnish. When you purchase your house, just tell us what kind of a contract you want and we will draw it up in such a manner that it will absolutely protect your interests and yet the contractor will be very glad to work under its fair terms.

Buying Satisfaction

It is these things plus the *absolute assurance of satisfaction*, which is written into our Guaranty, and the knowledge that when you pay the price quoted you are absolutely assured of getting enough material of the grades as specified to build the house, which are the real secrets of Gordon-Van Tine values. These are the qualities you get in the GORDON-VAN TINE HOMES. You do not simply buy so much lumber and millwork and hardware and paint—so many thousand shingles and so much lath and the rest of the material. What you buy is a HOME. What you buy is SATISFACTION. Look at your purchase in this way. Compare prices if you will—but do not forget the most important part of the bargain —GORDON-VAN TINE SERVICE.

Real Service That Insures You Satisfaction

THE MACHINES THAT SAVED

The contrast in these two pictures tells the story. Four men with this great machine can do the work of 40 men with handsaws.

HERE are a few of Gordon Van Tine's wonderful wood-working machines. Substituting machine work for expensive hand labor has saved Gordon Van Tine customers conservatively over $100,000.00.

Compare these machines and the work they do, also illustrated here, with the old-time hand-saw-and-chisel way of preparing the materials. The contrast is the proof of the savings our customers make.

The big gang trimmer, shown above, can eat its way through a car of lumber, trimming both ends square, as fast as four men can pile lumber on it. It is pneumatically controlled, has a dozen saws, one in each slot. They fly up when the man at the key board presses the lever. Thus a board can be cut into 12 pieces at one operation, if necessary.

The door mortising machine is a wonderful example of the time and money saved by the Gordon Van Tine System of Construction. With it, we mortise a door ready for the lock in less than a minute. It takes a good carpenter at least half an hour to mortise one door with brace, bit and chisel. This is a small thing—but it is typical.

The illustration below shows material for kitchen case assembled for shipment. Note that fronts are set up, doors are completely built and ready to hang, drawer sides are dovetailed, plowed and rabbetted for bottoms

Doors Mortised For Locks.

It takes a carpenter 30 minutes to mortise a door for a lock with chisel and brace and bit. Our wonderful mortising machine does the job perfectly in less than two minutes. All doors in Gordon Van Tine Homes mortised for locks.

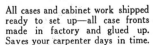

All cases and cabinet work shipped ready to set up—all case fronts made in factory and glued up. Saves your carpenter days in time.

HOMEBUILDERS OVER $100,000

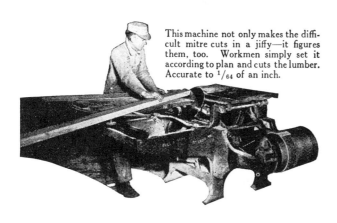

This machine not only makes the difficult mitre cuts in a jiffy—it figures them, too. Workmen simply set it according to plan and cuts the lumber. Accurate to $1/_{64}$ of an inch.

and ends. All your carpenter has to do is to set them up, nail into place and attach the hardware which we furnish.

Instead of spending days to build the cases he has them set up in a few hours—and you get a better job.

Above at the left is illustrated one of our mitre saws. With this machine difficult angles and bevels are calculated and cut in a few seconds. Such cuts are very difficult to figure on the job—they waste time and material.

One of our wonderful window frame machines is shown at the right. It plows, dadoes, bores the pulley holes and cuts the pockets in our window frames. All frames are shipped all ready to set up. The illustration below at the left shows a side jamb for window frame the way it comes to you—plowed, dadoes, bored for pulleys and pockets cut. Other parts of the frame have all cuts made and are ready to set up. It takes but a few moments of a carpenter's time to set up one of our frames and their machine cutting insures perfect fitting windows and doors. Frames are shipped bundled, pulleys, weights and sash cord included but not in place.

Below is shown the rafter machine which bevels both ends of the rafter and at the same time cuts out the notch to seat it over the plate with a single downward stroke of a foot lever. Six cuts in one operation. A striking example of time-saving.

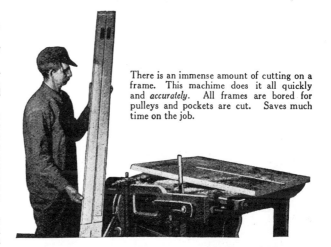

There is an immense amount of cutting on a frame. This machine does it all quickly and *accurately*. All frames are bored for pulleys and pockets are cut. Saves much time on the job.

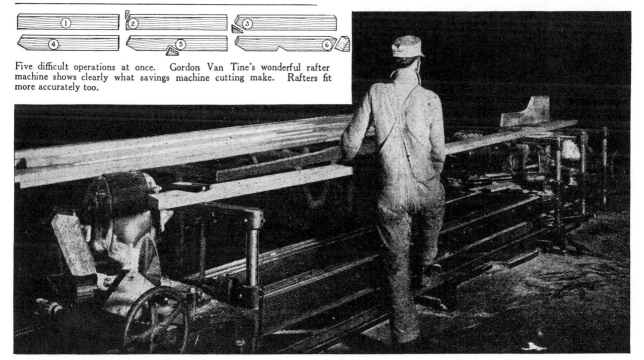

Five difficult operations at once. Gordon Van Tine's wonderful rafter machine shows clearly what savings machine cutting make. Rafters fit more accurately too.

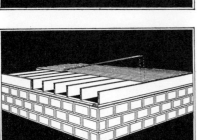

Plates ready-cut and fitted, are laid on top of the foundation and fit exactly.

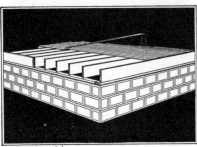

The joists cut to proper length laid on top of foundation and girders. Sub flooring laid on top of joists.

Gordon - Van Tine notched plates, all ready-cut and fitted, laid on top of sub flooring.

Ready-cut studding shown fitting into notches in plates.

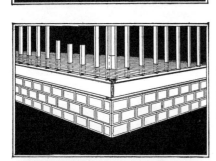

The studding in place—top plates being laid on studding. Notice headers and trimmers for window opening all cut and fitted. Notice also double studding at corners and double top plates.

THE GORDON-VAN TINE
Saves You Up to 17% on Lumber Waste—And 30%

NINETY-SEVEN per cent of the lumber that goes into a house must be cut at one or both ends—*an average of more than two cuts on each piece.* In the days of cheap labor this work was all done by the carpenters on the building lot. Stock lengths and sizes of lumber were sawed and ripped up to fit by hand-saw and elbow grease.

You remember passing a building lot where a new house was to be built and seeing the carpenters sawing up the lumber?

If you were interested enough to observe closely, you no doubt were impressed by the fact that although the carpenters always seemed to be working steadily, the actual construction seemed to progress by fits and starts—about two days working on the ground and at the benches, and one day's nailing, on an average. Those carpenters were working all the time, but they were making such slow progress because they had to spend so much time *preparing the material for use.*

And when those carpenters were through, remember how the yard around that house looked? Littered about knee deep with short sawed-off pieces of lumber—from 5 and 6 feet long on down to trimmed ends, wasn't it? A whole cellar full of kindling wood when it was piled away—terribly expensive kindling wood.

30 to 50% Carpenter's Time — 17% Lumber—Saved

Experts estimate that this old-fashioned way of making whatever the local dealer has in stock do, and sawing it up to fit on the job by hand, *wasted from 30 to 50 per cent of the carpenter's time, and an average of 17 per cent of the lumber*—and the time and the lumber that are wasted, cost just as much as the time and lumber that are used.

In the good old days when we thought our forests would last forever, and lumber was dirt cheap—those days when a carpenter got thirty cents an hour and was glad to get it, this toll of waste may not have mattered so much. But now-a-days, $75.00 to $300.00 in hard cash, going into the cellar to start fires with, and $150.00 to $500.00 excess carpenter's bill for pushing the hand-saw is a big enough total to be pretty seriously considered.

The GORDON-VAN TINE Ready-Cut method of construction has eliminated all but a little less than 2 per cent of the lumber

Skyscraper Construction

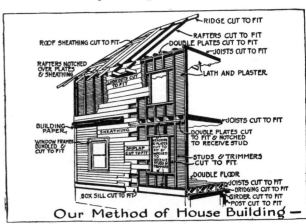

Our Method of House Building —

As you know, the modern skyscraper is all ready built in the great steel mills which turn out its framework. The big girders are all prepared there, and even the rivet holes bored to fit. Everything is marked in accordance with the plans, and the erectors simply put the giant structures together. Now all this results in tremendous economies, because the steel mills substitute machinery for slow hand work, and also in accuracy,

READY CUT SYSTEM
Material by Eliminating
on Construction Cost

Ceiling joists cut and beveled laid on top of double plates. Everything fits to perfection.

waste (the necessary waste in mitering, beveling and squaring up —and the sawdust), and has made possible savings in construction cost which our customers say average up to 43.2 per cent.

It Sounds Impossible—But We Do It

To those skilled in the old method of construction this no doubt sounds impossible. But if you could step for a minute into one of our three great Ready-Cut Factories at St. Louis, Missouri, Chehalis, Washington, or Hattiesburg, Mississippi; if you could see the great machines at their work—their flashing saws eating into the lumber as fast as the conveyors can bring it to them, cutting the largest and smallest pieces accurately to a sixty-fourth of an inch, so fast that the eye can scarcely follow their work—you would begin to realize how this wonderful saving is made.

To see a truck load of lumber, which would require half a day's time to cut by hand-saw, whisked through the great pneumatic control gang trimmer in five minutes, for instance; or to watch the rafter machine as it trims both ends of a rafter at once and at the same time cuts the notch to fit it over the plate; to see these things is to be everlastingly convinced that the Ready-Cut System is the only way to prepare lumber.

Care in Marking, Bundling, Loading, Make Building Easy

And then if you could inspect this cut material as it is assembled and loaded into the cars, noting how every piece is marked just as the plans are marked and see the care taken to load the cars so that each bundle will come out in the order in which it is to be used; if you could follow the shipment through and see how our complete and thorough instructions show the workmen just how to unload and pile the lumber so it will all come to hand as needed; and then if you could stay there for three or four days to a week and see them frame that house up; see the carpenters without spending a minute to saw, take that perfectly cut and fitted material and make the frame of a house of it just as fast as they can drive nails, see everything fit to perfection, making a right, tight, ship-shape job that is a joy to a good mechanic—in short, if you could follow through a Ready-Cut House from start to finish you would be just as throughly convinced and as enthusiastic as other GORDON-VAN TINE customers are—for seeing is believing.

Rafters and lookouts cut, notched and beveled fitting into place perfectly.

Ready-Cut System makes this merely a matter of nailing up. Cut on the job it is a work of days.

The <u>Notch</u> that Compels Accuracy

Our experience and the volume of our business has made possible certain refinements in construction which are peculiar to GORDON-VAN TINE Ready-Cut

Methods Applied to Homes!

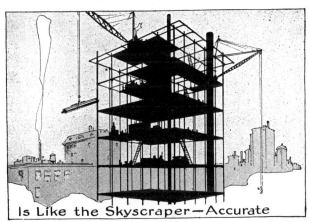

Is Like the Skyscraper—Accurate

because exact science takes the place of human guesswork and human mistakes. Well, what the steel mills do for the skyscraper, our mills do for the *modern home.* Our machines do in a few hours what it would require hand labor days to accomplish. This saves for you, and the *accuracy* with which the work is done gives you a *house of no mistakes.*

Ready-Cut sheathing, both wall and roof sheathing, being nailed in place. Not a saw on the job and the house ready for siding and shingling. These pictures show why the Ready-Cut System saves you big money.

The Speedy Economical Way to Build

Homes. First and foremost among them is the now famous GORDON-VAN TINE notched plate.

Each upright stud rests on a plate and is capped by a plate. *We notch those plates.* Each stud fits into its own notch. There can be no deviation—the walls must be set accurately. No measuring is necessary—accuracy becomes automatic. The notch compels accuracy. This is simply one of the means which we have taken to insure satisfaction and time saving in GORDON-VAN TINE Ready-Cut Homes.

And of course doing a big volume business as we do and standardizing this business has enabled us to lower our costs and consequently our prices to you. Quantity manufacture is the secret of low costs in all business. We have applied it to house building to your advantage.

Complete, Easily Understood Book of Instructions Furnished Free

The GORDON-VAN TINE Ready-Cut System is the acme of simplicity. To insure that everything will go right and you will gain all the savings possible we furnish you free with your order, not only complete plans, but a Book of Instructions, telling you just what to do from unloading the car to setting the ridge board. Particularly important are the instructions on piling the materials. We exercise great care in packing it in the car so that it is unloaded in rotation, and instructions tell you just how to pile it so that every piece will be handy when you need it. Every step of the way, everything is clear and plain.

For the Man Who Is in a Hurry

The home-builder wants quick results and ease of erection, and sometimes the season of the year makes it necessary to build in double-quick time. The Investor and Real Estate Operator must get their houses built *quickly* to avoid extra interest and expense, and to get their money earning dividends as soon as possible.

Our "Ready-Cut Homes" fill the bill in every case, because they make it possible to build quickly and economically, and at the same time produce *finished* results, which will satisfy the most exacting man.

For the Man Who Does His Own Work

A man who is handy with tools can build one of our "Ready-Cut Homes." This is a broad statement, but it has been proven by actual experience that it is not difficult for a handy man to follow our complete plans and directions and nail this material in place. However, unless a man has had a fair amount of building experience he will usually profit by having a carpenter on the job to show him the numerous effort and time-saving "tricks of the trade" that only come from experience.

For the Carpenter

The contractor or carpenter who undertakes to build a Gordon-Van Tine "Ready-Cut Home," reaps the benefit of the work which we do in our factory. It is money in your own pocket to take advantage of our factory facilities. It is only reasonable to say that studs, joists, rafters and sheathing can be cut on a power-driven saw more cheaply than they can by hand work.

The method of construction is standard—just like any carpenter is accustomed to. There is nothing new to learn, to study over, or to estimate on. The material comes on the job in such shape that it goes right where it belongs.

If You Order Your House Not Ready-Cut

You can buy any Gordon-Van Tine home with lumber Not Ready-Cut if you desire or find it necessary, with the exception of industrial cottages, summer cottages and garages which are only sold Ready-Cut.

If you order your house Not Ready-Cut the lumber shown on the specification pages 9 and 10 marked Cut-to-Fit will be furnished in standard mill-run lengths, selected so they can be cut to best advantage by carpenters on the job, but not ready-cut at our factory.

Remember, however, that you still get the advantage of Gordon-Van Tine plans; that all window and door frames will be shipped cut-to-fit, bundled and marked; all linen cases, kitchen cases and stair work will be shipped cut-to-fit, ready to set up, case fronts glued up; all doors will be mortised for locks and all hardware, tin work, nails, paint, etc., will be furnished.

The Gordon-Van Tine Not Ready-Cut home represents a great step forward from the usual material bought of the local lumber yard and the savings, while not as great as though you bought Ready-Cut, **are** still very important.

These Photos show how ready cut home No. 544 saved $250.00 for A. G. Kittell, Editor Nebraska Farm Journal.

Material piled on building site—foundation in—November 3rd, 3 P. M.

Two days later—November 5th—two men on the job ready to start sheathing

November 7th. Rafters and dormer in place. Most of roof sheathed.

November 10th, 1:30 P. M. Porches up—roof sheathed—nailing on shingles and siding.

The House completed, altho starting in November and handicapped by carpenter shortage, Mr. Kittell was able to move into his home before cold weather overtook him. He estimates that he saved at least $250.00.

Specifications

Note their Completeness and the Uniform High Grade of Material Furnished

For Not-Ready-Cut Construction See Note at Bottom Page 8

READ these specifications of Standard High Grade Lumber with the utmost care. These are the most important pages in this book. They tell the *facts* about the *quality* of Gordon-Van Tine Homes. There is no camouflage here— no attempt to make poor material sound good by using fanciful names.

Every item in these specifications is of the *highest* grade practical to use. You cannot buy better material. Others may offer to beat Gordon-Van Tine prices. They cannot do so if they match Gordon-Van Tine *quality* and furnish *all* the material we do. Match any other specifications with ours, and detect the *jokers*. And remember—what you really want is a good home—the best your money can buy—a home that will last for your lifetime and your children's. Such a home these specifications insure you.

Girders, Box Sill, Wall Plates, Joists, Studding, Rafters and all 2 inch dimension lumber including plates, headers, blocking, cripples, cornice return, stair landing and horses are all No. 1 yellow pine, surfaced and edged *Cut-to-Fit. Every piece marked.* Bundled when necessary for easy sorting and handling. We guarantee every piece of framing lumber is of proper and sufficient size and strength for its purpose. See illustrations for actual size of principal members.

All Studding spaced 16 inch on center, *Cut-To-Fit.* Single plate at bottom and double plate at top of *all walls* and partitions.

Sub-Flooring, 1x6, No. 2 yellow pine, tongued and grooved, *Cut-To-Fit,* and marked. Sub-flooring is furnished for first floor in all houses.

Finish Flooring, for first and second floors, 1x4 (3¼-inch face), clear flat grain yellow pine. This flooring is clear—no knots or defects of any kind.

Bridging 1x3 for 2x8 and 2x10 joists on all spans of 12 feet or over, cut to fit, bundled and marked.

Lath for all inside walls and ceilings, No. 1 soft short-leaf yellow pine; guaranteed to make a first-class job. 85 per cent of these lath are 4 feet long, 15 per cent are 32 inches long. (No lath furnished for cellar or attic.)

Cellar, Grade and Attic Stairs, furnished complete.

Roof Boards, 1x4, No. 2 yellow pine, surfaced two sides, *Cut-To-Fit,* bundled and marked and properly spaced to insure longest life of the shingles. All angles for hips and valleys cut exact.

Wall Sheathing, 1x8, No. 2 yellow pine shiplap, surfaced two sides, *Cut-To-Fit,* each section tied up in bundles and marked. Angles cut for gable sheathing.

Roof Shingles, extra clear 5 to 2 Washington Red Cedar, a high grade standard shingle. Wall shingles, where shown are 6 to 2 Star A Star Washington Red Cedar. All roof shingles laid 4½ inches to the weather.

Attic Flooring, No. 2 yellow pine, tongued and grooved, for all houses having an attic stair. *Cut-To-Fit* and marked.

Outside Finish, clear grade suitable for exposure to the weather. This includes corner boards, facia, outside base, frieze, porch beams, belt, porch steps and risers, lattice frames, porch ceiling, cornice ceiling, etc., as shown. (See below for frames and mouldings.)

Siding, clear Louisiana red cypress or California Redwood, spaced 4½ inches to the weather. This siding is absolutely free from knots or defects. Siding is furnished for all houses except where the illustration and description shows shingles or stucco on the outside walls.

Building Paper, AA Brand red rosin to be used between double floors and under the siding and under and around all door and window frames.

Outside Mouldings, such as Crown, Bed, Belt, Watertable and Cove moulding, are clear white pine or fir.

Porch Columns and Rail (where shown). Clear Washington fir. Top and bottom rail with square balusters, cut to convenient lengths.

Porch Flooring, 1x4, clear edge grain Washington fir.

Byrkitt Patent Sheathing Lumber furnished for all outside walls of stucco houses, *Cut-To-Fit.* This patent sheathing furnishes a firm key for the outside stucco or cement, and there is no metal to rust. This is the most approved method of construction for durability and warmth, and is endorsed by the best architects and contractors.

Outside Frames for all windows, sash and doors, *Cut-To-Fit,* bundled and marked. Window jambs plowed and grooved and bored for pulleys. Door jambs rabbetted for doors. All made of clear white pine.

Windows and Sash are made of clear white pine, glass set in and puttied. In windows over 24x28 we use double strength glass. All two-light windows are check rail and made to hang on weights.

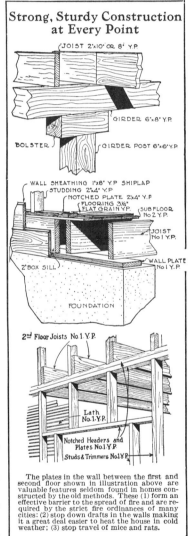

Strong, Sturdy Construction at Every Point

The plates in the wall between the first and second floor shown in illustration above are valuable features seldom found in homes constructed by the old methods. These (1) form an effective barrier to the spread of fire and are required by the strict fire ordinances of many cities; (2) stop down drafts in the walls making it a great deal easier to heat the house in cold weather; (3) stop travel of mice and rats.

What We Furnish—

Such Complete Specifications Furnished Only by Gordon-Van Tine

Doors—All interior doors are of two panel design, having white pine stiles and rails and beautiful slash grained Douglas fir panels. Front doors are of handsome design suitable to the house. Six-panel Colonial front doors for all Colonial houses. Glazed doors provided for rear and grade doors. All doors are strictly "A" quality and mortised for locks.

Inside Finish, clear slash grain Douglas fir, Craftsman pattern in casings, base and mouldings. Ends squared, bundled and marked. Picture moulding furnished for all rooms except bath, kitchen and upper halls. Chair rail furnished for bath room. All interior finish is selected for beauty of grain and is properly machined and *sanded* ready for varnish or stain.

Blinds, Window Boxes, Lattice and Trellis are furnished where shown in illustration.

Mantel Shelf, Dome Damper and Ash Trap are furnished when fireplace is shown on floor plan.

Main Stair in all 1½ and 2-story houses, clear slash grain Douglas fir, *Cut-To-Fit,* bundled and marked. 1⅛-inch treads, ⅞-inch risers, tongued and grooved together, stair stringers housed out for treads and risers. Newels, rail and balusters, furnished (except where shown between walls) in handsome Craftsman design. All complete and machined ready to set up.

Kitchen, Pantry and Linen Cases clear slash grain Douglas fir, *Cut-to-Fit,* bundled and marked. Fronts of these cases are put together and shipped set up. Kitchen or pantry cases have flour bins, towel drawers, and small doors below countershelf, with doors and shelves above. All counter shelves are clear hard maple, the sanitary wood. Linen cases have large linen drawers, doors and shelves. Towel cabinet furnished for bath room in all houses not having a linen closet. See color pages for illustrations.

The following miscellaneous material is furnished: **Scaffolds and braces, tar paper for covering lumber, grounds for guides to plastering around doors and baseboards, backing strips and hardwood thresholds for all outside doors.**

HARDWARE

Mortise Lock Sets are furnished in our bevel edge Regal Design, antique copper finish. Front door locks are solid bronze with night latch. Rear and grade door locks are solid bronze. Inside locks are plated on steel. All locks have heavy bevel, giving them a handsome massive appearance. They are strictly first-class in mechanism and finish.

Hinges, with loose pin, are furnished. Mortise hinges of proper size for each type of door. **Sash Lifts and Sash Locks,** Regal Design, for all windows. **Cabinet and Kitchen Case Hardware,** including all catches, pulls, loose pin hinges, etc. The above items are furnished regularly in our antique copper finish.

Bathroom Hardware is All Nickel Plated.

Miscellaneous Hardware, complete for all details, including cellar sash sets, closet coat hooks, maple base knobs, sash cord, sash weights, door bell, etc.

Nails, proper sizes for all purposes, such as common nails for framing, casing nails for outside finish, finish nails for interior woodwork, lath nails and galvanized shingle nails.

TINWORK

Gutters, Valleys and Flashings are all furnished in heavy grade of tin, painted both sides. A special mineral paint is provided for the final coat.

Down Spouts, made of corrugated galvanized iron, are supplied to assure proper drainage from main and porch roofs. Elbows, shoes and necessary hooks are included.

PAINTS, OILS AND VARNISHES

Quality Brand Mixed Paint furnished for *three coats* for all outside work. Special paint furnished for porch floors. Unless otherwise instructed, we will ship paint in colors as shown in plan descriptions.

Shingle Stain is furnished for all shingles on outside walls (where shown) for two brush coats. (No stain for roof included.)

Quality Brand Spar Varnish furnished for all porch ceilings, natural finish, together with one coat boiled oil for priming.

Quality Brand Fine Interior Varnish for two coats, on all interior finish. Three coats of Quality Floor Varnish for all finished floors.

Putty, Pure Linseed Oil, Pure Turpentine, are included as required.

Sandpaper and Steel Wool are furnished for smoothing all interior floors and finish, rubbing down varnish, etc.

White Enamel Finish for five-coat work is furnished for wainscot and woodwork in all bath rooms; we furnish two coats white enamel, two coats of undercoating and one coat of hard oil.

Important Additional Information—Read Carefully

FIR LUMBER FOR THE NORTHWEST—Shipments for North Dakota, South Dakota or states west of these are made from OUR MILL AT CHEHALIS, WASHINGTON. In these shipments Douglas fir is furnished throughout in place of yellow pine for all framing lumber, flooring, sheathing and outside finish. Siding is clear red cedar, free from knots or defects. Inside finish and doors clear slash grain fir. Fir products from our Western Mill are the highest grades manufactured. Only No. 1 fir is used—even where No. 2 yellow pine is found in general specifications.

CHANGES IN CONSTRUCTION—Different climatic conditions prevailing in different parts of the country sometimes make alterations advisable in stock specifications. Where desired, these changes can be made and we will be glad to submit you revised prices.

If you live in the extreme Northern part of the country you may want to back plaster and put building paper under the roof shingles for warmth. If you want to make such changes, we will be most glad to tell you just how much they add to or subtract from the price of any home in this book.

MASONRY—Don't ship plaster, lime, cement, brick, etc., with lumber. Freight charges on such a car are much higher than on a straight car of lumber and millwork. We do not furnish such items for that reason, so would advise that you buy them locally. All plans covering masonry, etc., are furnished with each house, free of charge.

PLUMBING, HEATING AND LIGHTING—Our plans show the location of all plumbing fixtures. On the last pages of this book, we show prices on all plumbing and fixtures for each home.

PLANS—We furnish one complete set of blue prints for each house sold. Should you desire an extra set, let us know, and we will gladly furnish it.

REVERSED PLANS—Any plan can be furnished with plans reversed (opposite location of all rooms) without extra charge.

CEILING HEIGHTS—All houses have first stories nine feet high, second stories eight feet, except where otherwise noted in the description of the house. These measurements are in the clear between floor and ceiling. Basements where shown are six feet eight inches high.

A few houses in this book are of unusual architectural type, the harmony of which requires different heights of ceilings. In these few cases a note of story height is given in the description of the house.

Screens and porch sash are not included, but are priced for every home at the back of the book.

SHIPMENTS—All lumber shipments are made from our Lumber Mills at St. Louis, Mo., Chehalis, Wash., or Hattiesburg, Miss. *Prompt shipments* and lowest freight rates are thus assured no matter where you live.

Highest Quality of Material Proven

Here is What Our Customers Say About the Goods They Got

The foregoing color pages convey an excellent impression of the unsurpassed beauty of Gordon-Van Tine homes after they are completed. But the strongest assurance of quality of the material which goes into them is, we believe, the voluntary testimony of those who *have built* them and are now living in them.

Below are excerpts from a few letters taken from thousands in our files which tell you better than we can of the *super-quality* of the materials that go into Gordon-Van Tine Homes.

There is no skimping in grade, dimension or workmanship. Nothing is omitted that will make for sound, lasting construction of longer life. Quality goes *all through*. Read these letters and then read pages 9 and 10 and you will realize why Gordon-Van Tine Homes are so far superior to the ordinary house.

Studs—Joists—Lumber

We were more than pleased. The joists ran nearly all clear, and the studding were three-quarters clear and straight—*I. A. Barker, Indianapolis, Ind.*

The framing material is much heavier and more substantial than is usually put into houses in this locality—*Mrs. Rose Wright, Hooker, Okla.*

I have a first class contractor putting up these houses and he says he has used material from several other "ready-cut" factories and he likes your material and the manner in which it is cut and fitted much better than he has ever seen yet—*J. A. Compton, Coshocton, Ohio.*

My carpenter says it's the finest bill of lumber he ever saw—*Geo. W. Golay, Minden, Neb.*

The studding and joists could not be better—*John W. Earich, Prospect, Ohio.*

They are the best I ever saw put in any building in Newport—*J. E. Doharty, Newport, Ark.*

It is all first class goods, lots of it and some to spare—*Jacob H. Shuman, Inlay City, Mich.*

Built-in Features

My sister never gets through talking on the convenience of the house—*C. H. Baker.*

I want to thank you for the excellent quality of the material you sent me, and the fine workmanship—*John L. Scanlon, La Salle, Ill.*

I am very well satisfied. I especially like the kitchen, which is so handy. The built-in cupboard is much handier than a pantry, and is very attractive—*Mrs. J. P. Gunzenhauser, Humeston, Iowa.*

I have found the Gordon Van Tine home arranged very conveniently. The closet room, linen closet and kitchen cabinets are particularly satisfactory—*Mrs. M. H. Paull, Barre, Mass.*

I think my little home is just perfect, and every one who sees it admires it, too. Everything is so convenient. The cabinets in the kitchen and bathroom are just grand. I would not part with it for any money in the world—*Mrs. Charles Hendries, Bessemer, Mich.*

Electric Fixtures

I didn't believe such nice fixtures could be bought for the money—*F. L. Ball, Davenport, Iowa.*

I bought my plumbing, electric fixtures and shades from Gordon-Van Tine at a great saving—*C. W. Horn, Grinnell, Iowa.*

Siding

My carpenter said he had been siding houses for 25 years, and he never put on as good siding—*J. M. Barrett, Davenport, Iowa.*

The lumber measured up beyond my expectations. I could not find a single knot in the siding—*Geo. A. Cummings, Ednia, Mo.*

Every piece of material that came in sight when the building was ready for the painters was absolutely clear—*C. H. Baker.*

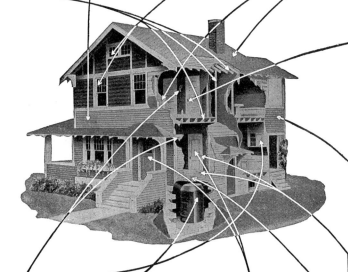

Furnaces

I would not have that heater taken out for $1000 if I could not get another—*A. D. Craig, Riverside, Iowa.*

The Fire King Pipeless Furnace arrived in good condition. I easily set it up myself and thus far it has given splendid service—*E. A. Myers, Eureka, Utah.*

Thank you for your prompt shipment. The furnace is doing good work with comparatively little fuel—*R. A. Lawrence, Pine City, Minn.*

Installed the furnace ourselves and had an abundance of everything. Am well pleased with the furnace—*C. E. Campbell, Jansen, Nebraska.*

Weather 22 degrees below, but house has been good and warm. Furnace has given entire satisfaction—*Fred A. Zorn, Mason City, Iowa.*

Windows and Frames

I never saw such nicely furnished window frames. The workmanship can't be beat—*H. N. Huss, Exira, Iowa.*

Sash were in perfect condition and am well pleased with them—*Jos. Swodden, Jr., Caseyville, Ill.*

Was very much surprised that you put such good stock in your sash—*Wm. T. Wormer, Metichen, N. J.*

Doors

Such doors could not be bought here for double the money—*J. S. Payne, Parker, Kansas.*

The doors are the nicest I have seen—*S. E. McFarland, Hermosa, South Dakota.*

The sash and doors were all A-No. 1 quality—*D. F. Barts, Watsontown, Pa.*

The fir trim and doors are beautiful—such pretty grain—*John Fernandes, Springfield, Ill.*

My five-cross panel doors are the admiration of all who have seen them—*W. S. Browne, Winchester, Ky.*

I am particularly pleased with the clearness and high polish of the glass, and the beautiful grain running through the wood of your doors—*Wm. L. Fisher, Philadelphia, Pa.*

Shingles

My carpenter said he never laid better shingles than the ones I got—*W. F. Caan, Grand Junction, Iowa.*

They are good A-No. 1 shingles, just as represented, if not somewhat better—*H. L. Berbin, Swanton, Ohio.*

Lath

Your lath cannot be duplicated anywhere—*Fred A. Zorn, Mason City, Iowa.*

I have never seen any better lath than those you sent me—*J. Belchambeau, Fox Lake, Wis.*

Hardware

The material was everything you claimed for it, from hardware to paint—*John Gleason, Illiopolis, Ill.*

Am well pleased with the quality. As to quantity I find the material ample to complete the job—*Geo. H. Woolman, Republican City, Nebr.*

Paint

We are more than pleased with the way your paint is wearing—*Albert Brown, Mechanicsburg, Ohio.*

Used your paint two years ago. I have been watching it, and like the lumber, millwork, hardware and furnace, it is standing the test and giving good satisfaction—*C. F. Godfrey, Roseville, Ill.*

The painters said that yours was the best varnish they had ever used—*L. R. Parish, Decatur, Ill.*

Mouldings

The interior woodwork is beautiful—*Mrs. Rose Wright, Hooker, Okla.*

The mouldings have given great satisfaction—*W. E. Schwarts, Camden, Me.*

Your windows, doors and mouldings are of excellent quality—*A. J. Carroll, Elliott, Ia.*

Flooring

I cannot say enough about your flooring, the quality as well as the milling was the best I ever saw. I have laid thousands of feet and have never seen any nicer flooring in my life—*E. E. Swarm, Clio, Ark.*

The flooring is the nicest I ever had—*M. S. Brown, Pinton, Mass.*

You do certainly handle good stuff—*William Van Emburgh, Easton, Pa.*

Everything was first class and plenty of it—*D. E. Roth, Pontiac, Ill.*

It is as good as anyone could get from any source—*Geo. Croudace, Rochester, N. Y.*

Gordon-Van Tine Home No. 535

Fine Sleeping and Sun Porches in This Home

This House Furnished with Siding or Shingles on Outside Walls Instead of Stucco. Write for Prices.

THIS beautiful home is certain to continue a favorite with the discriminating home-builder. It will prove, wherever built, one of the community's most substantial units. Should your need suggest, and your desire permit the construction of this exceptional home, then select this plan with all the comfortable assurance that goes with it.

There is small need, if any, to impress upon you the beauty, the convenience, and excellence of this home. The exterior could not be more imposing or pleasing—it is indeed a beautiful home, inside and out.

The impressive features of the exterior are the fine proportions obtained—the broad eaves, the big stucco pillars, the heavy brackets supporting the quaint hood over the entrance; the attractive front door and side lights, the two quadruple casement sash on either side, with the two flower boxes set below them, are welcome additions that serve to intensify the fine harmony that prevails throughout.

Notice particularly the fine balance contained in proportioning the windows of the second floor. Hold in mind, as you study this plan, the living comforts afforded by the sun porch and sleeping porch.

The living room and dining room are spacious and perfect in light and ventilation—opening from the sun porch are our beautiful French doors. You will always appreciate the fireplace with its cheer and warmth. The kitchen is a model, equipped with our kitchen case, style "D" and so handily arranged it will always be appreciated as a perfect room in a perfect home.

Through the service hall the basement is easily reached. Here there is space for the ice box and a convenient closet. Notice how easily we have arranged the approach to the second floor stairway—either from the front or rear halls.

Four bedrooms, a bath, a sewing room, with the sleeping porch provide an ideal arrangement upstairs. Besides a closet for each bedroom, we have furnished our linen closet as shown on the colored insert. Entrance to the sleeping porch is made from either chamber.

Prices for sectional sash for sun porch will be quoted on request.

PAINT—Unless otherwise instructed, we will furnish white paint for trim. The walls are stucco, for which we furnish Burkitt patent sheathing.

For Prices on This Home, See First Page.
Read Pages 9 and 10 for Full Description of Materials.

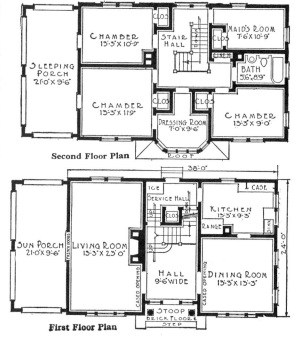

Second Floor Plan

First Floor Plan

For Plumbing, Heating, Lighting for This Home, See Last Pages of Book

Gordon-Van Tine Home No. 608

A Rarely Distinctive Bungalow Home

For Prices on This Home, See First Page. Read Pages 9 and 10 for Full Description of Materials.

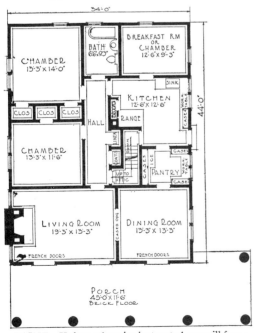

PAINT—Unless otherwise instructed, we will furnish white paint for body and trim. Green shingle stain for wall shingles above belt and in gable. We do not furnish stain for roof shingles.

HALF the pleasure in a home lies in its exterior attractiveness and harmony of design, and from that standpoint, too, this house must surely win admiration.

It stands for sun and light and cheer, inside and out. The 11-foot pergola porch supported by large stucco pillars, and the deep French doors are an assurance of this. The long, broad bricked porch floor laid in pattern design, with concrete border and the dormered roof are features that you will like also. By the way, there are windows in the gabled ends which you cannot see here, assuring ample air circulation for the attic.

You have observed the charm of the outside. What about the interior? Come in. From the front porch you enter the big living room, where the full French doors admit a flood of sunlight. This room is distinguished by the big fireplace with small windows above on either side. Can't you see a big, comfortable couch nearby, where you can get just the rest you need in time of tension? The dining room is no less attractive, and the pantry between the dining room and kitchen keep the latter entirely apart.

This service room is especially well equipped, affording a place for everything, even your refrigerator. Our

specially designed cases equip it perfectly, while in the kitchen additional cupboard facilities are provided.

Opening from the kitchen is the outside entrance, the passage to the basement, and also the door to a cozy breakfast room, a time and labor saving feature that will be used and appreciated every day in the year. This room may also be used for maids room or emergency bedroom.

With all its roominess there is a commendable compactness about this house. A door leads from the living room into the long hall, which connects the two big chambers and the bath. It also gives access to a convenient coat closet, to the kitchen, and also to the stairs leading to the floored attic, extending over the entire house.

The bedrooms are large, with three closets between them, and two and three windows each. From either it is just a step to the bath, which is complete with everything conveniently arranged.

The basement extends under the entire house proper and is well lighted with the seven cellar sash we include in our bill We also furnish shingles for sidewall above belt line.

Think it over, and see if your house choosing problem is not most satisfactory settled here.

For Plumbing, Heating, Lighting for This Home, See Last Pages of Book

Gordon-Van Tine Home No. 521

A Very Popular 4-Bedroom Bungalow

For Prices on This Home, See First Page.
See Pages 9 and 10 for Full Description of Materials.

PICTURE to yourself the pleasure of owning and living in a home as charming as this. A more attractive exterior would be hard to imagine. It is artistic and homelike in every line. Everything about this house bespeaks well balanced architecture that emphasizes the home feeling.

The appearance of this house is emphasized by the finish. The timbered front dormer and the projecting bay window in the dining room wall are added features.

This home is delightful throughout its interior also. From the big comfortable arched porch with its view unobstructed by many pillars, one enters the friendly well planned living room. A wide opening beyond invites one to the comfortable dining room, lighted by the group of triple windows in the bow, which forms one entire side of the room—an especially attractive window arrangement.

The kitchen is an unusual model of convenience. The sink and work table are each under a window, and arranged in the most convenient manner, with the sink to the left of the table and the large built-in case, design "D," to the right. This is shown on the color pages. The rear door, which is on the same level as the walk, serves as a rear entrance to the house and to the roomy basement below.

The central hall gives direct access to a large coat closet, dining room and living room, bed rooms and bath. From here the stairs lead to the second floor, where there are two more bed rooms and an attic, well lighted by the windows in the dormer. These three rooms all open from the upper hall.

All the first and second floor bed rooms are well provided with closets of good size, and with plenty of furniture space. It is quite unusual that a home occupying no more ground space

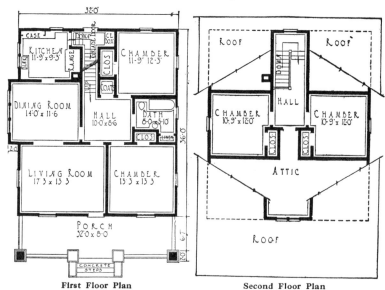

First Floor Plan   Second Floor Plan

than this bungalow should offer four splendid sleeping rooms, with even a well lighted attic space besides.

You must be agreed that the entire plan of this house is most charming. Imagine owning this beautiful little home and then plan to get it. A family intending to invest in a home would be well repaid for sacrificing a bit in order to own such a house as this.

PAINT—Unless otherwise instructed, we will furnish seal brown paint for body and white for trim. We do not furnish stain for roof shingles.

For Plumbing, Heating, Lighting for This Home, See Back of Book

Gordon-Van Tine Home No. 506

Fine Sized Rooms in This 4-Bedroom Home

For Prices on This Home,   See First Page.
Read Pages 9 to 10 for Full Description of Materials.

THE design of this house has proved itself admirable in all parts of the country—it is substantial, handsome and well arranged.

The broad effect is emphasized still further by the design of the porch. The brick pedestals and newels, the good lines of the porch columns and the square balusters are all pleasing.

A glance at the floor plan shows this to be unusual.   The living room and dining room extend across the entire front of the house, commanding a splendid view in almost every direction. These rooms are made practically one by the wide opening between them.

No room is taken up by a stairway at the front of the house.   But instead it opens off the passage way, making it equally convenient to the living room, kitchen or den. Notice the room that may be used as a den or downstairs sleeping room.   It is of good size with windows well placed.

The kitchen has surely been designed as a labor saver.   Our kitchen case design "B", and space for the sink occupy the outer wall, and assure the worker of excellent light.   We want also to call your attention to the fact that the 54-inch space that has been left for the range, is ample for even the largest of ranges.

From the kitchen one passes to the rear porch through a good sized entry which could easily be used for a refrigerator room or wash room.   Or one may leave the kitchen by means of the grade door just under the stairway leading to the second floor

Upstairs there are three fine chambers each with a big closet.   Can you imagine three better planned bedrooms than those shown here?

Two or three windows for each sleeping room in a house are surely unusual, but here they are to be found and plenty of wall space for the proper placing of furniture besides.

The stairway leading to the house sized attic, the bath and the linen closet—like the one shown in the colored section—all open from the second floor hall also.   The attic is floored and well lighted and ventilated by the windows in the dormer.

As you consider this house, picture your own comfortable furniture on the inside, and certainly you will decide that here indeed is much to attract and satisfy you at an exceedingly low cost.

PAINT—Unless otherwise instructed, we will furnish clear gray paint for the body and white for the trim of this home.

First Floor Plan

28'-0"

STOOP

DOWN

GRADE DOOR

Ice Box ENTRY

CHAMBER 11'-6"x13'-3"

KITCHEN 11'-3"x9'-6"

RANGE

CASE

SINK

28'-0"

LIVING ROOM 15'-3'x13'-3"

60 CAS OPG

DINING ROOM 11'-3"x13'-3"

PORCH 23x8'

First Floor Plan

Second Floor Plan

DOWN

BATH 7'-4"x7'-6"

CHAMBER 11'-6"x12'-0"

HALL

LINEN

CLOS

CLO SETS

CHAMBER 15'-3"x12'-0"

CHAMBER 11'-3"x14'-9"

ROOF

Second Floor Plan

For Plumbing, Heating, Lighting for This Home, See Last Pages of Book

Gordon-Van Tine Home No. 614

A Charming Dutch Colonial Home

For Prices on This Home, See First Page.
Read Pages 9 and 10 for Full Description of Materials.

THERE is a hospitable "homey" feeling about a Dutch Colonial home which has endeared it to countless persons. Perhaps that explains the ever-increasing popularity of the type. When a true Dutch Colonial is designed with such care and skill as that shown above, it becomes an ideal home for country, suburb or city. The wide 8 inch siding gives a most pleasing exterior appearance.

Notice that the big porch is cut across the entire front of the house instead of at the side, thus permitting this home to be built on a 40 or 50 ft. lot without crowding.

The front door leads into a beautiful reception hall which has a fine coat closet at the right. The living room is 21 ft. 6 in. by 12 ft. 3 in. inside, not including the bay window, a beautiful feature which enhances both the interior and exterior of the home. Placing it opposite the fireplace balances splendidly and makes this one of the most charming of living rooms. Notice that there are six big windows to give plenty of light and ventilation, but that there is also plenty of wall space for all the usual pieces of furniture.

The big closet to the right of the fireplace can be used for storing extra wraps, as a place to put the children's toys, or for countless purposes. It is a much appreciated addition.

A wide cased opening leads into the finely proportioned light dining room. The size and shape of this room permits the best arrangements of the usual dining room furni-

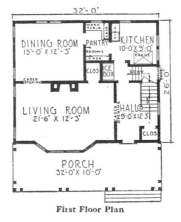

First Floor Plan

Second Floor Plan

ture, and means that 12 or 14 people can be served comfortably without crowding, around the expanded dining table.

The pantry with its two cases, work table, and the little cupboard for brooms, etc., is an extremely handy arrangement. The cases are of special design unusually roomy and complete. Notice that although direct passage is had to the kitchen, the doors are so placed that guests cannot see from the dining room into the kitchen. The kitchen is light and compact—just the size for the most efficient accomplishment of the work to be done. Space is provided in a recess in a back hall for the refrigerator where it is handiest to pantry, kitchen and outdoors, where the ice man can get at it without going through the rest of the house.

Upstairs we find four fine bed rooms. The owner's room in front is an exceptionally large and airy room, and all of the bed rooms have windows in two walls furnishing cross ventilation. The bath is centrally located—accessible to all bed rooms.

The linen closet opens off the main hall and there are three large shelves and two drawers providing ample room for the usual supply of bedding, towels, etc.

For a thoroughly modern, fine looking four bed room home, providing ample room and the utmost convenience, we do not believe this beautiful Dutch Colonial can be improved upon.

PAINT—Unless otherwise instructed we will furnish gray paint for body and white for the trim of this home.

For Plumbing, Heating, Lighting for This Home, See Last Pages of Book

The Entrance

FROM HOME 574

THE charm of the Colonial Home depends largely on the handling of the entrance, for the plain, often severe, lines of true Colonial architecture need the relief of graceful entrance detail.

Entrances to other Gordon-Van Tine Colonial Homes are similar to this one, while homes of other architectural types in this book have just as hospitable and carefully worked out entrances as the one shown above. Invariably the attractive appearance is gained by good design, and without the aid of costly material. The front door illustrated is furnished for all Colonial homes. Other types of architecture have beautiful glazed doors of harmonious design.

Wherever blinds are shown they are furnished as shown above; solid for the lower windows; slatted for the second story. Sidelights and window boxes as illustrated are furnished whenever they are shown on any plan.

This, and the following illustrations, emphasize the beauty and the completeness of all Gordon-Van Tine Homes. The smallest and most inexpensive house in this book is designed carefully as well as economically.

The Entrance Hall

FROM HOME 604

THE skill and taste of our architects is not expended entirely on the handsome exteriors of Gordon-Van Tine Homes. If anything, more care is taken with the interior effects, of which the hall of Home 604, shown above, is an instance.

We want particularly to call your attention to the fine stairway. The newels, balusters and rail are the same as are furnished with every Gordon-Van Tine Home wherever a stairway is shown. Note the handsome banded design of the woodwork around the cased opening leading into the dining room. This is our Craftsman design, furnished with every Gordon-Van Tine Home. The electric fixture is the hall light from our "Moraine" set.

The hall and stairs of the other homes differ from this only in size and arrangement. All designs of material are exactly like those shown above.

The Living Room

FROM HOME 602

THE dominant note in this, as in every Gordon-Van Tine living room, is comfort. A beautifully proportioned room, every part of it well lighted, yet the wall space permits an ideal arrangement of furniture. All the details of millwork shown are regular stock designs, such as are furnished with every Gordon-Van Tine Home. For instance, wherever French doors are shown on any plan, a pair like these are furnished. In each home where a fireplace is indicated we furnish a well proportioned wood mantel shelf, like the one shown above.

It is on such items as these that Gordon-Van Tine saves greatly for you, and at no sacrifice of beauty or originality. Such items as these are usually made up to special order at great expense. Our method of standardizing designs enables us to furnish them to you at stock millwork prices, and still retain all the beauty which fine designing and superior workmanship can give.

Picture moulding is furnished for every home just as shown here. From the woodwork around the cased openings you get a very good idea of the beauty of design and grain of the celebrated Douglas Fir finish in our Craftsman design, which is used in every Gordon-Van Tine Home. For those who prefer it, an optional price is offered for fine clear Oak Doors, Woodwork and Flooring.

The Dining Room

FROM HOME 599

THE proper arrangement of doors and windows to give light, ventilation and easy access, together with good proportion without using up all the wall space, is the essence of good planning. This dining room is an example of the care devoted to these details by Gordon-Van Tine architects. Plenty of room is provided for the buffet and there is space in another corner for tea wagon or serving table, yet the dining room is very light and spacious.

The door shown leads to the pantry. Every Gordon-Van Tine Home is furnished throughout with doors like this—a beautiful two-panel design. In all our homes, the door which opens from the dining room into the pantry, or kitchen, is equipped with a double acting hinge, which permits it to swing either way. The brass push plate shown is always furnished for all double acting doors. The electric fixture shown is from our "Moraine" set, with brass finish.

A Bedroom

FROM HOME 563

THIS light, cheerful room is the right-hand front bedroom of Home No. 563 and opens on to the sleeping-porch through the door seen at the left of the picture. Wherever a sleeping porch is shown the door leading on to it is glazed full length with divided lights just as this door is.

In planning a bedroom our architects always have in mind light, cross ventilation and the proper wall space for the necessary articles of furniture. As you look through this book note particularly the care which has been put in the planning of the bedrooms. You will find that there is always room for bed, dresser, chairs, etc., and that the matter of convenient arrangement, proper light and good ventilation has always received consideration.

All bedrooms have a picture mould as shown in this illustration. The light fixture in this room is from our Moraine set.

The Kitchen

FROM HOME 602

THIS illustration shows a typical Gordon-Van Tine kitchen. Imagine the real pleasure of preparing a meal in this light, cheerful room. Note the convenient arrangement of the cases—how the windows are placed to make this a light and pleasant place and how the proximity of both cases make it easy to do the work with the least effort.

The kitchen cases are two of our four stock designs. Type D is shown at the left—Type B at the right. Types A and C are similar to these but include slightly different combinations of cupboards, etc., A being the same as B but without the extension on the table, and C the same as D, but with top section two doors wide. These cases all have hardwood tops, removable hardwood mixing board, divided utensil drawer, tilting flour bin, as well as drawers and cupboards galore. Each home has at least one of these cases.

The illustration at the left shows the dinette or Pullman Dining Nook furnished in a number of our plans. This particular one is from Home No. 581.

Bathroom and Linen Closet

FROM HOME 607

HERE is shown a typical Gordon-Van Tine bathroom equipped with our Washington fixture set. You will note that the door is our stock two-panel design white enameled. The hardware, such as door lock set, sash fasteners, window catches and window lifts are all nickel plated. The light fixtures also. We furnish the chair rail—also enough white enamel to finish every Gordon-Van Tine bathroom five coats. The fixtures, such as towel bars, soap dish, cup holder, mirror, etc., are not included in the stock specifications, but you will find them listed and priced in our Building Material Catalog.

In nearly every Gordon-Van Tine Home a linen closet is furnished. This is built right into the wall as illustrated here and as you see has plenty of room for linens, towels, bedding, etc., and all those odds and ends that are so often scattered through every bureau in the house. It is furnished with the front framing all set up, the doors ready to hang, the drawers ready to be put together. All hardware is furnished.

The Porch

FROM HOME 535

THIS beautiful sun porch is a faithful reproduction from Home 535, tastefully furnished. Throughout the book you will find many homes with porches similar to this—some larger and some smaller—but all with just as great possibilities. Neither screens nor sash for porches are included in the price quoted in the front of the book. The prices on either or both will be furnished you on request. This porch is screened only. By using sash also it could be made just as cheerful and comfortable for winter as for summer. This home is stucco and consequently the walls and ceiling of the porch are finished just like the outside of the house. Many of the homes have clear beaded wood ceiling for porches.

These eight typical views of Gordon-Van Tine Homes give you an idea of how all the other homes in this book appear when built. The same woodwork, hardware, doors, etc., are used in every home in the book as are shown in these illustrations. When you want to know what a room in any particular house looks like, turn to the illustration of the similar room in this color section and except for size and arrangement you will find them identical.

Gordon-Van Tine Home No. 545

A Farm Home of Dignity and Comfort

For Prices on This Home, See First Page.
Read Pages 9 and 10 for Full Description of Materials.

JUST what it appears to be—an impressive farm home for the large family. The merits are many—too numerous to give particular mention in the limited space, so we ask you to study the plan very carefully. You are certain to recognize many features which, very likely, are just what you need.

Skill is reflected in every line of this big home—the skill that means perfection. From the number of prosperous farmers who have built this home, we assume it will continue to solve that most vexatious of all problems—the right house for a big family. You will appreciate the comfort it offers—and that, after all, is the most important feature.

The big front porch with its massive triple columns setting at rail height on masonry piers is a substantial addition that relieves any suggestion of severity. All through your survey of the fine exterior of this home you will find a simplicity of design and perfect balance of proportion—this knowledge gives you the welcome assurance that this home will endure—never will look old-fashioned.

Especially desirable is the wash room to which direct entrance is made by the grade door. The basement stairs also lead down direct from this entrance. The kitchen porch is roomy and has space for the ice box. Lattice for this porch is furnished.

The pantry has two big special Gordon-Van Tine kitchen cases provided with shelves of generous size cutting boards and a work table. The large kitchen will also be appreciated by the housewife.

All rooms are spacious with perfect light and ventilation. There are plenty of closets, each bed room has one—in addition there is an extra hall closet and the Gordon-Van Tine linen closet furnished with this home. The stairway is accessible from the living room, kitchen and down stairs bed room.

Careful study of this plan will convince you of its desirability—every provision has been made in making this the ideal home where room and lots of it is needed.

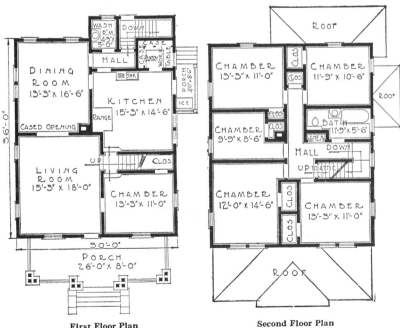

First Floor Plan   **Second Floor Plan**

PAINT—Unless otherwise instructed, we will furnish light gray paint for body and white for trim. We do not furnish stain for roof shingles.

For Plumbing, Heating, Lighting for This Home, See Back of Book

Gordon-Van Tine Home No. 609

A Big Comfortable Colonial Home

For Prices on This Home, See First Page.
Read Pages 9 and 10 for Full Description of Materials.

HOW often we have admired those simple, dignified old homes in our histories. The home pictured here retains all the features which made this style so popular a century ago, while added to it are all the most modern improvements which make life easier and more enjoyable. The inviting entrance, with its full length bevel plate door and side lights, the big side porch and the windows, so finely proportioned, all make a distinct appeal.

The long hall and imposing stairway leading to the first landing from the front hall and rear entry is an exceptionally attractive arrangement, creating a homelike and spacious appearance. The living room with its cheery fireplace and seven windows, and broad dimensions carries a conviction that here is indeed solid comfort.

The old Colonial atmosphere is carried out very consistently in having the hall separate the living and dining room. This arrangement is unusually pleasing in the larger home, since the living room has no need of borrowing the effect of space from the dining room.

The kitchen is roomy and well lighted. Our big kitchen case style "D" is included. The housewife is certain to appreciate this ideal, roomy kitchen. The basement stairs lead down direct from the entry. Notice there is space in the entry for the ice box. Also notice the closet just inside the rear door. There is another closet at the stair landing which will be most convenient.

Upstairs the arrangement is perfect. Four good sized bed rooms each with a fine closet afford ample accomodations for the average household and a guest room besides. Notice the big linen closet in the hall. This is furnished without extra cost and is similar to the design shown on the colored insert.

To build this home reflects your good taste and assures you of the utmost in real home-value.

PAINT—Unless otherwise instructed, we will furnish white paint for the body and trim, and bright green for the blinds of this home.

Second Floor Plan

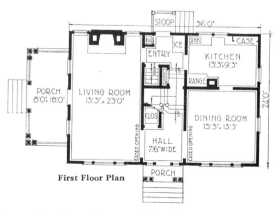

First Floor Plan

For Plumbing, Heating, Lighting for This Home, See Last Pages of Book

Gordon-Van Tine Home No. 612

A Striking Three-Bedroom Bungalow

For Prices on This Home, See First Page.
Read Pages 9 to 11 for Full Description of Materials.

Floor Plan

PAINT—Unless otherwise instructed we will furnish seal brown paint for the body and white paint for the trim of this home.

THERE is an unusual air of hospitality about this home. The big porch extending outward invitingly and the substantial air of it, makes this fine residence uncommonly attractive. The design of the roof with three intersecting gables is unusual and remarkably effective in this type of home. The broad eaves supported by timber brackets, the wide 8 inch siding and the craftsman barge boards serve to enhance the low hanging lines of this true bungalow.

The porch with its solid rail can easily be screened and makes a wonderful outdoor living room as it is exposed on three sides.

The door into the living room opens at the side. This is a splendid big room, full 23 ft. by 13 ft. 3 in. inside measurements. The fireplace in the middle of the front wall is flanked on each side by two big windows and a large window in the side wall makes this an extremely sunny and pleasant room in winter and unusually airy and cool in summer. Notice also that there is ample wall space provided for the usual pieces of furniture, without obstructing any opening. There is a closet for coats which opens from this room opposite the fireplace.

A big cased opening leads into the dining room which is perhaps the most attractive room in the house because of its splendid bay window. The proportions of this room are excellent and permit seating twelve to sixteen people at the central dining table without crowding. The wall

space is ample for buffet, serving table, tea cart and the usual pieces of dining room furniture.

To the rear of the dining room is the kitchen. Notice that a big built-in case (Type B—see color section) is furnished with work table, which connects with the sink. Both sink and work table are placed under the twin windows making a sunny and pleasant place to work.

At the rear of the kitchen there is a recess which can be used as a breakfast nook if desired. We will be glad to quote prices on the benches and table, such as are shown in the color section, to properly fit this out if you will write us. Notice that there is a closet for brooms near the dining room door. The rear entry provides room for the ice box, above which is a built-in case of special design. We furnish all material ready to build in for all cases at no extra cost. The entry arrangement was a particularly happy idea. It permits access to the rest of the house without going into the kitchen. It makes it possible for the refrigerator to be iced without tracking up the rest of the house, and it provides two doors between the kitchen and the outdoors, insuring warmth and comfort in winter.

The central hall connects all three bed rooms and the bath room. Notice there is a linen closet at the end for which we furnish all shelves, drawers, doors, etc. Each bed room has its own closet and each is well lighted and opens from the central hall from which also opens the bath room, making it possible to reach the bath room or any other room in the house without passing through either of the other bed rooms.

As you look at this plan you will perceive that each inch of space has been used to the best advantage by the architects. It is a splendid example of fine planning and gets and unusual amount of living space into a home which is not large. This is particularly gratifying because it keeps the cost down to an unusually low figure for a three bed room bungalow.

For Plumbing, Heating, Lighting for This Home, See Last Pages of Book

Gordon-Van Tine Home No. 529

A Colonial Home with an Ideal Floor Plan

For Prices on This Home, See First Page.
Read Pages 9 and 10 for Full Description of Materials.

THE beauty of this Colonial type of house is in the simplicity of its lines and is emphasized by the attractive Colonial entrance. The walls are shingled laid 8 inches to the weather in double courses. The blinds, flower boxes and trellised entrance are touches that give the house an appearance of hospitality and comfort.

The floor plan gives the most compact arrangement of six large rooms, and all conveniences that we have ever devised.

Passing through the vestibule the hall is entered, which is really a part of the living room and shares with it the glow from the fireplace and the view through the French doors at the opposite side. The coat closet to the left of the vestibule is a handy feature—it is lighted by a sash. The relative arrangement of the living and dining room window assures one of a summer breeze or winter cheer at meal time. And the wide opening between these rooms means that together they command air and light from three directions—the living room even from four.

The kitchen is compact and most conveniently arranged. We include our kitchen case style "B" at no extra cost. The twin window over the sink and work table admits of plenty of light and air. Note also the handy broom closet.

Notice the stairway to the second floor is easily accessible to the kitchen by means of the door to the reception hall. So, too, is the front entrance. The three comfortably sized bed rooms all have cross ventilation, unusually good wall space and adequate closet room. The additional linen closet is well placed handy to all bed rooms and bath.

The entire house is neat, dignified, comfortable and comparatively inexpensive to build. It is the type of New England's Old Colonial Mansions adapted to fit the needs of the present generation by keeping all the desirable features of the early home and adding present day improvements.

Lattice is furnished for front porch.

PAINT—Unless otherwise instructed, we will furnish silver gray shingle stain for the body, white paint for the trim and bright green for the blinds of this home.

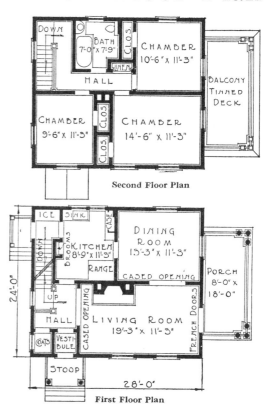

Second Floor Plan

First Floor Plan

For Plumbing, Heating, Lighting for This Home, See Last Pages of Book

Gordon-Van Tine Home No. 590

America's Best 6-Bedroom Farm Home

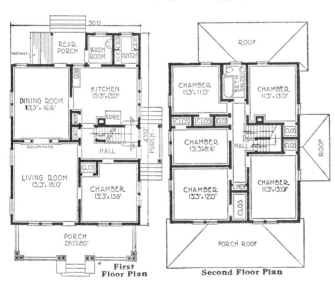

First Floor Plan

Second Floor Plan

For Prices on This Home, See First Page.
Read Pages 9 and 10 for Full Description of Materials.

THIS big nine room house embodies all the features which make a farm home attractive, convenient and comfortable. It results from a combination of architectural skill and a thorough knowledge of the needs of a farm home.

The exterior with its three porches bespeaks a comfortable roomy interior. Even the dormers add to this effect. And the floor plan which shows nine rooms and bath confirms the impression.

The outstanding feature of the house undoubtedly is the central hall. Because of it, access may be gained to all rooms from any room or from the outside without need of passing through any other rooms. Study the floor plan and consider what this means.

The sleeping rooms are equally accessible from the kitchen, the porch or the living room. And these bed rooms leave nothing to be desired, so light, airy and conveniently arranged are they.

Besides the linen closet opening off the upstairs hall there is an additional storage closet. From this hall, stairs ascend also to a splendid attic, which extends over the entire house. The uses to which this can be put are in reality too many to name.

To return to the first floor: the living and dining room extend from the front to the back of the house. These rooms are separated only by a Masterpiece bookcase colonnade.

The coat closet opening at the foot of the stairs is just outside the living room door, and at the same time convenient to the side entrance. The downstairs bed room opens from the living room also, as well as from the hall. It has a closet of its own.

Not least important in this splendid farm home is the kitchen with the convenient pantry and wash room opening from it. There is room here for everything needed in a kitchen, and room to put away everything else. The broom closet and the pantry with its two "A" cases and work table and the basement stair near at hand are all examples of this.

And withal it is a cheery kitchen, with three big windows at the side and additional light admitted from the wash room. These windows afford a view in at least three directions. The best feature of the wash room by the way is that one can reach the dining room from it, by merely crossing the back porch.

And near to the porch is the hatchway leading to the basement.

PAINT—Unless otherwise instructed, we will furnish clear gray paint for the body. white for trim and green shingle stain for the wall shingles of this home.

For Plumbing, Heating, Lighting for This Home, See Last Pages of Book

Gordon-Van Tine Home No. 536

A Beautiful Suburban Home

This House Can be Furnished with Siding or Shingles on Outside Walls Instead of Stucco.   Write for Prices.

For Prices on this Home, See First Page.

**Read Pages 9 and 10 for Full Description of Materials
Furnished for This Home.**

THE simplicity of good taste, the charm of fine design have made this home a "show place" in fine residence districts in scores of cities. The walls are stucco, starting from the low foundation line, giving the home a substantial appearance.

The casement windows in the front downstairs rooms, the broad eaves and the recessed entrance with the projecting bay above it are all fine examples of good architecture.

The effect as you enter the front door is especially attractive.   To right and left are wide cased openings leading into dining room and living room, and before you the open stair case—a combination which gives an impression of comfort and space.

The living room is all that the name implies, with the big fireplace and the living porch opening from it.   Notice the amount of wall space—no difficulty in arranging your furniture here.   The living porch is finished on the inside for stucco finish, while the ceiling is of beaded material and the floor of fir.

The dining room, nearly 14 feet square, is ample for all requirements.   Three windows flood the kitchen with light and yet permit plenty of space for our case design "D".   Notice with what care the kitchen equipment has been placed to make the work easy.

The rear entryway is one of the best features of the whole plan. It provides a place for your ice box, out of the way, yet convenient, and it also allows for a duplex stairway—a short flight leading to the main stairs from the kitchen.   The cellar stairs lead down from the entry and there is also a fine broom closet here.

The second floor plan is so arranged to provide an abundance of closets. Each of the three bed rooms has one, there is one in the bath room, a big linen closet in hall and a fine closet in the sewing room. The twin windows at the rear of the upstairs hall make it as light and airy as each of the big attractive rooms. The sewing room with its closet is an other special feature.

A substitution of shiplap, building paper, siding and paint for Byrkitt sheathing for outside walls, can be made for a small additional cost.   Write for prices.

PAINT—Unless otherwise instructed, we will furnish white paint for the trim of this home.   The walls are of stucco.

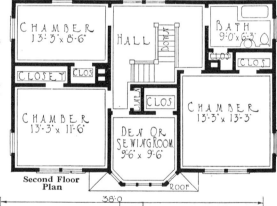

Second Floor Plan

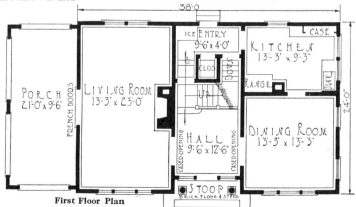

First Floor Plan

For Plumbing, Heating, Lighting for this Home, See Last Pages of Book

Gordon-Van Tine Home No. 596

An Ideal Home for Town or Farm

For Prices on This Home, See First Page.
Read Pages 9 and 10 for Full Description of Materials.

THIS house has been very carefully designed and will make an attractive home, It has been planned primarily for the farm, since we believe that there is no reason why good architecture should be confined to the cities.

This neat bungalow shows how very pleasing the small house can be made. The bracketed cornice, the shingled walls and the porch each add their part.

In fact, probably the most pleasing characteristics of the exterior are its porches. The columns of the front porch are pictured of field stone—which will be easily procured locally, and be both practical and durable.

This is a plan working out extremely well in point of housekeeping convenience. A study of the floor plan shows the living rooms properly placed on one side, and the bed rooms with bath conveniently arranged between on the other.

And the closets alone are worthy of special mention. There is one for each bed room, a linen closet like the one shown in the illustration off the bath room, and an additional closet opening from the dining room.

The size of the dining room itself is not to be overlooked. Its size and good wall space mean that practically any number of people can be seated here. The cased opening separating the living and dining room gives a spacious effect to both and provides extra room in either when needed.

Perhaps even more attention, if that is possible, has been given to the kitchen arrangement than to any other part of the house. At one side is the well lighted storage pantry, affording a place for all supplies. There are specially designed cases having 8 doors above the counter shelf and 5 drawers, 3 doors, 1 bin and a cutting board below.

Beneath the twin windows in the rear kitchen wall is a splendidly light place for a big work table, while under the other window opening onto the side porch is the space planned for the sink. Just next to this is the wash room, an always desirable feature in the farm or city home. Notice that a good place for a lavatory has been planned here.

The doors connecting the dining room, kitchen, porch and wash room are arranged so that there need be no traffic through the busiest part of the kitchen when the outside help comes in to meals.

The plans call for a basement under the entire house. There will be access to it, both from the kitchen and by way of the outer hatchway. We supply basement sash as well as materials for these. The outside stairs, however, are planned to be of concrete.

All in all viewed from a standpoint of attractiveness and good arrangement it cannot be improved upon.

PAINT—Unless otherwise instructed, we will furnish silver gray shingle stain for the shingles on the side walls, and white paint for the trim of this home.

For Plumbing, Heating, Lighting for This Home, See Last Pages of Book

Gordon-Van Tine Home No. 613

3 Bedrooms and Sun Room All on One Floor

This Home Furnished With Siding or Shingles on Outside Walls Instead of Stucco. Write for Prices.
For Prices on this Home, See First Page.
Read Pages 9 and 10 for Full Description of Materials Furnished for This Home.

THIS attractive bungalow has three fine bed rooms, all with ample closets, living room, dining room, kitchen, bath room and sun room all on one floor, in a most compact and convenient floor plan. Its most inviting exterior is distinguished by the wide eaves supported by brackets, the recessed porch and the half timbering in the front gable which sets off to advantage the stucco walls. Although it contains six big rooms exclusive of the sun room, it is only 28 ft. wide and will go nicely on a 40 ft. lot.

Study this ideal floor plan carefully. Note the convenient arrangement of all the rooms. See how easy it is to get from any one room in the house to every other room, but notice at the same time that every room is separate and by itself—it is not necessary to go through any of the bed rooms for instance to reach another, or to reach the bath room. A fine central hall takes care of this feature.

Note also the excellent light and ventilation provided in this home, but a careful examination will show you that while the number of windows and door openings is unusual, plenty of wall space has been provided for all the necessary furniture.

The solid rail makes the front porch easy to screen if desired. One enters the front door, which is protected under the main roof of the house, directly into the well proportioned living room. The fine sun room is connected with the living room by a pair of French doors. A cased opening leads into the dining room. The fireplace is just opposite this

cased opening so its warmth and cheer affects both rooms.

A door at the rear of the living room opens into the central hall, just inside of which is a big closet for coats. At the end of the hall is a big linen closet for which we furnish all material including doors, shelves, drawers and hardware, all ready to set up (see color section for illustration). Note also that there is a small closet which opens off this hall for mops, brooms, dust cloths, etc. The housewife will find this a great convenience.

All three bed rooms open from this hall, which also connects them with the bath. Note the enormous closet off the left hand rear bed room. The other two bed rooms each have a fine sized closet also. The two rear bed rooms have three windows which are arranged to give cross ventilation. Twin windows light and ventilate the middle bed room very effectively.

Notice that there is a door from the kitchen into this central hall making it possible to reach the sleeping quarters of the home direct from the kitchen, and at the same time making it possible to reach the front door from the kitchen without passing through the dining room.

The kitchen itself is the acme of convenience. Notice that two cases are provided, the one above the sink (Type A) and the other on the outside wall (Type B) where the light from the windows shines directly on the work table. For illustration of these cases see color section. A closet is also provided in this kitchen, which can be used for any number of purposes. The compact size and good arrangement make it possible to do the work here with a minimum of effort. One needs to take but few steps when preparing a meal. Space for the refrigerator is provided in the rear entry hall. The steps go down into the cellar from this hall and door leads into the kitchen. Notice that this arrangement of two inside doors insures a warm pleasant kitchen no matter how cold or stormy the weather may get.

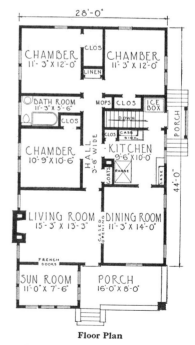

Floor Plan

PAINT—Unless otherwise instructed we will furnish seal brown paint for trim of this home.

For Plumbing, Heating, Lighting for this Home, See Last Pages of Book

Gordon-Van Tine Home No. 574

Beautiful Colonial Home With Ideal Plan

For Prices on This Home, See First Page.

Read Pages 9 and 10 for Full Description of Materials.

First Floor Plan

Second Floor Plan

THE Colonial style of architecture of which this home typifies the best always appeals to people who want a home bespeaking a quiet dignity and reserve. It is modeled from a famous old New England home.

The plain gables, the shuttered windows and the hooded stoop are distinctly Colonial. The open porch at the side is a further part of the harmony of this plan, and an important factor when comfort is considered.

For the outside walls we furnish clear 6 to 2 cedar shingles to be laid 5¾ inches to the weather, every third course doubled. The walls are shingled clear to the grade line to prevent the design from appearing too high—an effect which would be apparent if the foundation were exposed.

Once inside you will be even more delighted for you will find it a modern Colonial home, in truth. Every desirable feature of the old Colonial house has been retained, and to these have been added the comfort and convenience of the most modern design.

The wide hall, with its open stairway, connects the two principal rooms and still permits them each to keep their own individuality. The wide open stairway is an especially attractive feature here, with the open balustrade in the hall side. The stairs ascend both from the front hall and the kitchen. The coat closet opens on the landing.

How attractive the view from the dining room across the hall and living room to the splendid big porch beyond. French doors open onto it, while to the right and the left are big Colonial windows. Of course, the especial feature in this family room is the fireplace. Everyone loves an open fire, when the air is a trifle crisp outside.

The dining room is spacious and airy and well arranged. The affairs of the kitchen are kept comfortably out of mind by the butler's pantry between. This pantry has two of our "B" cases, and a place is provided for a refrigerator so arranged that it can be iced from the platform in the rear.

The kitchen is also equipped with our "C" case, with the broad work table extending beneath the window.

The upstairs rooms open from four sides of the almost square hall; and the door to the bath is not far from any of them. The owner's large bed room has two closets. There are closets for the other two bed rooms and sewing room also. This room can easily be used for a sleeping room, as it has a door leading into the hall and a closet opening from it. The large linen closet opens from the hall near the bath. Six cellar lights are provided for the basement which extends under the house proper.

The dignified aspect, the excellent proportions and the attention given to comfort and convenience mark this house as unusual in its desirability.

PAINT—Unless otherwise instructed, we will furnish silver gray shingle stain for the body, white for trim and bright green for blinds.

For Plumbing, Heating, Lighting for This Home, See Last Pages of Book

Gordon-Van Tine Home No. 503

America's Most Popular Farm Home

For Prices on This Home, See First Page.   **Read Pages 9 and 10 for Full Description of Materials.**

THE publishers of a well known farm journal recently inquired of their subscribers the type of house best adapted for use on the farm. More than a thousand letters with suggestions were received, and the above house is the result of those suggestions.

A careful study of the first and second floor plan shows beyond question every feature and detail of this house covers adequately the requirements of a modern farm home. The fact that the above house has been built so often speaks well of its popularity.

Because of its broad and massive lines it will show up particularly well from the road. A hasty glance from the passerby gives an impression of comfort and a desire to see the interior arrangement.

A large comfortable kitchen, a large dining room and a wash room for the men folks are absolutely necessary on the farm A downstairs bed room is very convenient. Or, for the farmer who prefers an office in his home to a downstairs bed room, this offers a possible solution.

The handsome cased opening between the living room and dining room adds spaciousness and comfort to both the rooms. This opening has been designed particularly wide so as to have the living room space available during threshing time, when the dining room is overcrowded at the noon day meal.

Only one stairway to the second floor of a farm house is needed if it is directly accessible from all parts of the house, as well as from the out doors. Our arrangement of the hall stair and side porch is ideal, and completely does away with the necessity of taking extra steps, and in bad weather is a protection to the freshly cleaned kitchen floor.

The hall and side porch arrangement also make it possible for the men to enter the dining room without having to pass through the kitchen or other rooms. This means that the housewife, busily engaged in the kitchen, need not be inconvenienced by persons passing

First Floor Plan

Second Floor Plan

through so frequently. Notice the good table space in the kitchen also.

What is better than plenty of pantry space? On the side walls of the pantry are cases consisting of doors and shelves clear to the ceiling and at the end walls beneath the window is a work table with drawers and a flour bin below.

This house has an abundance of light in all rooms. Upstairs we have four bed rooms, a bathroom and plenty of closet space in every

bed room. There is also a linen closet most conveniently located. Turn to the color section and see the design. The attic stairway opens from the hall. The attic extends over the entire house. The plans are for a house size basement reached by the cellar hatchway, and also by the inner stairway, which is just under te one going up from the second floor.

Unless otherwise instructed, we will furnish white paint for both body and trim of this home.

For Plumbing, Heating, Lighting for This Home, See Last Pages of Book

Gordon-Van Tine Home No. 610

Special Features in This Ideal Farm Home

This House Can Be Furnished With Siding or Shingles on Outside Walls Instead of Stucco. Write for Prices.
For Prices on This Home, See First Page.   **Read Pages 9 and 10 for Full Description of Materials.**

First Floor Plan

Second Floor Plan

THE farm home must be practical as well as big enough to meet the requirements—in addition there should be the desire to build a home that is also attractive.

In this ideal farm home, the interior affords a wealth of room, comfortable living quarters with the greatest convenience. The exterior has been given unusual attention and is decidedly attractive. It is a beautiful home.

Always welcome is the big front porch. On this home it adds to the attractive exterior.

The excellent placing of the windows gives each room in the entire house cross ventilation. This home will be cheerful and pleasant—always well-lighted and ventilated—because of the fine proportion of the windows.

Points of special interest in this home are the many excellent features provided. The wash room, directly accessible from the rear porch and convenient to the kitchen and dining room. The inter-connecting hall permitting direct passage from one room to another—in fact connecting all rooms.

The stairway—up or down—from this hall. The big dining room, a welcome necessity at threshing time. The handy coat closet in the hall just off from the dining room.

There's the big kitchen and the pantry with the big Gordon-Van Tine kitchen case, style "C". The linen closet in the upstairs hall handy to the bed rooms and bath. The grade door permitting direct entrance to cellar or kitchen. The big attic which is floored and well-lighted by twin windows in each gable and the dormer window.

This home in its entirety is a ready answer to the farmers, home problem.

The more you study this plan, the better you will like it. After you check up on our money-saving price you will decide to build it, and from that day on you'll have a perfect home on **your** farm.

PAINT—Unless otherwise instructed, we will furnish white paint for the trim of this home.

Gordon-Van Tine Co., Davenport, Iowa.
   Gentlemen: In answer to your inquiry about our house, will say that we are very well pleased with the quality of lumber that you sent us. The carpenter said it was as fine a grade of lumber as he ever worked with, and the painter said it was the first house he ever painted that he did not need any shellac to paint knots.
   W. C. Howenstine, Schenectady, N. Y.

For Plumbing, Heating, Lighting for This Home, See Last Pages of Book

Gordon-Van Tine Home No. 615A and 615B

A Charming English Half-Timbered Design

This Home Furnished with Siding or Shingles on Outside Walls instead of Stucco. Write for Prices.
For Prices on This Home, See First Page.
Read Pages 9 to 10 for Full Description of Materials.

A FEATURE of first importance of this home is the fact that it is only 22 ft. wide and therefore can easily be built on the 40 or 50 foot city or suburban lot.

The steep lines of the roof suggest the English type while the panelled gables of both porch and house proper carry out the effect in a most pleasing and harmonious manner.

Step into the well lighted, comfortable living room with its cheery fireplace in the center of one end. Opposite it is an open stair at the foot of which is a handy closet for coats and wraps. In the corner is a door leading to the kitchen, grade entrance or cellar. This passage makes it unnecessary to pass through the kitchen on the way to the garage and makes all parts of the first floor readily accessible to every other part.

You pass through a cased opening into the spacious dining room with its twin window and well arranged wall space. Notice that there is ample room for buffet and china closet in the corners nearest the living room, leaving the way to the breakfast room clear and unobstructed.

Imagine a breakfast here in early June with the fragrant morning air drifting through the open windows. We'll venture that you'll not only breakfast here but enjoy the other meals here as well for many months of the year. The location makes this room handy to either kitchen or dining room, yet the latter are directly connected by a swinging door.

The kitchen is planned that all useless steps may be eliminated. Type B kitchen case, with its work table right under one of the twin windows provides plenty of storage for pots, pans, knives, spoons and all utensils. The rear door opens on to a convenient porch.

Note the very handy space for the refrigerator near the grade entrance. It is close to the kitchen yet can be reached for icing from the grade door. Don't overlook the fine closet for brooms, mops, dust pan, etc., just off the hall connecting dining room and kitchen.

The front bed room with its three large windows and two deep closets leaves nothing to be desired. Each of the rear bed rooms has plenty of light and air, two good size closets and a door opening on to the sleeping porch. Should the larger of these two bed rooms be given over to guests, the sleeping porch can be utilized by members of the family, using the entrance from the smaller bed room.

One of our fine linen cases (see color section) is placed in the central hall within easy reach of all bed rooms and the bath.

For exterior, beauty, compact yet convenient arrangement, this plan offers a wonderful value in a home only 22 ft. wide.

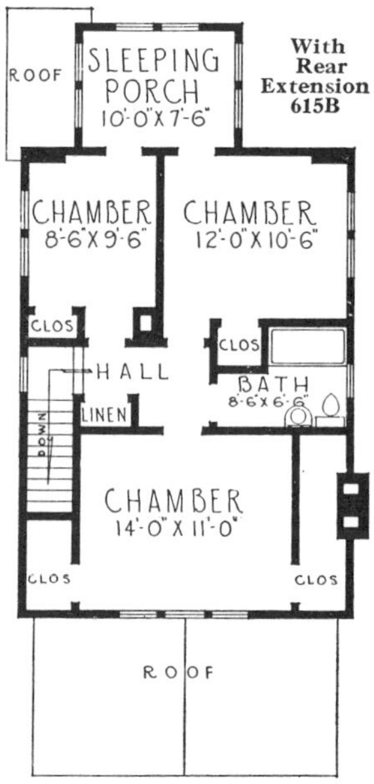

Second Floor

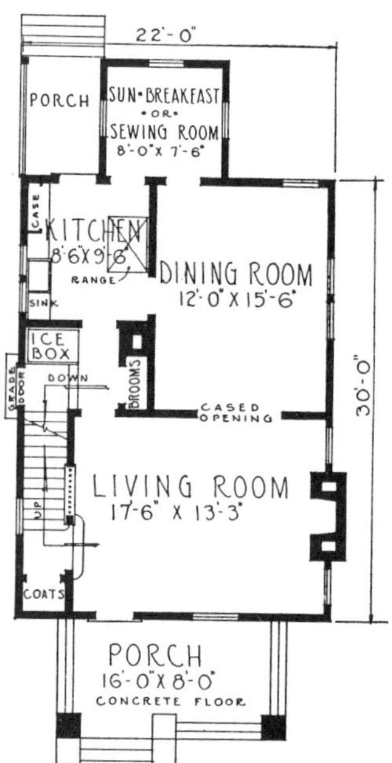

First Floor

Plan No. 615B is exactly as shown above. No. 615A omits the rear extension; the doors shown leading on to sleeping and sun porches are changed to windows, and a small stoop is furnished in place of the entry porch.

PAINT—Unless otherwise instructed we will furnish seal brown paint for the trim of this home. The walls are stucco.

For Plumbing, Heating, Lighting for This Home, See Last Pages of Book

Gordon-Van Tine Home No. 517 and 517-B.

This Charming Bungalow Has 4 Bedrooms

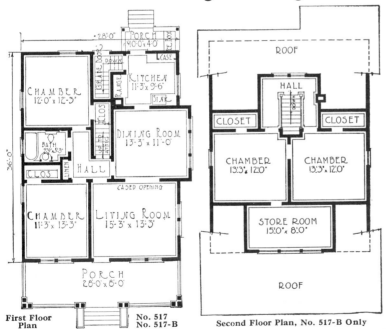

First Floor Plan   **No. 517**
     No. 517-B

Second Floor Plan, No. 517-B Only

PAINT—Unless otherwise instructed, we will furnish brown shingle stain for the wall shingles and white for the trim of this house.

For Prices on This Home, See First Page.

See Pages 9 and 10 for Full Description of Materials.

This home is priced in two ways. First, with the downstairs only finished off—the upstairs simply floored to be used as an attic. Second, the downstairs finished off complete and the upstairs also as is shown in the second floor plan indicated to the left.

ALL the appealing features of the bungalow are included in this charming home. The broad, low lines of the roof, with its dormers in the front and the rear, the heavy brackets, and the wide cornice, give it a distinctive touch.

In studying the side walls an unusual and attractive feature is instantly noticed, produced by carrying the shingled side walls down to the grade line.

The front porch has a stateliness about it that makes an instant appeal. The architectural effect is secured by proper grouping of the pillars.

The interior is especially cheerful and cozy. The window arrangement has much to do with this as well as with the good furniture spaces throughout.

The bed rooms and bath have a privacy always desirable. The closets are of unusual size. The linen closet off the downstairs hall is like the one shown in the center color pages.

Careful attention has also been given to the kitchen. The cabinet is the one shown on the colored insert as design "B." This is not far from a large window, in this way providing a light and sunny place for work.

A glazed door leads to the boxed up rear porch. There is also another outside glazed door at the cellar stair platform which is on the same level as the walk. Entrance to the kitchen, therefore, can be secured either from the grade door or from the rear porch.

Our plans call for a house sized basement. You will notice that we have provided the necessary windows. A well constructed house can never have too large a basement, because you may wish to provide a furnace room, a vegetable room and a laundry.

For Plumbing, Heating, Lighting for This Home, See Last Pages of Book

Gordon-Van Tine Home No. 531

Beautiful Sweeping Lines in This Bungalow

This House Can be Furnished with Siding or Shingles on Outside Walls Instead of Stucco. Write for Prices.

For Prices on This Home, See First Page.

Read Pages 9 and 10 for Full Description of Materials.

HERE is one solution of your problem of how to get the best results on the investment of your money. In this house you will have the compactness of the bungalow and still retain the privacy afforded by a second story.

The exterior walls are the popular stucco upon Byrkitt patent lath, while the dormer and roof are covered with Clear Red Cedar shingles. The Colonial windows, the full length of porch with its broad steps, and the projecting bay window hood are all attractive architectural features. This bay window which breaks up the straight exterior also gives a space for a window seat within.

The pleasing impression gained from the outside is kept upon entering, for to the right is the big fireplace, and to the left the opening into the den.   This room, by the way, has a closet, and upon necessity could easily be converted into a bed room.

The living room and dining room are practically one because of t h e plaster colonnade. Don't you see in, imagination, this great big cheery light room stretching from the front to the back of the house, with windows on three sides and a cosy little den opening off of it? Directly across from the front entrance is another door, leading to the stair hall and the kitchen.

The compact and convenient kitchen is just the right size to make work easy and still not give the feeling of being over crowded.   Notice the proximity of the space for the ice box in the entry to the kitchen case and sink.   The kitchen case is our design "B" as shown on the colored insert.   And by no means overlook the splendid closet just behind the rear entry door which opens on the ground level.

Upstairs are two nice bed rooms—rather different in shape from many—the linen closet, and the bath room in the rear.   The bed rooms have closets, plenty of windows, and can have a direct draft on hot summer nights because of the bath room and hall windows. Notice, too, the large floored attic. Indeed you will have a comfortable and convenient house if this is your choice.

First Floor Plan **Second Floor Plan**

PAINT—Unless otherwise instructed, we will furnish white paint for the trim of this home.

For Plumbing, Heating, Lighting for This Home, See Last Pages of Book

Gordon-Van Tine Home No. 588

A Skillfully Designed and Planned Bungalow

For Prices on This Home, See First Page.   **See Pages 9 and 10 for Full Description of Materials.**

IN this home you see another fine bungalow—one of the many excellent plans which have been so carefully developed by our skillful designers. You need only to study the floor plan and illustration to find those things which are so necessary to your venture—the sterling qualities which guarantee success—style, beauty, economy, convenience, comfort.

The outside walls are made most attractive by covering with shingles. The broad sweeping lines of the gable roof, continuing over the front porch, bears out the pleasing outlines most prominently.

Banding the house, just below the eaves, is a belt-course that also serves as a head casing on all outside frames, creating a suggestion of solidity and perfect harmony each part being one of the other.

In the shortened ridge line of the roof and subsequent treatment given in the battered gable ends there is an effect which is decidedly unique, and which is very popular because it so greatly adds to the charm of the exterior.

Over the dining room projection is placed a quaint hood giving protection and contributing to the beauty of the home.

In addition to this fine exterior we show you a floor plan that has proven the most popular in homes of this size.

The rooms are all well proportioned and of good size. All have windows in each outside wall, which permits cross ventilation. These rooms will be very pleasant —plenty of air and light everywhere. The front and rear doors are glazed bungalow doors of beautiful pattern.

The cased opening between the living and dining rooms gives to these rooms a very spacious appearance. If desirable, a pair of beautiful French doors can be set in this opening at a very small cost.

Every housewife who studies this plan will be interested in the perfectly arranged kitchen—notice particularly our big kitchen case, style "C," as shown on the colored insert, which is included at no extra cost. Notice also we furnish our Linen Closet in this home—here it is most conveniently placed in the hall between the two bedrooms and bath and just a step from the dining room.

The bedrooms and bath are separated from the living rooms by the hall—you will easily understand the advantages of this planning. Each bedroom has a big closet—there is also a handy coat-closet in the hall just as you enter from the dining room.

From the rear stoop, entrance is made through the entry, in which there is space for the ice-box, into the kitchen. Leading directly down from the entry is the cellar stairway—accessible from the kitchen or outside direct.

The front porch is but three steps high— the house is built low to intensify the low-down effect, conforming to bungalow construction.

The cellar sash are partly below grade —set in open areas which are to be drained into footing drain-tile.

This is a modest, thoroughly comfortable home—withal it is right-up-to-the-minute in design. You are sure to be favorably impressed, if it is a bungalow you want.

PAINT—Unless otherwise instructed, we will furnish brown shingle stain for wall shingles and white paint for trim. We do not furnish stain for roof shingles.

For Plumbing, Heating, Lighting for This Home, See Back of Book

Gordon-Van Tine Home No. 607

A Dutch Colonial Home of Rare Charm

For Prices on This Home, See First Page.
Read Pages 9 and 10 for Full Description of Materials.

SOME houses are just houses; others proclaim the fact that there is a home within. This home announces itself at first glance, and expresses the idea of cheer and hospitality. The entrance bespeaks a much warmer greeting than that given by the one time custom of carving "Welcome" over the house door

The true Dutch Colonial gambrel roof, the shingled walls, shuttered windows, and wide porch make this one of the most charming of places. And you need never worry that the home of your neighbor will darken your rooms, when your house is built with the long walls facing the front and rear.

Each detail of this home has been planned by men and women of practical experience, who have kept every possibility for comfort and pleasing appearance in mind.

From the attractive stoop one enters a vestibule having a large coat closet to the left. This arrangement leaves the hall proper, free from drafts, unencumbered and usable as a part of the living room when so wanted. This hall space sets off the open stairway most splendidly also.

A large fireplace occupies the center of the outside wall of the splendid living room, with French doors at the right of it, which lead to the comfortable living porch. The position of the porch at the side insures greater comfort and privacy.

Besides these French doors, there are in the living room, three large Colonial windows of the type found throughout the downstairs.

The dining room is equally well lighted, carefully planned and cheerful. It is of a size suited to the needs of this house.

The kitchen is a representative Gordon-Van Tine kitchen, well arranged with our special built-in kitchen case, design "D" (see color pages) and even a built-in broom closet. Three steps bring one down to the space for the refrigerator and the rear grade door, where the ice man can enter.

Upstairs are the bath, linen closet and three chambers, besides the hall which is well lighted by the windows on the stair landing. The bathroom as well as bedroom has unusual closet space. All the upstairs ceiling heights are eight feet in the clear.

You, of course, will build a basement under the entire house. Our blue prints provide for it and we furnish enough windows to give proper light and ventilation.

All lattice necessary to construct porches as shown is furnished. A mantel shelf, ash trap and dome damper are furnished for fireplace.

Second Floor Plan

First Floor Plan

PAINT—Unless otherwise instructed we will furnish silver gray shingle stain for wall shingles, white paint for trim and green paint for blinds. We do not furnish stain for roof shingles.

For Plumbing, Heating, Lighting for This Home, See Back of Book

Gordon-Van Tine Home No. 602

The House Beautiful

This House Furnished with Siding or Shingles on Outside Walls Instead of Stucco. Write for Prices

Second Floor Plan

First Floor Plan

For Prices on This Home, See First Page.
Read Pages 9 and 10 for Full Description of Materials.

WITHOUT a doubt this is one of the most beautiful houses in America today. Even in the illustration this house must appeal to you for its distinctiveness and for its absolute harmony in every detail. As you look at it, you feel that the long sloping roof, the dormers, the French windows and entrance, are all especially suited to one another, and to this house in particular.

The low set stucco walls without an exposed foundation, the area ways for the basement windows, the porch to the side and rear, all further the effect of the French style of architecture.

A glance at the floor plan here gives you an idea of its unusually fine arrangement. The immense living room with its French windows opening in three directions, its fireplace and the porch beyond leaves nothing to be desired. The library just back of this splendid big room is secluded as such a room should be, and because of its location can lend itself to various uses. It is easily accessible to all parts of the house, and has a closet of its own.

One of the especial features of this home is the excellent plan for the reception hall, which is left free to be what its name implies, because of the vestibule and two coat closets opening off of it. One entire side of the hall is given to the beautifully designed stairway, a pleasing idea in this particular style of house.

The kitchen has two big built-in cases, our designs "B" and "D" with the sink and work table each under a window. Ceilings downstairs are 8 feet 4½ inches high.

The plan of the back hall is worthy of especial attention. Here is a place for the refrigerator, next the kitchen door, a broom closet and clothes chute, and from here one reaches the maid's bath, the basement stairway, as well as the rear flight of the duplex stairway, an entrance to the library and the outside door.

The rectangular upstairs hall brings one to four unusually attractive rooms, the bath with its linen closet and trunk room. The clothes chute opens here also. The room to the left, almost as large as the living room, is equally well lighted and has two good sized closets, as has the next largest chamber. The room in the center front is particularly attractive because of the triple window extending almost across one entire wall. The maid's room has not been neglected either in light, closet space or cross ventilation.

Blinds are furnished for windows as shown.

PAINT—Unless otherwise instructed, we will furnish white paint for trim and green paint for blinds. We do not furnish stain for roof shingles.

For Plumbing, Heating, Lighting for This Home, See Back of Book

Gordon-Van Tine Home No. 584

Bungalow Home of Rare Charm

For Prices on This Home, See First Page.

See Pages 9 and 10 for Full Description of Materials.

IF the outside of a house shows the character of the people who live within, we venture to say that no one could do better than to let this house be representative of its occupants. The chief secret of the appearance of a house is usually found in the part the roof treatment plays in the harmony of the whole. Here the dormer window breaks any possible monotony that might result from an entirely plain over-hanging roof, and the roof in turn is one of the chief causes for the friendly aspect of this particular bungalow.

The effect is furthered by the attractive grouping of the Colonial window and the set-in porch with its broad steps and substantial columns, which are shingled like the house walls. This porch at once makes you think of the welcome shade it will afford you in the summertime, and the protection offered by it during any unpleasant weather. Notice that even this fine sized porch does not darken any of the rooms, for all three rooms looking onto it, also have a group of windows facing into the open.

The spacing in the large living room is especially good, and the fireplace is ideally placed where its glow can be enjoyed from the adjoining rooms also.

The cosy den, just off the living room, is large enough to be used as a bed room, when emergency requires, since the French doors between can be effectively curtained.

The dining room at the front of the house gives a splendid street view, and when its many windows at the side are open, admit much air and light into the living room, also through the open French doors connecting the two.

As the hostess in the average small house knows to her sorrow, it needs much ingenuity in seating guests at the dining table to place them so that they are not continually conscious of the happenings of the kitchen. This is usually not due to any fault in the arrangement of the dining room, but rather to the closeness of the kitchen. This difficulty is done away with here, by the pass pantry equipped with a work table, and wall case for china. Then, too, think how much pleasanter it would be to work in the pantry on a hot summer morning than to stand next to the lighted range in the kitchen.

The arrangement of the kitchen itself is excellent. The sink and work table have the best of light, and at the same time are near to the built-in case and pantry which is similar to the illustration shown in the color pages. The ice box has its proper place in the entry. A broom closet opens from here also, as do the basement stairway and the rear door. Kitchen case "D" is provided for the kitchen while our stock case "A" is furnished for the pantry.

The bath and two chambers are reached through the small hall opening from the living room. Off this hall is the linen closet also. Each chamber is well-lighted and ventilated and has unusual closet space. Notice that there are two closets for the room to the right.

Floor Plan

Nine cellar windows light up the entire basement which extends under the house proper, providing more than the necessary floor area for furnace and coal bins, fruit cellar and laundry.

We suggested that you would be willing to be judged by the exterior of this house if it were your home. And we know we are right in assuming that since you have become better acquainted with the house, you will want it for your home, for you surely recognize the comfort it can afford you and the excellent value it offers.

Mantel, dome damper and ash trap are furnished.

PAINT—Unless otherwise instructed, we will furnish brown shingle stain for side walls, and white for trim.

For Plumbing, Heating, Lighting for This Home, See Last Pages of Book

Gordon-Van Tine Home No. 537 and 537B

Furnished as Either a One or Two Floor Home

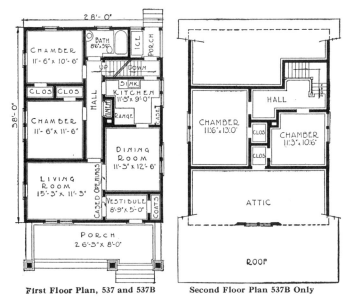

First Floor Plan, 537 and 537B **Second Floor Plan 537B Only**

PAINT—Unless otherwise instructed, we will furnish cream paint for the body, white for trim and oxide red for the wall shingles of this home.

AFTER SIX YEARS

Gordon-Van Tine Comapny, Davenport, Iowa.   Pueblo, Colo., Nov. 1, 1916.
Gentlemen: In April and May, 1910, I purchased of you three carloads of lumber to be shipped to Numa, Colo., for building houses and barn for myself and Mr. A. R. Widick, of Ordway.   My dealings with you at that time were so satisfactory and your prices so reasonable, and the quality of your material so good that I naturally think of you at this time as I am in the market for a lot of millwork for my home and garage, which I am now erecting in Pueblo.
W. L. Hartman,
(Hartman & Ballreich.)

For Prices on This Home, See First Page.

Read Pages 9 and 10 for Full Description of Materials.

A VIEW of the outside of this house at once gives you the impression that this would be a most livable place. It's a home that attracts the passerby because of the lines of the long sloping roof, the quaint dormer window and the effect of the shingles and siding divided at the belt course. The use of cottage windows, a corresponding door and the boxed-in porch are all characteristic of good design.

When someone comes in on a stormy, windy night the occupants of the living room will appreciate the fact that entrance is made into the vestibule. And the coat closet at the right of the vestibule is the most appropriate and convenient place for wraps either in winter or summer.

The living room has splendid ventilation and excellent light. Opposite the twin windows it offers a balancing wall space for davenport, piano or another correspondingly large piece of furniture.

The effect of space in this room is heightened by the wide cased opening into the dining room. This almost throws these two rooms into one, and still does not bring to view the kitchen door, often known to open at inopportune moments. The dining room, which is also well lighted by twin windows, has an unusual amount of unbroken wall space.

The kitchen is compactly arranged so makes many steps unnecessary. The working space is compact and our "B" design case makes the work itself easy.

The distance to be covered by the housewife in a day's work could in this kitchen be reduced to the minimum. There is splendid refrigerator space on the rear porch.

The arrangement of the hall is an excellent feature—it communicates with every room, except the dining room, which, however, is easily accessible. The linen closet off the hall is large enough to hold various supplies, all within easy reach of the places where needed.

Steps ascend from the rear to the upstairs. In No. 537 the upstairs is simply a floored attic. In 537B the upstairs is finished off as shown in the upstairs floor plan.

One of the very satisfactory features in this bungalow is the location of the bath. It is near to all the sleeping rooms and still apart from the living room. The bath room itself is well planned offering another convincing evidence of the general convenience here.

The basement is light and airy, is under the entire house, and has ample room for a laundry and general basement in addition to the furnace and fuel room.

For Plumbing, Heating, Lighting for This Home, See Last Pages of Book

Gordon-Van Tine Home No. 604

A Distinguished Colonial Home

**For Prices on This Home See First Page.
Read Pages 9 and 10 for Full Description of Materials.**

THERE is a restful charm, a sort of quiet, well-bred dignity unaffected by time or style that distinguishes the Old New England Homes, and has made them models of real home architecture—a note which the architects were fortunate enough to catch and preserve in this excellent example of a modernized New England Colonial Home.

The quaint dormers throw light and ventilation into the attic, at the same time adding in attractiveness. And the shuttered windows also present a double argument for beauty and utility.

The outside walls are shingled—laid in alternate courses of 7 and 2 inches each—adding greatly to the harmonious exterior of this house.

The massive pillars supporting the roof of the trellised porches, are of the same design as the stately columns of the hooded entry.

This entry leads into a vestibule having a coat closet to the left, and at the right of the entrance to the hall proper there is another splendid closet.

The wide open hallway, with its cased openings into the adjoining rooms makes really one splendid big room of the entire front of the house.

The large living room is both individual and artistic. It has such an unusual number of especially attractive features—the French doors on both sides of the fireplace, the casement windows at either end and also the excellent wall space for furniture. The dining room also has the broad casement sash, besides two additional windows on the adjoining wall, all placed to the best advantage for the arranging of dining room furniture of any size.

The passage from the dining room is through the butler's pantry to the kitchen. Do not overlook the great number of cases in the kitchen and pantry. In the kitchen you find both our case "B", "A" and special "C" case, as well as the convenient broom closet and in the pantry two "B" cases with only a slight variation.

The ice box can be iced from the rear porch if placed as planned in the butler's pantry. Here it will be accessible to the kitchen and dining room as well as the pantry, and likewise have the coolest spot in the house. This entire department is thus kept separate. The duplex stairs ascend from the kitchen as well as from the front hall—the accepted, best practice.

The hall on the second floor is large and light. The linen closet, as shown on the colored plate, is here. The bedrooms are almost equally large and light and well supplied with closet room. Two of them open through French doors onto the splendid large porch—a real haven on warm summer nights. And the little sewing room next to it is a most convenient feature.

From the upper hall an open stairway leads to the attic, which is floored. It is house size and of equal height with the other ceilings, for its entire length and for 10 feet in width—a splendid big room.

Blinds, window boxes and trellis are furnished as shown.

Second Floor Plan

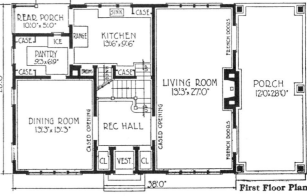

First Floor Plan

PAINT—Unless otherwise instructed, we will furnish silver gray shingle stain for body, white for trim, and bright green for blinds.

For Plumbing, Heating, Lighting for This Home, See Last Pages of Book

Gordon-Van Tine Home No. 563

An Impressive Colonial Home

First Floor Plan   Second Floor Plan

For Prices on This Home, See First Page.

Read Pages 9 and 10 for Full Description of Material.

THIS is a 365 day in the year house, one that assures you annually of twelve months of pleasure and satisfaction.

The plain substantial lines, the broad shuttered Colonial windows, the living and sleeping porch, all bespeak a house that is built with comfort in mind. Since there is always a fondness for Colonial architecture, this house will remain equally satisfactory as time goes on.

The Colonial entrance, with its red brick steps, attractive hood and ornamental brackets, is most inviting, and well in keeping with the general scheme of the house.

From the hall one gets a charming view across the wide living room, and through the French doors to the sun porch, on the other side. The hall itself is spacious, and so arranged as to leave much space available for the furniture. The big light living room with the fireplace making cheerful the gloomy days and cold evenings of winter, is in keeping with the rest of the plan. It is of ideal proportions and the wall space is ideally arranged to take care of the larger pieces of furniture and leave plenty of room for bookshelves, etc. The large coat closet at the left of the fireplace is a convenience that will be appreciated.

The unique feature of this plan, and the one which has endeared it to builders in all parts of the country is the porches. The liv-

ing porch, with French doors opening from both living room and dining room gives an air of spaciousness unusual in a home of this size. It practically doubles the size of the living room and makes an ideal breakfast porch at the same time.

The large dining room with excellent window and wall space, permits of an excellent view in three directions

The butler's pantry between this and the kitchen keeps kitchen sights, sounds and odors well removed. The pantry case is a special design, extending around two side of the pantry from floor to ceiling. The kitchen itself will prove to be a comfortable and convenient place in which to work.

The hob nails of the ice man's boots need give no terror here, for the refrigerator can stand on the back porch or in the inner hall. Also note the broom closet here. From the kitchen a combination stairway leads up to the main stair landing. Under these stairs is a grade door, leading both to the kitchen and the basement. There is also a door, leading into the front hall and stairs to the second floor go up from this hall also.

The basement is extended under the house proper, assuring ample room for furnace, coal and wood rooms, fruit cellar and laundry, while seven cellar sash, which we furnish, promise ample light.

Upstairs are four well lighted rooms and plenty of closet space. Light and ventilation have been given equal attention everywhere, for each room has two exposures. The sleeping porch is unusually large and airy, and can be reached from two of the chambers.

The ready-cut linen closet is also conveniently placed. From the square upper hall, stairs lead to the attic, which is all floored, and well lighted by the dormers at the front and side.

The price quoted on page 1 does not include sectional sash and hardware for the sun and sleeping porch. Additional prices on these items will be quoted on request.

PAINT—Unless otherwise instructed, we will furnish white paint for body and trim and green paint for blinds. We do not furnish stain for roof shingles

For Plumbing, Heating, Lighting for This Home, See Back of Book

Gordon-Van Tine Home No. 600

Sleeping Porch and Four Bedrooms in This Ideal Suburban Home

For Prices on This Home, See First Page.
Read Pages 9 and 10 for Full Description of Materials.

SOLID, substantial worth is the immediate and lasting impression one gets of this home. Any possible severity of line is at once dispelled by the beautiful and extremely hospitable entrance. Just inside the door is a vestibule on either side of which are convenient coat closets. Beyond, is a centrally located reception hall from which direct access is had to all parts of the house. Straight ahead is a passageway to the rear entrance providing a means of getting to and from the garage without going through the kitchen.

Step into the spacious living room. At the far end, so that its warmth and cheer are felt throughout the room, is the fireplace, flanked by a window on either side. Plenty of unbroken wall space permits of most advantageous placing of furniture. Two pairs of French doors lead to the broad comfortable porch.

This porch with its solid boxed rail is easily screened and will form a delightful retreat on hot summer evenings.

From the opposite side of the reception hall one enters the large, well lighted dining room. Notice the ideal location for buffet along the rear wall.

Study the plan of this wonderfully compact kitchen for a moment. Large windows admit a flood of light from two directions; two of our complete and convenient kitchen cases provide out-of-sight storage for all necessary utensils and supplies. There is plenty of room to work in, yet everything is close at hand. Almost within the kitchen itself our architects have devised a nook for the refrigerator. A handy clothes chute is just outside the kitchen door. Can you imagine a better arranged or more convenient and labor saving kitchen than this one?

Our architects have even found room for a toilet and lavatory on the first floor—a most unusual feature in a house as moderately priced as this one.

Four good sized bedrooms and a sleeping porch insure comfortable and ample sleeping accommodations for even the larger than average family. Each of these bedrooms has a fine closet with shelf.

One of our linen closets with shelves and drawers is built into the hall wall within easy reach of the bath and all bedrooms.

The bath is notable because of its unusually large size, which is in keeping with a home of this character.

Space permits only a brief outline of the attractive features of this home here. As you study the plan and picture this home on the lot you have in mind, its beauty and comfort become more and more apparent. From any viewpoint, it is the ideal home for city suburb or small town.

PAINT—Unless otherwise instructed, we will furnish white paint for body and trim and green paint for blinds. We do not furnish stain for roof shingles.

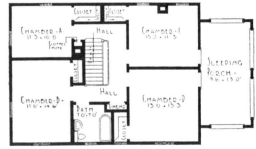

Second Floor Plan

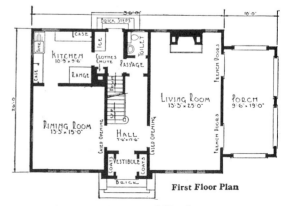

First Floor Plan

For Plumbing, Heating, Lighting for this Home, See Last Pages of Book

Gordon-Van Tine Home No. 505

An Extremely Popular Home—
Note the Two Porches

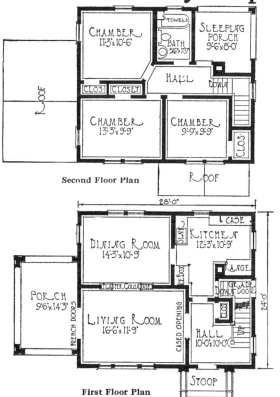

Second Floor Plan

First Floor Plan

For Prices on This Home, See First Page.
Read Pages 9 and 10 for Full Description of Materials.

IN a certain mid-western city there are no less than eighteen examples of this identical home. And every owner is enthusiastic, proving that this is a house not only good to look at but also to live in.

The exposed rafter ends, the hooded stoop, and the San Diego front door add greatly to the exterior appearance, as does also the sun porch. This and the sleeping porch in the rear are especial features.

The entire interior is compact and convenient. The coat closet off the reception hall is one illustration of this. It would be hard to secure an equal impression of space from an equal number of feet except by the arrangement of the cased opening between the living room and hall, the French doors just opposite, leading to the sun porch, and the plaster colonnade—which connects the living room and dining room. Illustrations of the French doors and colonnade appear in the colored section.

The compact well arranged kitchen is equipped with our kitchen case "D", that provides room for all kitchen equipment. The hallway connecting the front and rear porch of the house offers a convenient place for the refrigerator without making it necessary for the iceman to cross the kitchen. Below the steps leading from this hallway, the rear and grade doors are combined—a saving in space and money.

The inner hall is in truth one of the especially convenient features, for it makes possible passage to the front door, or the second story without crossing the living or dining room.

Upstairs there are three chambers with spacious closets opening off of each, bath and sleeping porch all under the same roof.

Prices on sash for the sun porch will be quoted on request.

PAINT—Unless otherwise instructed we will furnish brown stain for the wall shingles and white paint for the body and trim.

For Plumbing, Heating, Lighting for This Home, See Last Pages of Book

Gordon-Van Tine Home No. 593

Comfortable, Prosperous Looking Farm Home

Options That Will Save You $158.50

Deduct the above amount from the regular price on this house if you are willing to buy it with the following changes from regular specifications:

6 to 2 Star A Star Red Cedar Shingles instead of 5 to 2 Clear; plain square edge casings for doors and windows instead of Craftsman design; all subflooring and kitchen case omitted.

For Prices on This Home, See First Page. See Pages 9 and 10 for Full Description of Materials.

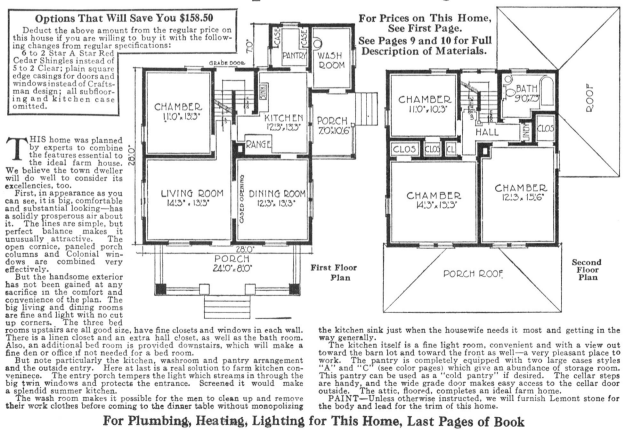

First Floor Plan

Second Floor Plan

THIS home was planned by experts to combine the features essential to the ideal farm house. We believe the town dweller will do well to consider its excellencies, too.

First, in appearance as you can see, it is big, comfortable and substantial looking—has a solidly prosperous air about it. The lines are simple, but perfect balance makes it unusually attractive. The open cornice, paneled porch columns and Colonial windows are combined very effectively.

But the handsome exterior has not been gained at any sacrifice in the comfort and convenience of the plan. The big living and dining rooms are fine and light with no cut up corners. The three bed rooms upstairs are all good size, have fine closets and windows in each wall. There is a linen closet and an extra hall closet, as well as the bath room. Also, an additional bed room is provided downstairs, which will make a fine den or office if not needed for a bed room.

But note particularly the kitchen, washroom and pantry arrangement and the outside entry. Here at last is a real solution to farm kitchen conveniece. The entry porch tempers the light which streams in through the big twin windows and protects the entrance. Screened it would make a splendid summer kitchen.

The wash room makes it possible for the men to clean up and remove their work clothes before coming to the dinner table without monopolizing

the kitchen sink just when the housewife needs it most and getting in the way generally.

The kitchen itself is a fine light room, convenient and with a view out toward the barn lot and toward the front as well—a very pleasant place to work. The pantry is completely equipped with two large cases styles "A" and "C" (see color pages) which give an abundance of storage room. This pantry can be used as a "cold pantry" if desired. The cellar steps are handy, and the wide grade door makes easy access to the cellar door outside. The attic, floored, completes an ideal farm home.

PAINT—Unless otherwise instructed, we will furnish Lemont stone for the body and lead for the trim of this home.

For Plumbing, Heating, Lighting for This Home, Last Pages of Book

Gordon-Van Tine Home No. 598

A Charming Colonial Bungalow

Read Pages 9 and 10 for Full Description of Material.

**For Prices on This Home,
See First Page.**

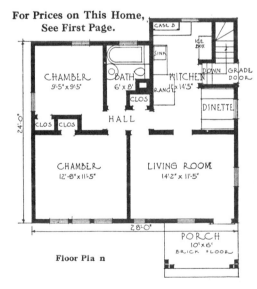

Floor Plan

THE grace and dignity which designers of Colonial times imparted to the homes they built in the Golden Age of Architecture is faithfully portrayed in this beautiful bungalow home.

Building it low to the ground gives it that substantial, inviting look which is the great charm of the Colonial—a feature which is accentuated by the low sweeping roof lines and battered gable ends.

The shingled walls and flower box soften the lines and complete the beauty of the exterior.

Inside this compact home is the comfort and convenience which comes only from skillful planning and the addition of every modern housekeeping help. Notice how the small central hall connects every room and yet gives absolute privacy to the bedrooms. You can go straight to the room you want to reach without passing through another and disturbing its occupants.

Notice the kitchen with its convenient arrangement of sink, range and pantry case and that handiest feature

of modern planning, the dinette, provided in a nook of its own. Space for the ice box is provided right in the room, and the use of the grade door for both kitchen and cellar door is a money-saving convenience.

Can't you see how **easy** the housework is in this most convenient of homes? Imagine preparing a meal in this handy kitchen. Why you can almost sit on a stool in the center of the room and touch sink, ice box, kitchen case and range without moving. You can set the table and attend to your cooking at the same time—and to reach any part of the house is only ten steps. Note the fine size of the rooms—the closets (including the convenient one in the hall), the splendid arrangement of windows that gives you fine ventilation and yet saves plenty of wall space. It isn't the amount of ground a house covers, it's the planning that determines the amount of living space there is in it—and this bungalow has more usable space than many homes of twice its size—at a corresponding saving in cost to build, to heat and to keep up.

PAINT—Unless otherwise instructed we will furnish green shingle stain for wall shingles and white paint for trim of this home.

For Plumbing, Heating, Lighting for This Home, See Last Pages of Book

Gordon-Van Tine Home No. 603

A Typical Colonial Home with Sun Porch

For Prices on This Home, See First Page.
Read Pages 9 and 10 for Full Description of Materials.

THIS is an example of distinction in the practical residence.

The gambrel roof and the cut off gable ends are reminders of Old Dutch Colonial architecture. The entrance with its gabled hood, supported by round pillars adds dignity, and gives just the desired protection to the hall.

The entrance separate from the living porch is always an advantage. Thus the porch is left, to be used almost as a room, and not also as a passageway. This placing of the porch also leaves the living and dining room windows free to air, light and sun.

The plan is open on one side through the dining room, on the other across the hall and living room beyond, to the sun porch, affording house width ventilation and view. The coat closet at the rear of the hall is conveniently situated, practically out of view of the living rooms, but near to them, and also to the front entrance.

The well proportioned big family room, made to seem even larger by the wide opening into the hall, and French doors onto the sun porch, has ample furniture space. This room is unusual in that it receives light and air from practically four directions. The sun porch can easily be made a real part of the house, at only a slight additional expense.

The kitchen is a handy work room,

with its built-in kitchen case and work table, conveniently placed in regard to both the sink and range.

This case is quite similar to our design "C." The table is immediately under the window, a fact which assures plenty of light.

The outside rear door and basement stairs lead from the entry off the kitchen, where there is also space for the refrigerator, easily accessible from the kitchen and the outside door, to the delight of both the ice man and the housewife.

While discussing the accessibility of the basement, it is worth while to know that it extends under the entire house, thus assuring plenty of room, not only for the furnace and coal rooms, but for fruit cellar and laundry as well. These rooms can be well lighted with the six cellar sash that we supply.

The upstairs hall which takes up no unnecessary room brings one to the bath, linen closet and three well sized bed rooms, all with good closet space. The linen closet is of our stock design. The bedroom to the right affords three closets, an unusual luxury, indeed. It has also been especially favored with windows in three directions.

For all practical purposes, the second floor rooms are of full height ceilings, except for a small portion in the win-

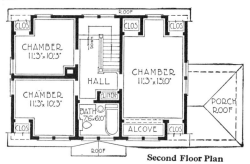

Second Floor Plan

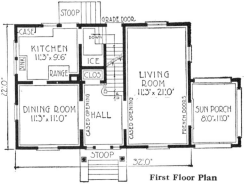

First Floor Plan

dow projection where it drops to a point of 7 feet from the floor. Clever planning provides for an air space overhead, and so assure cool rooms on hot days and nights.

The attractive shingled walls add greatly to the appearance of this home. Shingles are spaced 6 inches to the weather to secure wide Colonial effect.

PAINT—Unless otherwise instructed, we will furnish silver gray stain for wall shingles and white paint for trim. We do not furnish stain for roof shingles.

For Plumbing, Heating, Lighting for This Home, See Back of Book

Gordon-Van Tine Home No. 601

A Thoroughly Satisfactory Home

This House Furnished With Siding or Shingles on Outside Walls Instead of Stucco. Write for Prices

For Prices See First Page.   Read Pages 9 and 10 for
Full Description of Materials.

Second Floor Plan

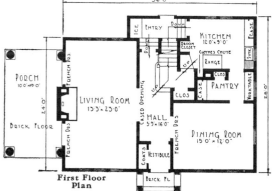

First Floor Plan

THE charm of the true Colonial is perennial. Born in a day when "home" meant comfort, and good living and open hearted hospitality—this distinctly American type has survived the horrors of the Mansard era and the Victorian period with its turrets and fretwork and iron dogs in the front yard, and comes down to us more than ever firmly established as the accepted standard of good taste.

The example of this splendid type shown above is remarkably correct in design and detail, retaining all the dignity and grace and vigor that distinguishes the true Colonial, yet embodying the modern ideas of comfort and convenience in which we have progressed so wonderfully.

The stucco walls, flower boxes under the triple downstairs windows and the wide porch are all modern ideas that will be appreciated.

The plan is thoroughly modern, and one of the most satisfactory we have ever designed. Note the fine porportion of the big living room, and the volume of light it receives from the two triple windows and the French doors on either side of the fireplace. The dining room, too, is excellent in proportion and wall space.

The planning of the hall is a real achievement. Back of the dining room it is offset enough to allow a passage down to the grade door, thus permitting one to go directly into the house from the garage or to go directly down cellar or out of the back door without passing through the kitchen. This arrangement of hall and stairs also permits a combination stairway so that one may go directly upstairs from the kitchen. There is a hall closet from this stair landing—also a coat closet off the vestibule. The pantry is fitted with a fine case and worktable and a closet as well. Note that it is lighted with a window right over the worktable. The kitchen has a big case extending from floor to ceiling, such as is shown on the color pages, and a broom closet as well. There are three windows in the kitchen. The refrigerator is placed in the rear entry, where it is cool and where the ice man can get at it without disturbing the kitchen.

Note the four fine sleeping rooms upstairs, and the big bath room. A large linen closet is provided, big closets for each bedroom and a clothes chute opening right besides the bathroom door. There is also a closet on the stair landing.

In design, in arrangement, in equipment, this comes very near indeed to our ideal of what a real home should be.

PAINT—Unless otherwise instructed, we will furnish white paint for trim and bright green paint for blinds. The walls are stucco for which we furnish Byrkitt patent sheathing.

For Plumbing Heating, Lighting for This Home, See Last Pages of Book

Gordon-Van Tine Home No. 512

An Unusually Well Planned Bungalow Home

For Prices on This Home, See First Page.
Read Pages 9 and 10 for Full Description of Materials.

THIS extremely homelike looking bungalow justifies our claim that it is a wonderfully complete six-room house. It appeals to the farmer as well as the city man. The lines given by the timbering, too, are rather unusual, and the brackets and exposed rafter ends add also.

The overhanging roof, the shingled walls and the large fireplace chimney, bespeaking a cosy living room, make their distinct appeal.

You can't help but like the shingled walls, stained either brown or green, with a white trim.

The porch is big and roomy, and whether surrounded by a shaded lawn or open to every bit of sun and air it will always be an inviting place. Such a porch protects the entrance from rain and snow, and prevents any concern to the housewife, caused by muddy feet coming in directly from the street or yard.

The porch rail and pillars are of a plain, substantial design, especially suited to the simpler style of home.

Not alone for its very attractive exterior does this bungalow commend itself—it is one of the best planned homes of the type. The large living room has a handsome fireplace, for which we furnish dome damper, ash trap and mantel shelf. The windows on either side of the fireplace, and the twin windows in the front make this an unusually light and cheery room. Notice the splendid wall space opposite the fireplace, where the largest living room furniture can be placed. The location of the coat closet is an ingenious bit of architecture.

The dining room is the light, cheery room that it ought to be, with space especially well planned. There is ample room for passage to the inner hall and kitchen, as well as for all the usual dining room furniture, even when the dining table has been extended to accommodate a large family.

The kitchen is conveniently equipped as all our kitchens are with a Gordon-Van Tine kitchen case, in this instance design D. The arrangement planned for the other kitchen furniture is excellent also.

The closet off the kitchen is a welcome place for the garden hat and basket, or for brooms and mops, if this be preferable, and the entry just across takes you to the basement and refrigerator, which can be iced from the outside, and still easily reached from the kitchen.

In many bungalows, the bedrooms open directly from the dining room and living room. Here, two of them are reached by means of a little inner hall—a much more satisfactory device. The stairway to the attic, which is over the entire house, ascends from this hall also. The door to the rear entry is glazed.

And though this house may appear only of average size, it affords two bedrooms and maid's room. The latter is entirely removed, but has been planned with no less care than the other chambers.

PAINT—Unless otherwise instructed we will furnish Brown Shingle Stain for the wall shingles and White Paint for the trim for this house.

Floor Plan

(Floor plan labels: STOOP 5'-0"x4'-0"; 28'-0"; DOWN; ICE; CLOS; CASE; KITCHEN 15'-3"x10'-9"; MAID'S ROOM 11'-3"x8'-6"; RANGE; CLOS; CHAMBER 11'-3"x10'-0"; SINK; DINING ROOM 11'-9"x13'-0"; HALL; BATH 7'-9"x5'-6"; LINEN; COAT CLOS; CASED OPENING; CLOSET; LIVING ROOM 15'-3"x13'-0"; CHAMBER 11'-3"x13'-0"; PORCH 18'-0"x8'-0"; 42'-0")

Grimes, Iowa.

Gordon-Van Tine Co., Davenport, Iowa.

Gentlemen: I received your letter asking me about the house. It is all completed. My carpenters tell me that I saved $300 by sending to you for the lumber. Am well pleased with the house. Had an abundance of everything to finish. Will send you a picture when I get one taken.

(Signed) Sadie B. Jack.

For Plumbing, Heating, Lighting for This Home, See Last Pages of Book

Gordon-Van Tine Home No. 527

Specially Designed for the Farm Family

For Prices on This Home, See First Page.   **Read Pages 9 and 10 for Full Description of Materials.**

First Floor Plan   **Second Floor Plan**

Options That Will Save You $145.20

Deduct the above amount from the regular price on this house if you are willing to buy it with the following changes from regular specifications:

6 to 2 Star A Star Red Cedar Shingles instead of 5 to 2 Clear; Plain square edge casings for doors and windows instead of Craftsman design; all subflooring and kitchen case omitted.

WE have given much thought to planning houses that will prove entirely satisfactory for country homes. Our idea has never been to make them less attractive, but on the contrary more convenient and suitable for their purpose. The plan shown here is the result of well worked out suggestions received from the farmer and his wife.

The house is large and roomy and substantial and at the same time of pleasing aspect, resulting from a combination of the attractive and practical.

The two dormers both have large double windows which light the large roomy attic—an unusual present day feature.

The clear siding, the Clear Red Cedar Shingles, the Fir porch floors are some of the proofs of satisfaction in exterior construction. The interior trim is clear Fir. The front door is our Monterey design, glazed double strength. This door and the three large windows provide an abundance of light and air in the living room—a very desirable feature.

All the five nice large main rooms are spacious and comfortable—the dining especially so. The room planned for the library can readily be converted into a parlor or front bed room, if either is more to be desired.

Summer work can be made very comfortable in this kitchen, since fresh air can be admitted from at least three directions. It is big and well planned with ample wall space for an oil stove, as well as a range and a large work table and sink. The pantry also is large enough for a goodly stock of supplies and is provided with a splendid case of special design. Entrances from the wash room are so arranged as to give direct access from the outside to either the kitchen or the dining room. Access to the basement is gained directly from the kitchen and from the outside on the walk level. This grade entrance has been made especially wide, to permit the passage of barrels, boxes, and other bulky articles.

Many houses have four rooms on the second floor but few of them have four large well-lighted sleeping rooms that will prove always comfortable and pleasant, with a splendid closet opening off of each. The bath room is also on the second floor. A closet with five shelves in the hall provides a convenient storage for linen, etc. This, beyond a doubt, is a model farm home at a most nominal cost.

PAINT—Unless otherwise instructed, we will furnish white paint for both body and trim.

PRETTIEST HOUSE IN COALGATE

Gordon-Van Tine Company, Davenport, Iowa.   *Coalgate, Oklahoma.*

Gentlemen: I have my house finished and it is given out that I have the prettiest house in Coalgate, built with your lumber and painted with your paints. I am going to have some pictures made of my house soon, and will send you one, with a letter that will do you some good if you want to use it. Coalgate is going to build this year, both business houses and residences, so don't delay in sending books. Yours truly, J. F. Clark.

For Plumbing, Heating, Lighting for This Home, See Last Pages of Book

Gordon-Van Tine Home No. 599

A Beautiful and Most Practical Home

For Prices on This Home, See First Page.
Read Pages 9 and 10 For Full Description of Materials.

This Home Furnished with Siding and Shingles on Outside Walls Instead of Stucco. Write for Prices.

THERE is a feeling of the Colonial about this home. If we may be allowed such a term, we could call it a Modern Colonial. The severity of the straight lines of the roof and dormer are relieved by the graceful sweep of the quaint entrance. The spacing of the windows is very well planned and the side porch, besides being an important element in the plan, is really necessary to complete the exterior. The fan light above the panelled door is typically Colonial. The exterior of this home is stucco.

The promise of beauty and comfort given by the exterior is more than met by the splendid plan which our architects have worked out. One enters the hall through a roomy vestibule. At the left is a good sized closet for coats. The passage directly back leads on into the kitchen. To the right is the living room, and while it is not possible to visualize all the charm of this room from the plan, still one may get some idea. Note the splendid proportions of this room and the fine light contributed by the triple front window and the French doors opening on to the porch. A most beautiful touch is the fireplace recessed under the plaster arch. The floor is tiled under the arch and the grateful glow of the open fire seems to take on added beauty when seen in this cozy nook.

The dining room is large and very light. Note that it also opens on the porch, through French doors. Connecting it with the kitchen is a fine pantry. Notice that a work table has been provided under the

window and a large case against the back wall.

This case is like to that of the design shown in the color section and extends from floor to ceiling. A similar case is also placed in the kitchen. There is a large closet in the pantry and altogether there is room enough for all the china, linen and other supplies necessary.

Note the splendid plan of the kitchen. Three windows make it unusually light. The big case gives plenty of room to keep all equipment and supplies. The ice box is in a separate entry where it is handy yet out of the way and can be reached without entering the kitchen proper. The double door of this entry serves to make the kitchen unusually warm in winter. A door leads directly through to the front hall upstairs. The door into this little hall way leads down cellar or out through the grade entrance. Any part of the house can be reached from the kitchen in just a step. And do not overlook the broom closet which is provided and has ample room for all cleaning equipment, aprons and the other things so hard to dispose of.

Upstairs one finds four large bedrooms, each having at least two windows with cross ventilation. Even the smallest is a good sized room and the largest, 16 ft.-9 in.x12 feet is unusually big. This latter room has two closets—each of the other rooms have a closet and there is a big linen closet opening off the hall. The bath room is handy to all bed rooms.

There is no waste space in this house. There is not an element omitted to make it a fine home to live in and it has many convenience features which homes twice the size do not boast. It is one of the finest designs we know of and we recommend it as giving one hundred cents value for every dollar in a thoroughly beautiful, liveable home.

PAINT—Unless otherwise instructed we will furnish white paint for trim. The walls are stucco, for which we furnish Byrkitt patent sheathing.

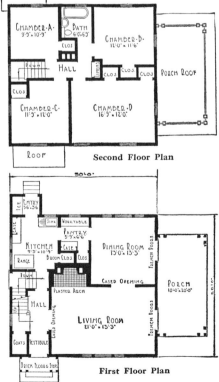

Second Floor Plan

First Floor Plan

For Plumbing, Heating, Lighting for This Home, See Last Pages of Book

Gordon-Van Tine Home No. 594

Real Comfort in this Farm Bungalow

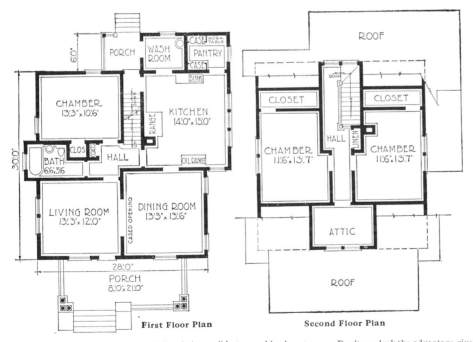

First Floor Plan

Second Floor Plan

For Prices on This House, See First Page.

Read Pages 9 and 10 for Full Description of Materials.

The front dormer is larger than the rear dormer—it provides pleasant space for a small sewing room. Twin Colonial windows are set in each dormer. The rear dormer window lights the upstairs hall and provides head-room for the stairway. Twin windows set in the gables of each side wall assure ample light and air for the two bed rooms upstairs.

Space is added to bath room and good proportion made possible in the center hall by the projection on the left wall over which is gracefully placed a quaint hood. On the right side the kitchen and pantry project 4 feet over which extends the slope of the main roof showing a continuous line.

The kitchen is really exceptional—the big triple window in the right wall assures good light and air. The cold pantry just off the kitchen also has an outside window and is equipped with the Gordon-Van Tine kitchen cases, styles "A" and "C." See these designs on the colored insert.

Note the wash room entered direct from the rear porch — the direct entrance to cellar from rear porch— also from the kitchen there is a door opening onto same landing. All outside doors are glazed doors of beautiful pattern.

BEFORE you is positive proof that it is possible to combine beauty and practicability in the farm home. Our designers in perfecting this exceptional home have found the happy medium where the need for room does not exceed the three bed rooms and usual living rooms. This story-and-a-half home is decidedly attractive, both inside and out.

The charm of the exterior is obvious—the big front porch always a welcome addition, with the two sets of round columns setting on brick piers at rail height, the walls sided to the belt course—this belt serves as the head casing on all outside frames—above the belt the gable walls and dormers are shingled. The top section of the side gables and the dormer gables are paneled. Brackets assist in the exterior decoration.

Don't overlook the advantage given in the plan by the center hall around which all rooms are grouped. Thus are all rooms made readily accessible from each other—the stairway leads up from this hall. Notice the handy coat closet at the end of this hall.

A study of the plan will show you many other points of interest which our limited space does not permit us to mention. Here is really a most desirable home for the farm or town, and at our low cost for the home complete, there should not be a moment's hesitation in choosing it.

PAINT—Unless otherwise instructed, we will furnish green shingle stain for the wall shingles and white paint for the remainder of the body and trim of this home.

For Plumbing, Heating, Lighting for This Home, See Last Pages of Book

Gordon-Van Tine Homes

Gordon-Van Tine Home No. 509

The Biggest Little Home You Can Buy

This house furnished with siding or shingles on outside walls instead of stucco.   Write for prices.

For Prices on This Home, See First Page.

Read Pages 9 and 10 for Full Description of Materials.

HERE is a home to please the most critical.   The picture hardly does it justice, for the wealth of room and ideal arrangement make this story-and-a-half bungalow suitable for the city or country.

The outside walls are stucco on Byrkitt lath.   Exposed timbers on the front porch, the graceful roof lines, and the handsome front door and the striking design of the windows all combine to make it a charming home.   Six big rooms besides bathroom and closets have been provided—all expertly arranged for convenience and comfort.

The living room is unusually light and cheerful.   The big open fireplace with its massive mantel shelf flanked by charming casement windows at once attracts your attention.   The wide cased opening into the dining room gives an unbroken view from the fireplace to the twin windows at the opposite side of the latter room, which has unusually good wall space.

The dining room is connected with the kitchen by means of a swinging door.   Here we find the same good arrangement in evidence.   Its well built kitchen case is our design "C", as shown in the colored insert.   A door leads to the cozy rear porch.   Another door connects with the basement stairway. This stairway as well as the cellar casement and sash are supplied.   Every room on the first floor, with the exception of the dining room connects with the central hall.   Note that the bath room opens from this hall, instead of from the bed room.   It is furnished with one of our towel cases, which not only has room for towels, but for toilet accessories, etc., as well, as is shown on the center color pages.

The stairway to the second floor is well designed, while the twin windows at the landing flood it with sunshine.   The upstairs plan provides for two comfortable rooms with twin windows in each.   The ceilings upstairs are 8 feet but of course they slope to the side walls, which measure 6 feet 6 inches.

Mr. John Fernandez, of Springfield, Illinois, who built this house, wrote:

"It is so well planned and the fir trim and doors are beautiful—such pretty grain.   And I saved 25 per cent by purchasing it of you and you have dealt with me in an honest business-like way all the way through."

You, too, will be glad that you selected this house, after you have moved into it and have found out what solid comfort and economy it spells.

PAINT—Unless otherwise instructed, we will furnish white paint for trim.

First Floor Plan

CHAMBER 11'-3" x 12'-3"

LANDING

PORCH 3'-3" x 4'-9"

KITCHEN 11'-3" x 12'-3"

HALL

BATH 11'-3" x 6'-0"

LIVING ROOM 15'-3" x 13'-3"

CASED OPENING

DINING ROOM 11'-3" x 15'-3"

PORCH 16'-6" x 8'-0"

20'-0"

34'-0"

Second Floor Plan

ROOF

CLOSET

DOWN

CLOSET

CHAMBER 11'-3" x 12'-6"

HALL

CHAMBER 11'-3" x 12'-6"

ATTIC

ROOF

ROOF

For Plumbing, Heating, Lighting for This Home, See Last Pages of Book

Gordon-Van Tine Home No. 589

An Ideal 3-Bedroom Bungalow

For Prices on This Home, See First Page.
Read Pages 9 and 10 For Full Description of Materials.

A FEW minutes study on your part of this exceptional home, will readily show you just why it has found so many friends.

It seems to have filled a universal need where the larger bungalow is desired. It is an excellent example of skillful planning. To build it in your community will reflect excellent judgment.

To have a "roof over one's head" is a pleasure, to be sure, but with this roof, with its many artistic lines all blending into a harmonious whole, over you and your family, you will rest perfectly content in the knowledge that you have built well. It takes no keen sight to see the dignified attractiveness of the exterior. Just let your eye follow the slope of the outline and you will be conscious of an impression most pleasing to you.

In the shingled walls, we have a rustic touch that is very popular. The straight-line effect of siding — although siding is substantial, too — is avoided.

Notice the fine proportion and balance of the entire exterior. The wide barge boards, brackets, exposed rafters are all typically true bungalow construction.

There is an added effectiveness to the planning of the front porch—the dining room projects, making a recess for the porch, which opens directly into the big comfortable living room.

You will immediately realize the fine position of the fireplace—it is the key to the whole living room setting.

The lighting and ventilating of this home have been given perfect treatment. The living room has a big window facing the porch and two of equal size in the side wall. The dining room has a twin window in the front wall with a flower box attractively set beneath, and two single windows of equal size in the side wall. The kitchen and bath have windows of ample size—plenty of daylight in these rooms. The two side chambers have windows in each outside wall which permits cross-ventilation. The chamber between has a twin window. The entry is well-lighted by the one-light Colonial sash and glazed door.

The sleeping quarters are conveniently kept to the rear, and are given the necessary privacy by the connecting hall. This hall is a big feature of this plan—note especially how easily it allows one to reach all rooms and direct from the kitchen, too—thus will many steps be saved by the housewife.

To the left of the fireplace is a handy coat closet—a most appreciated feature in bungalows. In addition to the three bed room closets, we include our linen closet at the end of the hall—handy to each room.

Between the living and dining room is placed a pair of our beautiful French doors—anyone can appreciate the added beauty these doors will give to the interior; then, too, they are practical—you can shut off the dining room when you wish to increase the heat in the living room.

In the hall is the attic stairway. The attic is floored and offers many possibilities in utilizing this extra space.

The kitchen is as compact and convenient as any kitchen can be. This room is equipped with two big Gordon-Van Tine kitchen cases, styles A and B, as illustrated in the colored section. The plan makes provision for a vent register to chimney flue—the air in the kitchen will always be clean and fresh, as odors are quickly passed off through this vent.

Like many of our bungalows this house is built low-down with cellar sash in open areas. Thus is obtained the desired effect. The front porch and side stoop are only two steps high—you are practically on the ground level.

The mantle, dome damper, ash trap and ash pit door for the fireplace are furnished as well as the attractive flower boxes shown.

We know you'll want to build this pretty, comfortable home and will gladly assist you.

PAINT—Unless otherwise instructed, we will furnish brown shingle stain for the wall shingles and white paint for the trim of this home.

Slitzer, Wis.

Gentlemen: We think we have a very nice home. The flooring all lay up fine and fit just right. We got this house about $300.00 less than we could have purchased it from the local yard. Our neighbor would like prices and circular of your furnace just like the one we got from you. Many thanks for being so prompt and making everything satisfactory.
Yours truly, F. B. Schmidt.

For Plumbing, Heating, Lighting for This Home, See Last Pages of Book

Gordon-Van Tine Home No. 507

Very Popular 4-Bedroom Bungalow

For Prices, See First Page.

See Pages 9 and 10 for Description of Materials.

THIS has proved to be one of our most popular bungalows both because of its attractive exterior and because of its convenient interior.

You'll like the Colonial design of the windows and the corresponding door and the friendly aspect given by the deep bracketed cornice and the front dormer. The heavy porch frieze, the outlined belt course, as well as the shed roof over the dining room windows, all add to the popular low, broad effect wanted in the bungalow.

This is made more pronounced by the shingles used above the belt course. By extending the siding to the grade line a much better effect has been obtained than could be had by exposing the foundation.

The living room is unusually light and is made more roomy by the broad cased opening into the dining room. The wall space well arranged for the placing of furniture. These same facts are true of the dining room made unusually cheerful by the window extension. The wall opposite offers just the proper place for the sideboard or buffet.

The kitchen is completely furnished with our splendid "D" design kitchen case. This as well as the space left for the sink have the best of light. The entire kitchen arrangement is the most convenient possible.

The ice box space in the entry is out of the way, and still close at hand. The arrival of the iceman need not concern the housekeeper as he does not enter the kitchen to fill the refrigerator.

The hall opening from the dining room connects all parts of the house. The bath and linen closet, which is like the design shown in the colored section, are easily accessible to all the bed rooms, for the stairway ascends from this hall and brings one directly to the three upstairs rooms. The sewing room with its triple windows is a cheery little work room that will make order

in the rest of the house less of a problem and offer an emergency sleeping place when necessary.

There is ample closet room for each of the four bed rooms that all admit of a various placing of furniture. All in all, an especial spirit of convenience and economy of space ruled when this house was being designed.

The basement is under the entire house and well lighted and ventilated. For this we provide six sash.

PAINT—Unless otherwise instructed we will furnish Body Paint, French Grey, Trim White, Shingles above belt course and Dormer Stained Grey.

First Floor Plan

Second Floor Plan

For Plumbing, Heating, Lighting for This Home, See Last Pages of Book

Gordon-Van Tine Home No. 587

A Compact and Convenient Suburban Home

The porch has a solid flat roof

For Prices on This Home, See First Page.   Read Pages 9 and 10 For Full Descriptions of Materials.

PROMINENT among our many fine bungalows is this plan which you are certain to find most interesting. It has many excellent qualities which you will readily recognize as being necessary to the new home you have in mind.

Study the exterior of this home—notice its friendly, inviting appearance. The shingled walls lend a rustic appearance that has become very popular. Notice also the odd touches in the design which make it disinctively different.

Strikingly attractive is the pergola effect in the front porch construction. Here the artistic treatment is emphasized in the look outs, the heavy cross-beam, the unique design of the balusters between the porch-posts, and the small brackets. Although this porch has all the appearance of a pergola it is nevertheless a protection in bad wather because of the solid flat tin roof. The porch is made more desirable by placing it in the recess made by the front projection of the dining room.

The new roof lines are odd but in perfect harmony with the design. The gable of the roof over the dining room abutting out in front of the gable of the main roof, creates a very pleasing effect. Notice also how the main roof is extended over the porch on the right side. In this design, you will notice how consistently the designer has held to a continuous outline, which always is very pleasing—it makes things stand out more prominently.

A careful study of the floor plan will reveal a treasure of desirable features—especially appeal-ing to the housewife. There never was a more convenient plan designed. Even the details are handled with a skill ordinarily found only in expensive homes — for instance, notice how the kitchen range is placed—the fireplace—the chimneys, two in one.

The rooms are spacious and ideally arranged. In the hall leading to the living room is the ever-handy coat closet—a most appreciated feature in bungalow construction. This hall is the out-standing feature of this plan—notice how easily and quickly you can go from one room to another. In this there are many steps saved for the housewife and we dare say she will appreciate the thought and skill that so carefully planned for her welfare.

The living and dining rooms are big rooms—with windows in each outside wall permitting plenty of fresh air and light. You can easily see how pleasant these rooms will be—the fireplace is a welcome addition to any home and you will see how well we have placed it.

The bed rooms are in the rear—separated from the living rooms. This is a most practical provision. Both chambers have windows in each outside wall—perfect cross ventilation. In the hall between the bed rooms is our big linen closet—a handy, appreciated convenience—one of the many which easily distinguishes the Gordon-Van Tine home.

Notice the ideal kitchen arrangement—the big Gordon-Van Tine kitchen case style "D", which is included at no extra cost. The work table extends under the big kitchen window, which is ample provision for plenty of light and air. And take special notice how easily the housewife can reach any part of the house in "just a couple of steps"—surely this house was planned for comfort and convenience. The glazed side door opens directly into the entry—to the right is space for the ice box—leading directly down is the basement stairs.

This house is built low to gain the desired effect so the cellar sash are partly below grade in open areas.

In this bungalow you find all the comforts of a big home costing three times as much or more. Just consider how perfectly well-contented you and your family would be installed in this excellent, distinctive home.

Floor Plan

28:0"

CHAMBER 13:6"x14:3"

CLOS

CLOS

LINEN

CHAMBER 11:3"x13:0"

ICE

COATS

BATH 7:9"x5:6"

HALL

DOWN

SINK

PORCH

42:0"

RANGE

KITCHEN 11:3"x9:6"

CASE

LIVING ROOM 13:6"x14:3"

CASED OPENING

DINING ROOM 13:0"x14:0"

PORCH 14:0"x8:0"

PAINT—Unless otherwise instructed, we will furnish silver gray shingle stain for wall shingles and white paint for trim. We do not furnish stain for roof shingles.

For Plumbing, Heating, Lighting for This Home, See Back of Book

Gordon-Van Tine Home No. 562

A Big 6 Room House at a Low Price

This House Can be Furnished with Shingles or Siding Above Belt Course.   Write for Prices.

For Prices on This Home, See First Page.

Read Pages 9 and 10 For Full Description of Materials.

THIS simple hip roof house stands out from the great number of hip roof houses because of its excellent lines and proportions.

The interior of this comfortable square house is just what the exterior represents it to be—airy, light and convenient. Every room has two exposures, assuring an abundance of air and light, something hard to secure in the longer narrower house.

The stucco above the belt course and the siding below adds to the modern present day exterior. The plain substantial porch columns, the broad windows and the wide cornice are additional features aiding in the same effect. The blinds as shown are included in the price of this house.

The large roomy porch creates a pleasing first impression with the newcomer. But what is really of vastly greater importance is that the porch assures a lasting impression of comfort with the occupants.

The closet at the right of the hall entrance is a most convenient place for coats, rubbers and umbrellas, and leaves the reception hall to be used as part of the living room. This room is entered through a wide cased opening from the hall. There is an unusual amount of living space gained through this arrangement of the first floor.

The fact that there is a direct passage from the kitchen to the hall, also makes the beating of a hasty retreat to the upper floor, when unexpected company arrives, a possibility for the hostess who is also her own maid.

The plan of the kitchen which places the sink and work table all near the windows, does away with the unpleasantness of working without a direct light.

Another fact that appeals to the worker here is that the sink and work table are arranged so that she always works from left to right—a real saving of effort.   The illustration on the colored pages of this book show case "B", the design used in this house. The ice chest placed away from the kitchen means that the ice supply is not affected by the necessary heat there.

The unnecessary expense of a back porch has been eliminated in this house as the door of the cellar stair platform will serve the purpose of an outside entrance just as well and also provides a means of easy access to the basement.

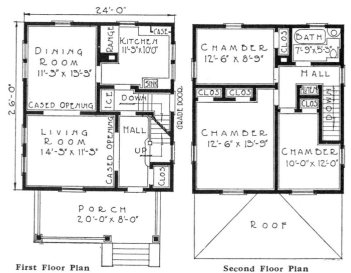

First Floor Plan   Second Floor Plan

A glance at the plan for the second floor convinces one that during the warm months the sleeping rooms must be cool.   And during the cold months it is always possible to raise a window in each room that does not admit the winter wind and snow.

The closets also must not be disregarded.   There is one for each room, two for one room and an additional linen closet in the hall.   You must agree that this house will make you, or your tenant, a pleasant convenient home.

PAINT—Unless otherwise instructed, we will furnish French gray paint for the body below the stucco, white for the trim and bright green for the blinds of this home.

For Plumbing, Heating, Lighting for This Home, See Last Pages of Book

Gordon-Van Tine Home No. 546

A Popular Gordon-Van Tine Bungalow

For Prices on This Home, See First Page.

Read Pages 9 and 10 for Full Description of Material.

HERE you can see how really attractive a bungalow may be. From the wide sloping roof, to the foundation upon which this house rests, it all creates the impression of a home that is different, yet comfortable and in perfect taste.

The recessed front porch seems to invite you to enter. Within there is a general change from the usual arrangement which affords you more air, light and between wall space than can often be found.

The generous broad flat lines, the wide eaves and exposed cornice all make you conscious at a glance of the undoubted air of hospitality. And you will find the plan of the interior one that is, even though unusual, at the same time, most truly homelike.

The house really consists of two portions joined by the living room. There is more living space thrown together than is often possible, for this big family room is unusually large. It has windows at both ends. The fireplace with two light windows on either side is opposite the entrance. This is practically the ideal location, for a glowing grate fire never seems more cheerful than when one enters from a blustering out doors, and is glad of this warm welcome

A coat closet opens off the living room, and to the left is the wide opening into the dining room—cheery and unusually well lighted. Its five windows almost make it a dining porch, and still experience has shown that this entire house is one that is easily heated though with all there are twenty-two windows

The kitchen is kept entirely apart by the service pantry between it and the dining room. Its arrangement is beyond a doubt ideal, with a built-in case and work table under the window each the full length of the pantry. The colored insert gives an illustration of our stock case which is similar to the one furnished for this home The kitchen itself is light and roomy, and access may be had to the basement and rear porch, where there is good space for the refrigerator.

One of the very special features of this bungalow is its three nice bed rooms and bath, all opening from the interior hall—and all having two or more windows. At the end of this hall there is a glazed door which gives light and also permits of connection between these rooms and the kitchen by means of the rear porch without passing through the living room.

These many attractive features have combined to make a most livable home of this bungalow, where all the money invested will bring comfort and satisfaction as the undoubted returns.

Mantel shelf, down damper and ash trap furnished for fireplace.

PAINT—Unless otherwise instructed, we will furnish seal brown paint for the body, and white for the trim of this home.

For Plumbing, Heating, Lighting, for This Home, See Last Pages of Book

Gordon-Van Tine Home No. 595

A Popular Bungalow Splendidly Arranged

For Prices on This Home, See First Page.   **Read Pages 9 and 10 for Full Description of Material.**

Options That Will Save You $170.00
Deduct the above amount from the regular price on this house if you are willing to buy it with the following changes from regular specifications:

6 to 2 Star A Star Red Cedar Shingles instead of 5 to 2 Clear; plain square edge casings for doors and windows instead of Craftsman design; all subflooring and kitchen case omitted.

THIS bungalow, especially suited to the farm, is distinctive in both appearance and floor plan.

You recognize it at once as a good sized and especially well planned farm bungalow. Its impression of size is increased by the wide cornice and half timbered effect of the big dormer and the gable ends.

The living rooms are large and airy with the best of wall space imaginable. The dining room is perhaps worthy of especial attention because of its ample size and splendid arrangement. Whether it is threshing time or the time of a big family dinner, there will always be plenty of room here. The coat closet opening just outside the dining room door to the hall, adds much in convenience to both these rooms.

We have indeed a right to point with pride to the kitchen pantry and wash room. And we cannot overlook the back porch. From the windows in this part of the house an excellent view can be had to both the side and the rear.

In the kitchen there is room for both a coal range and an oil stove as well as a work table, or other kitchen furniture. In the pantry are both our "A" and "C" cases and an excellent place for the refrigerator, also.

Between the kitchen and the rear porch—in the best possible location—is the wash room. Notice that it is of good size, well lighted with plenty of space for the hanging of out door clothes. Every detail in the arrangement of this room means a saving in work for the farm wife.

The hall which leads to the three sleeping rooms opens from the dining room. These chambers have all been planned with the placing of the bed room furniture well kept in mind. They have splendid closet space also. The door arrangement is such that direct access may be had to the kitchen from this part of the home.

The bath is compact and convenient, with a towel case like the one shown in the colored section.

The attic stairs ascend from this hall also. The house size attic offers a place for the many things for which a farm house attic is necessary.

Under the entire house there is a basement. This is easily reached by the kitchen stair or by means of the outside hatchway with its wide door and stairs. We supply both these stairways as well as the basement sash.

The outside walls are bevel siding to the belt line and Red Cedar shingles above.

PAINT—Unless otherwise instructed, we will furnish brown shingle stain for the wall shingles. Lemont stone paint for the body, and white for the trim of this home.

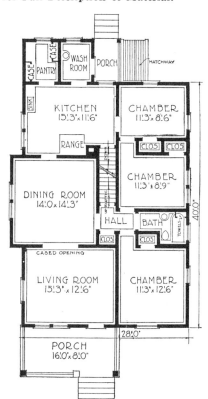

"I SAVED FIVE HUNDRED DOLLARS"
Gordon-Van Tine Company, Davenport, Iowa.   *Orville, Iowa.*
  Gentlemen: In the buying of my home selected from your catalog, I saved about five hundred dollars. In regards to material it was as good as I could have bought at home and some was better. If I was building again, I would do just as I did this time, regardless of home dealer. When you're on the market get as much for the money it is what I call good business. When it comes to fairness I was used as good as I would have been at home and probably a little better. Yours truly,   Jim Bernard.

For Plumbing, Heating, Lighting for This Home, See Last Pages of Book

Gordon-Van Tine Home No. 597.

Three Bedrooms in this Convenient Bungalow

For Prices on This Home, See First Page.   **Read Pages 9 and 10 for Full Description of Material.**

Options That Will Save You $103.50

Deduct the above amount from the regular price on this house if you are willing to buy it with the following changes from regular specifications:

6 to 2 Star A Star Red Cedar Shingles instead of shingle roll roofing; plain square edge casings for doors and windows instead of Craftsman design; all subflooring and kitchen case omitted.

A GREAT amount of careful thought was given to the designing of this house with the aim of securing a large kitchen, a large living room, three bed rooms and a bath and still confine the house to comparatively small, though sufficiently large outside dimensions. We feel that we have succeeded remarkably well.

The inside is especially suited to those who want convenience and compactness. In fact the room arrangement is ideal, and will do much towards lightening the day's work for the housewife. And, best of all, this house can be built for a very reasonable sum.

The exterior is practical as well as attractive. Especial features are the attractive effect produced by the combination of siding and shingles for the walls, and the preservation of the broad sweeping bungalow lines secured by extending the roof over the porch.

The kitchen must also make its appeal. There is ample space for the dining table and chairs away from the working space where the range, sink and kitchen case, our "B" design, are conveniently grouped.

On the opposite side of the sink is ample room for a cream separator if its location in the kitchen is necessary.

The large living room with windows on two sides, you will find has room for all the usual living room furniture and can be used for a combination living-dining room when so desired. The clever door arrangement at the rear means that while the bed rooms and bath are near to both, this room and the kitchen, they can be entirely closed off.

Each of the three bed rooms has two windows and a splendid closet. The bath room and an extra closet open from the hall. The bath room can be converted into a store room if this should prove more satisfactory.

The plan provides for a basement under the entire house. Its stairway is on the inside, convenient to both the kitchen and rear door.

The most satisfactory furnace to be used here, would be one with pipes leading to each room, though a pipeless furnace could be used to advantage if so placed that the register would be between the kitchen and hall doors.

PAINT—Unless otherwise instructed, we will furnish Lemont stone paint for the body, white for trim and brown shingle stain for the wall shingles.

This home has our famous Jap-a-Top shingle design, slate surfaced roll roofing over 1x6 sheathing laid tight together.

Floor Plan

CHAMBER 10'.0" x 10'.6"
BATH 5'.6" x 6'.9"
KITCHEN 15'.0" x 10'.6"
HALL
CHAMBER 12'.3" x 10'.6"
CHAMBER 9'.6" x 10'.6"
LIVING ROOM 12'.3" x 14'.0"
PORCH 14'.6" x 8'.0"

For Plumbing, Heating, Lighting for This Home, See Last Pages of Book

Gordon-Van Tine Home No. 508

Impressive Home—Economical To Build

For Prices on This Home, See First Page

Read Pages 9 and 10 for Full Description of Materials

THE simple lines and good proportion of this substantial looking house are specially set off by the big front porch, the wide box cornice and the dormer windows. It is the simplicity of design, carried out in the entire plan which in part has made this home so popular

The square floor plan, giving an equal chance for the best light and air in each room, has much to do in making this house so generally a favorite. Notice the arrangement of the numerous large windows. Even the entrance hall has not beenoverlooked, for in addition to the light admitted through the glazed door, the window on the stair landing provides more light. Another especial feature here is the closet for coats just to the right of the entrance. Surely this is a most satisfactory hallway.

The hall is made much more a part of the house, because the opening into the living room is so wide and well placed. And in turn the living room and dining room seem like one big room, stretched all the way from the front to the rear, with windows on three sides. This roominess is the result of the wide cased opening and the narrow partition between these two rooms.

We are proud of all of our kitchens since we know that they are well arranged and well equipped with our special built-in features. And this kitchen is another example proving the fact—notice the built-in case, design "B", shown on the colored plate in this book. And notice, too, the roominess and cheer in this kitchen with its two windows, something not always possible in a much more pretentious house.

The ice box can be placed near at hand, in the rear entry, where the iceman can easily reach it, since the outside cellar door is on a level with the sidewalk directly opposite.

The door into the front hall from here is a great convenience, too, especially in furnace time, for the basement steps are so easily reached from the front of the house in consequence. This door also makes the second floor so much closer to the kitchen.

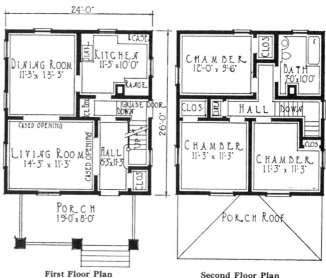

First Floor Plan   Second Floor Plan

A glance at the second floor plan shows you three well sized chambers of equal attractiveness each with two windows. The closets are ample in size and the linen closet centrally placed. This is like the one shown in the colored insert. The bath leaves nothing to be desired for it has been most carefully planned and is unusually large. No house is a bargain unless it's just what you want, but if this house is what you want you can do no better.

PAINT—Unless otherwise instructed, we will furnish lead color paint for body and white for trim of this home.

For Plumbing, Heating, Lighting for This Home, See Last Pages of Book

Gordon-Van Tine Home No. 502

A 5 Room Home–This is a Universal Favorite

For Prices on This Home, See First Page.

Read Pages 9 and 10 for Full Description of Materials.

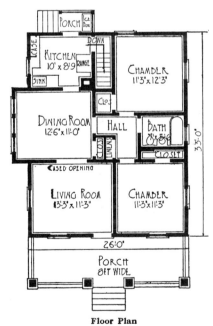

Floor Plan

THERE has been a steady and consistent demand for this home from discerning purchasers ever since we first offered it. The straightforward dignity of the exterior, and the comfort and convenience of the plan explain the popularity at a glance.

The exterior is sided with Clear Cypress Siding up to the belt course, which also forms the top window line. From belt course to cornice, Clear Red Cedar Shingles are used; while the wide cornice itself gives the pleasing low roof effect. The high piers, square columns, and broad steps of the inset porch are some of the other attractive features to be considered

Study the floor plan with care. The living and dining rooms can almost be considered together for they are nearly one room, because of the wide opening between them. They both are made most cheerful by the light received through the window extension in the dining room.

The coat closet just beyond the cased opening is accessible from the front door, and likewise from the rear of the house.

The kitchen leaves nothing to be desired. Our kitchen case "B" is furnished and space has been planned for the entire kitchen equipment. This room will be cool on warm summer days, because of the door and window arrangement.

Access is had to the basement directly from the kitchen. There is no necessity for stepping into a cold entryway, or for taking unnecessary steps when going to the basement. As in all our houses of this class, we supply cellar stairs and sash, girders and girder posts.

The hall opening off of the dining room brings one to the sleeping rooms, bath and linen closet. The latter is an addition not always to be found in a two-bed room bungalow. It is the case shown in the color section. The bed room closets are large, but at the same time cause no irregularities in the rooms themselves, and the two sleeping rooms with windows in adjoining walls are comfortable and cheerful.

You have long imagined the feeling of pride in ownership when you could point to your home. This feeling will be emphasized greatly when your home meets with the entire approval of yourself and family.

PAINT—Unless otherwise instructed, we will furnish Lemont stone paint for body, oxide red shingles stain for dormer and wall shingles above belt, and white for trim.

For Plumbing, Heating, Lighting for This Home, See Last Pages of Book

Gordon-Van Tine Home No. 554

Large Bedrooms in This Inexpensive Bungalow

This House Can be Furnished with Siding or Shingles on Outside Walls Instead of Stucco. Write for Prices.

For Prices on This Home, See First Page.

Read Pages 9 and 10 for Full Description of Materials

THIS is not an expensive house, but it has a most attractive exterior. Its lines are all simple and practical with nothing to detract from the harmony of plan. Good judgment has been used in achieving the bungalow ideals of simplicity and coziness and above all practicability.

Any possible monotony of line has been avoided by the dormer, which breaks the roof before it extends over the porch. Further variation has been introduced through the more abrupt slope of the house roof, as well as the hooded bay. This projecting window improves the exterior of the house, and at the same time adds a bit of space to the width of the dining room.

The exterior walls and the square porch pillar are stucco, for which we furnish Byrkitt patent sheathing.

The dormer walls are shingled, with rafter ends and cornice, like those of the main roof. The plainness of line is further emphasized in the outlined belt course and the porch rail and balusters.

A vestibule can seldom be arranged for in a house of this size, but here you find a vestibule and a closet for coats opening off of it. The all year round advantage of this arrangement needs no explanation.

You will like the living and dining room thrown together, with the two sets of twin windows, good furniture space, and pleasant outlook.

An absolute through draft can be gained at any time by opening the door that leads to the carefully worked out Gordon-Van Tine kitchen.

This is fitted with a kitchen wall case design "B". You will admit it is planned to make work simple and pleasant. The sink is placed between the work table and range. This conforms to the approved ideas of kitchen arrangement.

The rear entry provides a recess for the refrigerator which is thus out of the way and can be iced without the iceman's entering the kitchen. The basement stairs descend here to a full sized cellar lighted with six cellar windows.

A small inner hall opening from the dining room connects the two large chambers, each having twin windows, really unusually large closets, and well arranged wall space. Both are adjacent to the bath. For the bath, we furnish a wall towel case, as shown in the colored section.

From front to back door every foot of space has been economically taken care of, a fact that is vouched for by those who have already lived in this comfortable home.

PAINT — Unless otherwise instructed we will furnish white paint for the trim. The walls are stucco.

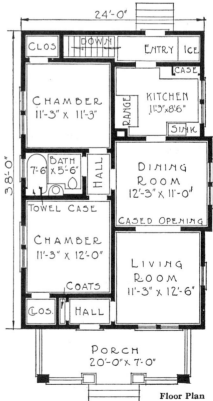

Floor Plan

For Plumbing, Heating, Lighting for This Home, See Last Pages of Book

Gordon-Van Tine Home No. 523

Note the Large Living Room and Fine Porch

For Prices on This Home, See First Page.   **Read Pages 9 and 10 for Full Description of Materials.**

Options That Will Save You $87.00

Deduct the above amount from the regular price on this house if you are willing to buy it with the following changes from regular specifications:
6 to 2 Star A Star Red Cedar Shingles instead of 5 to 2 Clear; plain square edge casings for doors and windows instead of Craftsman design; all subflooring and kitchen case omitted.

MR. HENRY BENSON, of Morristown, Minnesota, after building this house, wrote us: "We are very proud of our new home and everything we received from Gordon-Van Tine has been as recommended."

Pride of ownership results from building well planned houses, that prove a source of comfort and satisfaction to the owner. Mr. Benson found this house practical. So will you.

The simple gable roof with its closed cornices is broken by the quaint dormer which also serves a practical purpose in furnishing light for the bath room. A similar dormer breaks the roof line on the opposite side. The Monterey bevel plated front door is protected from the weather by a bracketed hood, while the stoop is flanked by boxed-in buttresses.

The side porch is excellently designed. Its sided rails and sturdy pillars supporting the shed roof give it an appearance of solidity and comfort. It is so built that it can be screened in and made a cosy place to spend the warm summer evenings.

Through the French doors opening onto this porch one is afforded a view of the well proportioned living room with its open stairway at the far end. A cased opening connects it with the dining room. A two panel door at the rear of the living room permits direct passage from the front door to the kitchen—a compactly arranged room with light and air admitted from two sides. The kitchen case consist of a flour bin, a set of three drawers and a compartment for storing utensils—our "B" design.

From the kitchen three steps take you to the Monterey door at the grade landing. This serves as a rear door also, thus saving expense and space.

You, of course, will have a cellar under the entire house. We supply plenty of windows to make it light and well ventilated.

Upstairs arrangements make use of every foot of space. The front room is commodious and well lighted, while the closet in the corner is a necessary convenience. The other two rooms are comfortably arranged and are supplied with good sized closets. Our towel case is a happy addition to the bath room. This you will find illustrated in the color section. The ceiling height of the second floor is 8 feet, except the corners where there naturally is a slope to the side walls, but the height is full 6 feet, 2 feet from the side walls.

After studying this plan you will agree with Mr. Benson. From the standpoint of appearance, comfort and economy it is the design which you will want. Perhaps we should add that the exterior is of beveled siding to the belt, and of shingles above, thus permitting of a three-color scheme of painting.

PAINT—Unless otherwise instructed, we will furnish gray stain for the shingles and white paint for the body and trim.

First Floor Plan
22-0
DINING ROOM 11-3"x 11-1"
KITCHEN 9-3"x 11-3"
CASE
RANGE
26-0
CASED OPENING
PORCH 8-0"x 14-0"
LIVING ROOM 17-9"x 13-3"
FRENCH DOORS
GRADE DOOR
UP DOWN
STOOP

Second Floor Plan
CHAMBER 9-0"x 11-1"
CHAMBER 9-3"x 11-3"
CLOS
CLOS
CLOS
BATH 5-6"x 7-2"
HALL DOWN
TOWELS
PORCH ROOF
CHAMBER 17-9"x 10-0"
CLOS
ROOF

ABSOLUTELY SATISFACTORY—SAVED $400.00

Gordon-Van Tine Co., Davenport, Iowa.   Burlington, Wisconsin

Gentlemen: I wish to say at the present time that your material for my home was absolutely satisfactory, both in regard to price and quality. Many people here at Browns Lake who know lumber say that it was the very best lot that ever came here. Even my contractor who has interest in getting lumber from the trust people said if he were building for himself again he would buy from you. My real friend on my job was Mr. Frank Lawson of Grays Lake. His opinion of your lumber and millwork was that I saved fully $400.00 by dealing with you. My house is as good or better than any on this lake and some cost nearly double.
                                                           T. W. Harrington.

Gordon-Van Tine Home No. 573

Comfort and Convenience for Little Money

For Prices on This Home, See First Page.   **Read Pages 9 and 10 for Full Description of Materials.**

THEY said we couldn't plan a six-room house to sell for as little as this one and have it livable. Here is our answer.

Three good bed rooms, a closet for each, bath, fine living room, big dining room, a real Gordon-Van Tine kitchen with a built-in wall case—front porch, back stoop, all of finest material, ready-cut at a very low price.

Scientific planning, quantity buying, large scale manufacturing tell the story. Note the skill with which this home is designed. Not an inch of waste space anywhere—not a wall that doesn't serve two purposes—six rooms in 36x24 space, and yet every room, because it is properly proportioned and the windows, doors and wall spaces properly handled, is livable—even impresses you as large when

you enter the house. This is the visible evidence of master-planning. Just as important was the figuring and scientific calculation which made possible the use of all stock materials and the elimination of waste —you can't see that, except in the price where it shows up as hundreds of dollars saved.

Don't you know just the lot where this lovely bungalow would look best—to you? Picture it built there—isn't making that dream come true worth a little effort? When you consider what an important word "home" is, and remember that it is an investment for a lifetime—not something you buy today and throw away tomorrow—when you realize these things you see an investment in a home in its true light.

PAINT—Unless otherwise instructed we will furnish brown stain for wall shingles and buff paint for the trim of this home.

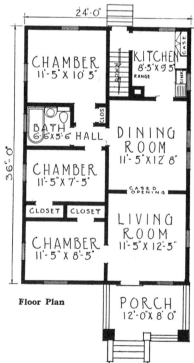

Floor Plan

Dear Sirs:
Just a line or two to lrt you know we got our house about finished up and it sure is a dandy. We are very much pleased with it. There isn't a house in that new town to look as nice as it is and everyone that sees it remarks about the nice fine lumber you carry. Our contractor said that was the very best of lumber and the house built to stand. We are especially pleased with our front porch, so nice and big. We had enough lumber left to build us a back screened-in porch and a shed. We are going to send the blue print plans back the first of the week, so this is all.
Yours truly,
Mr. and Mrs. John Stash, Virden, Ill.
P. S.—The next time we build you will get our order again no matter how small an amount it will be.

For Plumbing, Heating, Lighting for This Home, See Last Pages of Book

Gordon-Van Tine Home No. **501**

Simple Straight Lines Make This a Favorite

First Floor Plan   **Second Floor Plan**

For Prices on This Home, See First Page.

Read Pages 9 and 10 for Full Description of Materials.

THIS house has three outside doors, the front, grade, and rear doors are all glazed doors. The Colonial windows lend dignity and height. About the whole exterior there is a suggestion of substantial worth.

A survey of the interior shows how carefully the plan was developed. The big living room, the cheery dining room, and the convenient kitchen, all carry conviction in their general good qualities. The entire house is perfectly ventilated and lighted. The chambers have cross ventilation—a window in each outside wall. Two big twins and a single window at the foot of the open stairway light the living room. The dining room has a twin and a single window. The kitchen has one wide, short window in the left wall, and another in the rear wall directly over the work table.

With this house we furnish our kitchen case style "C" and our convenient linen closet. Both are very much worth while features.

Through the hall, which connects all upstairs rooms, the sleeping porch is reached. Nowadays the sleeping porch is not only a comfort but a necessity.

To build this house confirms the good judgment of many hundreds who have found in it real home-comfort. It is bound to please you because from every point you view it, there can only be one conclusion—perfect. Perfect in design, looks and material.

Note—Prices on sash for enclosing sleeping porch will be quoted on request.

PAINT—Unless otherwise instructed, we will furnish oxide red shingle stain for the wall shingles, cream paint for the body and white for the trim of this home.

PROMPT SHIPMENTS, AND SAVED $350.00 TO $400.00
Gordon-Van Tine Company, Davenport, Iowa.   *Wharton, New Jersey.*
Gentlemen: We are certainly pleased with all the material in our home which we bought from you, and all the neighbors think it is fine. And the saving was great. We saved about $350.00 to $400.00 from what it would cost around here. And you were so prompt in your shipments and everything came in such good shape. Well, this is from the Gordon-Van Tine Company Booster. I remain a satisfied customer. Mr. Chas. T. Lecher. P. S. You can send anyone here who wants to see a fine home.

"SAVED A NEAT LITTLE SUM"
Gordon-Van Tine Company, Davenport, Iowa.   *Marion, Iowa.*
Gentlemen: We are pleased with the material you furnished for our home. It is fine quality and first class in every respect; we also saved money by buying of you, although we cannot state the amount, we feel certain that it is a neat little sum. Very truly yours, C. L. Wahl.

For Plumbing, Heating, Lighting for This Home, See Last Pages of Book

Gordon-Van Tine Home No. 539

A Good Looking and Inexpensive Home

For Prices on This Home, See First Page. Read Pages 9 and 10 for Full Description of Materials.

Options That Will Save You $96.65

Deduct the above amount from the regular price on this house if you are willing to buy it with the following changes from regular specifications:

6 to 2 Star A Star Red Cedar Shingles instead of 5 to 2 Clear; plain square edge casings for doors and windows instead of Craftsman design; all subflooring and kitchen case omitted

T HOUGH you are not going to build an expensive house, you like to feel that you are building a house that will give you a lifetime of service, if you should not care to build again. So we bid you look carefully for what you want. We know that nowhere can you find a more pleasing and practical design than this, at so small a cost.

It is a remarkably attractive home, in which we have paid particular attention to the exterior design. We are pleased because it offers you numerous unusual features that are rarely found in any but costly houses. It is original, distinctive and good-looking wherever placed.

The unique roof treatment combines well with the style of living porch at the side, and still provides for ceilings 7 foot 11 inches from the floor, which of course assures good circulation.

The placing of the porch offers seclusion and comfort otherwise impossible, for it need serve only as an outdoor room, since the hooded stoop at the front shelters the entrance. The roof extending over the living room windows connects these two in a friendly fashion.

First Floor Plan

FLOWER BOXES AS SHOWN, ARE A SPECIAL ADDED FEATURE OF THIS HOUSE WHICH ARE FURNISHED WITHOUT EXTRA CHARGE.

kitchen case, design "B", situated so that the work table comes just under the window. The sink has an equally advantageous position.

The basement stairway enters the kitchen and is next to the outside door. This arrangement will often save the spotlessness of the kitchen floor. Plenty of room is provided in the basement as it extends under the entire house, and four cellar windows provide the light that is necessary.

In the upstairs you have a good sized bath and linen closet, and the chambers are all pleasant and livable.

PAINT—Unless otherwise instructed, we will furnish cream paint for the body and white for trim.

The architect has improved the appearance of this design by running the siding clear to the grade line—exposing the foundation would destroy the present pleasing effect.

The entrance brings one into the reception hall. Here there is a broad open stairway and in the rear a convenient coat closet. And don't overlook the fact that just back of it is its exact duplicate opening into the kitchen. It is hard to say which will give you the most service.

From the reception hall you have a view through the cased opening, across the living room, and then through the French doors onto the porch. Since there is a window just at the foot of the stairs this is an unusually light and airy living room, from which the dining room opens. This is nearly square, of the size most desired in the modern house.

The practically square kitchen has a

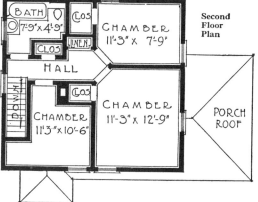

Second Floor Plan

Gordon-Van Tine Home No. 516

Unusually Handsome 5-Room Home

For Prices on This Home, See First Page.
Read Pages 9 and 10 for Full Description of Materials.

Floor Plan

PORCH | ICE BOX | CASE

CLOS

DOWN

KITCHEN
13'-3" x 9'-3"

RANGE

SINK

CHAMBER
9'-3" x 11'-0"

DINING ROOM
14"-6'" x 11'-0"

BATH
7'-0"x 5'-6" TOWELS HALL

CLOSET

CASED OPENING

CHAMBER
9'-3" x 10'-0"

LIVING ROOM
13'-3" x 11'-3"

34'0"

24'0"

PORCH
24'-0" X 8'-0"

HERE is a one floor five-room home that offers all the conveniences which modern planning give, a good-looking up-to-date exterior, all at a very nominal cost.

The gable roofed extension of the dining room adds to the pleasing effect of the exterior and the roominess of the interior at the same time. The beautiful round columns of the porch, and the simple lines of the hip roof, and the band above the twin windows in the gable end of the house are features that further attract your attention.

Step inside and find how truly liveable this house is. Notice how every foot of space is of use. No unnecessary hall or entryways but rooms practically square and all planned for comfort. Place your furniture in imagination and find this to be true.

A cased opening throws the living room and dining room into one. It is beautifully and appropriately designed adding greatly to the two rooms.

A door opening from the dining room into the hall provides a convenient passage to the sleeping rooms. The location of this door means that a trip may be made from kitchen to bed room practically unobserved by a guest.

The bed rooms are as entirely separated from one another as from the rest of the living rooms. The bath is equally near to both. The towel cabinet here and the good closet opening off of each room are convenient features that will be especially appreciated by those who live here.

The kitchen is a Gordon-Van Tine kitchen. That means it is convenient and practical for working. A window in each outside wall assures light and ventilation. The space planned for the range is near to the outside door and the basement stair. No matter where your fuel is kept it won't have to be carried a great distance. The sink, if you decide upon one, can be put where the dishes to be washed need not be carried far from the dining table. And our kitchen case, design "B", is well located.

You will find that the basement can be as conveniently arranged as any other part of the house. For it we furnish the stair and necessary sash. There is adequate space for a laundry, a fruit cellar and a furnace room. Since few homes are being built without making plans for a furnace, it must be a satisfaction to the purchaser to know that this house heats most easily.

PAINT—Unless otherwise instructed, we will furnish light yellow f or body paint and white for trim.

For Plumbing, Heating, Lighting, for This Home, See Last Pages of Book

Gordon-Van Tine Home No. 611

Unusually Well Planned Craftsman Bungalow

For Prices on This Home, See First Page.
Read Pages 9 and 10 for Full Description of Materials.

THE wide overhanging eaves, double front gable, timber brackets and shingle walls are all typical of the true craftsman bungalow. The brick pillars supporting the porch columns contribute a solid, substantial, well-rooted feeling to the whole home. The combination porch and open terrace is a particularly pleasing feature. The plan contains many unusual and pleasing features.

The living room is made cheery by the big fireplace at the end which is balanced by two windows. The wide cased opening gives both living room and dining room the advantage of the space and light of the other.

The den off the living room is a particularly pleasing arrangement and permits of a privacy not often found in the usual compact bungalow. Notice there is a closet for coats opening off the living room just at the rear of the den.

The dining room is of fine size and well proportioned. Triple windows furnish an abundance of light and there is plenty of wall space for buffet, serving table, chairs, etc. Notice particularly the little hall which opens from the dining room. This connects both bed rooms, bath room and kitchen. Every room is thus made entirely private, and yet accessible from

every part of the house. Notice there is a linen closet built in just opposite the door into this hall. We furnish for this closet, all the necessary shelves, drawers, doors, etc., and complete hardware, all ready to build into the wall.

The kitchen is splendidly arranged and is equipped with big built-in wall case (Type D—see color section) which connects with the sink. The big twin windows which are right above the sink and work table make this a very light and pleasant place to work. Notice that room for the ice box is provided in the entry, and that there is a closet for brooms opening into the kitchen. The combined rear and grade doors save room and an extra outside opening, and makes the cellar accessible from both kitchen and outdoors.

The bed rooms are both fine size and are light and have plenty of air. Each has its own big closet and they are both convenient to the bath room. Notice the front bed room also opens into the living room.

If desired the den can be used as an emergency bed room.

This remarkably complete and trim bungalow is a real bargain at the price quoted.

Floor Plan

PAINT—Unless otherwise instructed we will furnish gray shingle stain for the body and white paint for the trim of this home.

For Plumbing, Heating, Lighting for This Home, See Last Pages of Book

Gordon-Van Tine Home No. 540

Lots of Room in This Fine Home

This House Can be Furnished with Siding or Shingles on Outside Walls Instead of Stucco. Write for Prices.

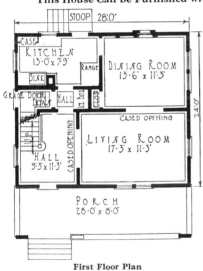

First Floor Plan

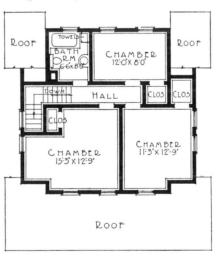

Second Floor Plan

**For Prices on This Home,
See First Page.**

**Read Pages 9 and 10 for Full
Description of Materials.**

The wide porch, over which the main roof extends, the solid boxed rail, the heavy timber brackets, the wide cornice, all tend to make this home appear massive. The shingled gables each have two big windows, which with the three front dormer sash and three full-sized windows in the rear dormer afford perfect light and ventilation to the three large bed rooms and bath. In the bath room is furnished our towel cabinet—a handy case with room for everything.

The big roomy living and dining rooms are well lighted. Each room has a twin window and a single window in cross position—there will be plenty of air and sunshine in these rooms. A glazed door opens into the large reception hall, with

FOR a city or suburban home this modified stucco bungalow is ideally designed. The unusual amount of room it contains is a constant source of surprise.

Both the exterior and interior are impressive. Front and rear dormers break the broad sweep of the roof lines and add to the second floor ceiling heights, which are in the main 8 feet except small spaces on each side of the dormers, where the heights are 7 feet, 4 inches and 5 feet 6 inches. But these cut off ceilings do not detract because the restricted space is so very small. In reality the upstairs rooms are very desirable, being of fine size, light and well ventilated.

the beautiful open stairway. Above the starting step is placed a large window—with another further up the stairs.

Direct passage from the hall to the kitchen is made through the small connecting hallway. Note the convenient recess here for the ice box—also the handy closet space in the dining room.

The kitchen will delight any housewife—big, square, well-lighted with two windows, one in each wall in addition to the glazed outside door. Our big kitchen case, style "C", is furnished in this kitchen. Entrance to kitchen is made either from rear or the glazed grade door at the side. From the grade level stairs lead direct to the basement.

Selection is a matter of judgment always. You will be delighted in your study of this home to find your desires so carefully anticipated.

PAINT—Unless otherwise instructed, we will furnish brown stain for gable and dormer shingles, and white for trim. Walls below belt are stucco.

For Plumbing, Heating, Lighting for This Home, See Last Pages of Book

Gordon-Van Tine Home No. 528

A Big Square Home—Four Bed Rooms

For Prices on This Home, See First Page.   **Read Pages 9 and 10 for Full Description of Materials.**

A TRULY beautiful home, dignified and spacious. Square lines and hip roof have always been popular but here again the touch of the expert is evident—his treatment of the outside walls removes this home from the commonplace square house.

The two belt courses breaking up the bevel siding, the wide closed cornice, the Colonial windows and stately porch blend harmoniously and give that character which is typical of Gordon-Van Tine Homes.

The feature of both the first and second floors is of course the big rooms—every inch is available. The commodious reception hall opens into the finely proportioned and well lighted living room. A large portion of the square dining room is visible through the cased opening. One pair of twin windows in the side wall and the single window in the rear wall add cheer while there is still much unbroken wall space for furniture.

Entering the kitchen through the double acting swinging door from the dining room, you are immediately impressed with the excellent planning. In the very lightest part of the kitchen, is our design "C" kitchen case (see color pages)—equally appropriate locations are given to the sink and range, and your ice box can be put on the rear latticed porch.

The central hall shows remarkable thought and skill. It contains a coat closet and directly opposite are the stairs leading up to the second floor or down to the grade door.

In this house we have planned a duplex stairway, by means of which one reaches the second landing direct from the kitchen.

Upstairs we have four fine chambers every one of which is supplied with a large clothes closet. There is also a complete built-in linen closet in the hall like the design shown on the colored insert in this book.

The two front chambers are unusually well lighted each being provided with one pair of twin windows and one single window while the rear chambers have a window in each outside wall thus assuring plenty of circulation in the hot nights of summer. As on the first floor, the designer, however, has not lost sight of the importance of having unbroken wall space for the placing of furniture.

Stairs lead up to the attic which is floored and well lighted by the front dormer.

If you want a big square home—space-saving and convenient, but combining the very best style of architecture you certainly cannot go wrong in building this home.

PAINT—Unless otherwise instructed, we will furnish cream paint for the body and white for the trim of this home.

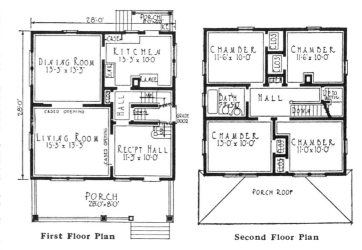

First Floor Plan   **Second Floor Plan**

Gordon-Van Tine Co., Davenport, Iowa.   Algona, Iowa.

Gentlemen: Some time ago I received a letter from Mr. H. B. Nelson requesting me to have a picture taken of my house plan and also one picture from the interior. I have complied with his request. The stairway is certainly as fine a feature as there is in any part of the house and the finish is certainly fine. I did the work on the case myself and most of the finishing.

I must say I am more than pleased with my home. Everybody that has seen the house expressed themselves more than pleased with the material and plans. You will remember Mr. Bert Peck of Algona has purchased material for a barn of your company, shipped to Comfrey, Minn. Mr. Peck is a business man, in the hardware business. I recommended your material to him and several others that will buy in the spring.   Mr. Geo. Koch.

For Plumbing, Heating, Lighting for This Home, See Last Pages of Book

Gordon-Van Tine Home No. 534

Distinctive Home, Exceptionally Well Planned

First Floor Plan   **Second Floor Plan**

For Prices on This Home, See First Page.
Read Pages 9 and 10 for Full Description of Materials.

A RT and economy are combined in this home. The gable roof and the siding shingles running to the second story window sills, cut off with the panels and siding below, make a pleasing treatment, while the stately entrance connected to the sun porch by the hood gives the necessary horizontal lines to lend perfect balance to the design.

The floor plan is an excellent arrangement. From the broad, spacious living room, entrance is made through the plaster colonnade into the big dining room. Directly opposite the front entrance is a door entering into the hall leading to the kitchen. Like all Gordon-Van Tine kitchens this one is ideally planned and

equipped with our big kitchen case, style "B," set in between the two kitchen windows.

In the hallway between the kitchen and living rooms is a recess for the ice box, just at the head of the stairs leading down to the grade door. The rear door opens from the kitchen onto a big back porch.

The spacious sun porch off of the living room is a very desirable feature. Entrance is made through a pair of French doors. The living and dining rooms are well lighted and perfectly ventilated. In the living room between the handy coat closet just inside the front entance, and over the open stairway, is a big window. In the front wall of this room is a big triple window. The dining room has a big window in the left wall and two smaller ones at each side of the rear wall. The flower boxes across the front add considerably to the beautiful exterior.

Sleeping porches are today considered a necessity in modern homes. Note the excellent provision we've made for this feature. In fact, the upstairs is ideal. Fine large chambers with cross ventilation and a commodious bath leaves nothing to be desired. Our handy linen closet is also included.

The more you look over this plan, the more you are convinced that here is an opportunity to combine individuality with a charming exterior, and withal a most convenient and comfortable interior.

PAINT—Unless otherwise instructed, we will furnish green stain for wall shingles and white paint for body and trim. We do not furnish stain for roof shingles.

For Plumbing, Heating, Lighting for This Home See Back of Book

Gordon-Van Tine Home No. 515

A Cosy, Comfortable Bungalow

For Prices on This Home, See First Page.
Read Pages 9 and 10 for Full Description of Materials.

Options That Will Save You $91.50

Deduct the above amount from the regular price on this house if you are willing to buy it with the following changes from regular specifications:
6 to 2 Star A Star Red Cedar Shingles instead of 5 to 2 Clear; plain square edge casings for doors and windows instead of Craftsman design; all subflooring and kitchen case omitted.

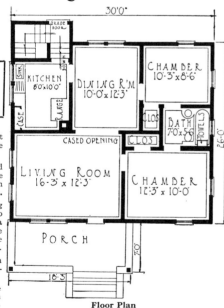

Floor Plan

THE overhanging roof of this shingled bungalow gives a sheltered effect to this cosy comfortable little home. The broad steps form a pleasing approach to the porch, which is unusually large.

This house illustrates especially well our careful planning of the interior combined with the greatest economy of space. The living room with four splendid windows, and the wide opening into the dining room lends itself to most artistic arrangement.

The clever placing of the dining room promises hot weather comfort even though there are windows only on one side, for these are in direct line with those on the opposite living room wall.

We especially recommend this kitchen to you for its compactness. The necessary articles of kitchen furniture are close together, which arrangement results in time saving and step saving to the housewife. Our kitchen case design "B" is of first importance. Work in this light, cheery little kitchen, can be done with all possible ease.

And notice that throughout the entire house the arrangement of windows and doors provides for excellent ventilation of every room.

The sleeping apartments here are arranged with the utmost economy of space in mind. The space often given to a hall in this type of a house has instead been converted into closet room, something always at a premium in the smaller home.

You will notice that the closets in these bed rooms are larger than the average and that the windows here are particularly well placed. Both of these bed rooms are especially comfortable.

The bath located between the two sleeping rooms lacks for nothing. It is large enough to permit of two entrances; which make possible a connection between the rear part of the house and the front chamber, without entering the living room—a much appreciated convenience.

This bath is equipped with one of our built-in towel cabinets, such as is illustrated in the colored inserts.

Note the happy arrangement of the entrance to the kitchen. Three steps lead you from this room to the grade landing and then to the basement. Here we have provided plenty of windows.

This rustic craftsman bungalow commends itself to you either as an all-year-round home, or as an excellent summer cottage for those who are looking for more comfort than is usually possible in such structures.

PAINT—Unless otherwise instructed, we will furnish brown shingle stain for the wall shingles and white paint for the trim of this home.

EVERYTHING A PERFECT FIT

Gordon-Van Tine Co.   *Louisville, Ohio.*

Gentlemen: In regard to my ready-cut home, I must say I am well pleased with my new home; so far everything fits to a perfect fit and I am more than satisfied with your ready-cut home. I am going to stick up for the Gordon-Van Tine Company if I lose my life. Yours for more Gordon-Van Tine homes.
(Signed) Mr. Roy Baughman

For Plumbing, Heating, Lighting for This Home, See Last Pages in Book

Gordon-Van Tine Home No. 586

Bungalow With Especially Attractive Features

For Prices on This Home, See First Page.
Read Pages 9 and 10 for Full Description of Material.

Options That Will Save You $99.20

Deduct the above amount from the regular price on this house if you are willing to buy it with the following changes from regular specifications:
6 to 2 Star A Star Red Cedar Shingles instead af 5 to 2 Clear; plain square edge casings for doors and windows instead of Craftsman design; all subflooring and kitchen case omitted.

THIS well designed economical bungalow is worthy of your attention. The extension of the main roof with its broad low lines and hooded dormer to cover the front and rear porches, is a new feature which makes the house stand out from the usual in design.

Consider the comfort that you will get in the shade of this roomy porch across the front. Its large, square built-up wood columns and broad steps are among its especially attractive features. These and the hooded dormer above all, help in giving the low broad effect always sought after in the bungalow. The shingled side walls add further to the homey, comfortable appearance.

The convenient and inviting arrangement of the attractive interior is carefully outlined in the floor plan of this page. The interior is delightful. The living room and dining room, both of good dimensions, with a handsome plaster colonnade between, are cheerful, well lighted rooms affording good furniture space.

A double action swinging door leads from the dining room to the kitchen. Viewed from every angle, this kitchen indicates that convenience has been the watchword. Both the work table of the kitchen case and the sink are each located directly under a window. This brings the kitchen case proper, which is our "C" design, equally near to both.

Another feature not always found in bungalows of this size is the convenient stairway to the basement. This is doubly convenient since it is just inside the door to the rear porch. The plans show a basement under the entire house. For this we supply the stairway and five cellar sash, assuring ample light and ventilation.

Look at the plan for the sleeping rooms and be convinced that this home has been carefully planned with a view to the requirements of those wishing a small home, conveniently arranged for utmost comfort.

Both bed rooms and the bath open from an inner hall. Each room has two windows and ample closet room; while off of the bath is a linen closet, such as is shown in the colored section.

Even when the door between the dining room and hall is shut, closing each part of the house to itself, excellent ventilation and air is still possible.

Often times a small house means lack of privacy and quiet. But this is not so here, for all the comforts and conveniences of a well ordered home are possible.

PAINT—Unless otherwise instructed, we will furnish brown shingle stain for the wall shingles and white paint for the trim of this home.

Cokato, Minn
Gordon-Van Tine Co., Davenport, Iowa.
About the material you shipped to me, I would say that everything was good throughout. Did not find anything defective and am very much pleased with the material.
Gust. Peterson.

For Plumbing, Heating, Lighting for This Home, See Last Pages of Book

Gordon-Van Tine Home Nos. 579 A and B

Five Rooms of Comfort in This Cozy Home

For Prices on This Home, See First Page.   **Read Pages 9 and 10 for Full Description of Materials.**

THE style and character of this up-to-the-minute bungalow set it apart and pronounce it a home of good taste wherever it is built.

And inside are literally five rooms of comfort. Compact, with every inch livable, all unnecessary space is eliminated, but every necessary feature is included. Imagine this cosy home just finished on the lot you have in mind. Step inside and let's see how easily and attractively it can be furnished and how convenient it is. Note how the wall space in the living room is planned so your piano or davenport goes in just the right place—and how tables and chairs can be arranged without being in the way as you pass through the rooms. The double window makes the dining room light and airy, and the doors are placed right where they ought to be to have things convenient, yet there are two spaces thoughtfully arranged for buffet and china closet.

The kitchen has fine light and ventilation, and is so conveniently arranged that the work almost does itself. Our splendid kitchen case "A" which is included at no extra cost is built in from floor to ceiling and provides space for dishes and supplies of all kinds above the worktable, and below has a cupboard for pans, a tilting flour bin, removable maple cutting board, compartment utensil drawer, etc., a whole pantry in itself.

The dinette and back porch are convenience features worth many times the cost, but can be eliminated and the alternate kitchen plan substituted at the saving shown on price page if you desire it.

The bed rooms are so planned that all necessary furniture can be placed in them without obstructing light or ventilation. Each has a fine closet. The bath room being connected with both is the most convenient arrangement possible. Note the inside cellar steps—a feature which is a great convenience.

How could you get more real livable home for the money? It can't be done—you can't get as much, except from Gordon-Van Tine—and the only reason we can do it is through our organization—which **knows how**—plus our big buying and manufacturing facilities, which hammer costs down to the bottom.

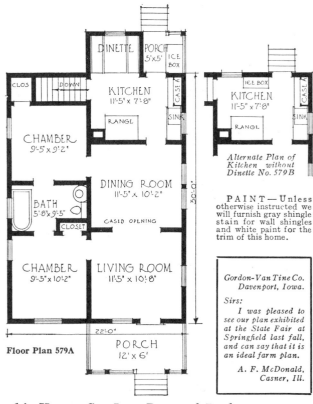

Floor Plan 579A

Alternate Plan of Kitchen without Dinette No. 579B

PAINT—Unless otherwise instructed we will furnish gray shingle stain for wall shingles and white paint for the trim of this home.

*Gordon-Van Tine Co.
Davenport, Iowa.*

Sirs:
I was pleased to see our plan exhibited at the State Fair at Springfield last fall, and can say that it is an ideal farm plan.

*A. F. McDonald,
Casner, Ill.*

For Plumbing, Heating, Lighting for his Home, See Last Pages of Book

Gordon-Van Tine Home No. 585

Specially Planned Farm or Town Home

For Prices on This Home, See First Page.
Read Pages 9 and 10 for Full Description of Materials.

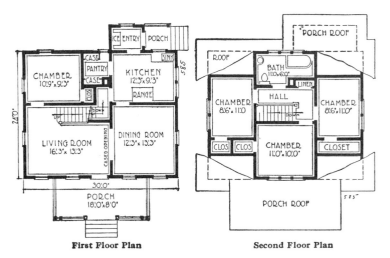

First Floor Plan   **Second Floor Plan**

PAINT—Unless otherwise instructed, we
will furnish white paint for body and trim.

EVERYTHING A PERFECT FIT

Louisville, Ohio.

Gordon-Van Tine Co.
   Gentlemen: In regard to my ready-cut home, I must say I am well pleased with my new home: so far, everything fits to a perfect fit and I am more than satisfied with your ready-cut home. I am going to stick up for the GORDON-VAN TINE COMPANY if I lose my life.

   Yours for more Gordon-Van Tine homes, (Signed) Mr. Roy Baughman.

Options That Will Save You $133.80

Deduct the above amount from the regular price on this house if you are willing to buy it with the following changes from regular specifications:
6 to 2 Star A Star Red Cedar Shingles instead of 5 to 2 Clear; plain square edge casings for doors and windows instead of Craftsman design; all subflooring and kitchen case omitted.

HERE is a design which will meet with great favor as a suburban home. Or it will prove equally profitable and satisfactory from any other point of view
There is nothing left to be desired either in appearance or convenience.

The large gabled dormers with their triple windows give not only an impression of size from the outside, but add greatly to the second story rooms.

Designed along low broad lines the use of perpendicular lines only on the front porch is another clever device which gives the needed appearance of height and affords an attractive approach to the house.

On the inside of this house likewise attractive features are not wanting. See the splendid stretch of space through the living room and dining room with its excellent furniture space. And note the compactness gained by the open stairway which ascends from the rear of the living room.

Just at the foot of these stairs is a door leading into the downstairs bed room or den. If the former this door brings it within easy access of the bath. This room has windows in adjoining walls and excellent closet space.

As is always true of the houses which we design especially for the country home, here we are particularly proud of the kitchen. It is light and roomy, with a splendid pantry opening off of it. The pantry cases are our "A" and "B" design, conveniently placed as to the windows. The space for the kitchen sink is also well lighted.

Just beyond the sink is a glazed door opening into the entry or washroom—something really a necessity on the farm.

On the other side of the kitchen next to the dining room door is a passage leading to the basement stairs, which descend directly under the front stairway, a great economy of space. For the basement we supply the stairs as well as sufficient cellar frames and sash.

Each of the bed rooms has two or more windows, each has an unusually large closet, and each has especially well planned furniture space, while off the hall is a linen case like the one shown in the colored section.

In this upstairs, as in the rest of the house, we have room arrangement with utility as well as comfort given consideration everywhere.

In fact here is your ideal town or farm home—convenient, compact and economical both from the standpoint of construction and that of lasting service.

For Plumbing, Heating, Lighting for his Home, See Last Pages of Book

Gordon-Van Tine Home No. 550

An Unusually Convenient Bungalow

**For Prices on This Home,
See First Page.**

**Read Pages 9 and 10 for Description
of Material.**

Options That Will Save You $96.85

Deduct the above amount from the regular price on this house if you are willing to buy it with the following changes from regular specifications:
6 to 2 Star A Star Red Cedar Shingles instead of 5 to 2 Clear; plain square edge casings for doors and windows instead of Craftsman design; all subflooring and kitchen case omitted.

BUNGALOW admirers will find their highest ideals sensibly incorporated in this attractive home. Both the exterior and interior arrangements show a strict regard for all that is modern in the way of conveniences, room arrangement, design and construction.

The sloping roof with the wide overhanging cornice and open rafters are only a few of the distinguishing features in this bungalow. The many advantages of the front porch are easily seen and appreciated.

A happy contrast is obtained on the outside walls by using the siding below the belt course with shingles exposed 5 inches to the weather above. The effective use of a belt around the entire house avoids any chance of a monotonous appearance.

The large, airy and well lighted living room is one of the outstanding features of the excellent interior. The front door is glazed with side lights to match. There is a handsome cased opening connecting the living room and dining room. The bed rooms are large, well lighted and have splendid closets with plenty of room which is always so desirable.

The bath is accessible from either bed-room and is provided with our stock towel cabinet shown in the color section.

The kitchen is particularly well planned with a careful consideration for convenience and light with the proper space allowed for our kitchen case "B" made up of a flour bin, drawers, large countershelf below and two doors and shelves above, extending to the ceiling. Refer to the color pages of this book showing picture of this work table and kitchen case.

The grade door arrangement will impress you with its convenience. The grade landing is ideal for the ice box.

There is a large basement under the entire house with plenty of space for your coal room, vegetable room, laundry and heating plant. Cellar windows are furnished and all materials in this house conform strictly with our standard specifications.

This bungalow when completed will prove a home of permanent satisfaction to you because of its unique interior arrangement and its attractive yet substantial outside appearance.

PAINT—Unless otherwise instructed, we will furnish Lemont stone for side walls up to belt, oxide red stain for wall shingles above belt, and white for trim.

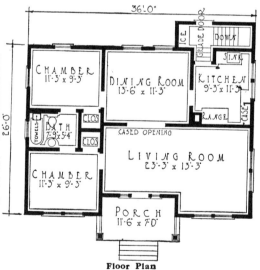

Floor Plan

For Plumbing, Heating, Lighting for This Home, See Last Pages of Book

Gordon-Van Tine Home No. 541

A Practical 6-Room Cottage, Cosy and Neat

For Prices on This Home, See First Page.
Read Pages 9 and 10 for Full Description of Materials.

Floor Plan

CHAMBER 11'3" x 8'6" · KITCHEN 11'3" x 11'3" · CASE · SINK · PORCH · ENTRY · ICE · RANGE · CLOS · CLOS · CHAMBER 11'3" x 9'6" · DINING ROOM 11'6" x 12'0" · LINEN · BATH · HALL · CLOS · CASED OPENING · CHAMBER 11'3" x 10'0" · LIVING ROOM 15'3" x 12'6" · 38'0" · 28'0" · PORCH 8'0" WIDE

Options That Will Save You $118.15 ·

Deduct the above amount from the regular price on this house if you are willing to buy it with the following changes from regular specifications:
6 to 2 Star A Star Red Cedar Shingles instead of 5 to 2 Clear; plain square edge casings for doors and windows instead of Craftsman design; all subflooring and kitchen case omitted.

IT is easy to understand why this home has been one of the best-selling homes we furnish Just study the floor plan and note the convenient and economical planning. Many of our friends have found in this one-story bungalow the very home they have in mind. The fact that so many people have built it suggests merit.

In this plan we show you a real, comfortable home with six big rooms and bath.

The exterior is very pleasing. The designer has made it most attractive by extending the hip-roof with its dormer, so as to cover the big front porch. In this is given to the porch an appearance of strength and solidity. Its close connection with the house is further brought out by the belt-course with the shingles above which extend in an unbroken line around the house. The belt serves as the head casing of all outside frames. This effect bears out prominently the continuous line of the outside trim. The dormer is glazed with a twin one-light sash.

The rooms are all well lighted. The living room has in addition to the glazed bungalow door, two big shingle windows, one in each outside wall. The dining room has a big twin window. The kitchen also has a twin window in the rear wall in addition to the glazed entry-door and glazed rear door.

Although the living room is given perfect lighting and ventilation, the wall space has not been sacrificed. Notice the fine possibilities here in placing your furniture and changing it about when desired.

The bed rooms are also provided with plenty of light and ventilation. Each bed room has two windows—the front and rear chambers have one in each outside wall, while the chamber between has a big twin window. You will notice also that the bed rooms are separated from the living rooms by the hall. This is a very desirable arrangement. In this hall conveniently placed is our handy linen closet. The rear bed room opens directly into the kitchen which will probably prove quite convenient at times. The two rear chambers are inter-connecting.

The kitchen is large and like all Gordon-Van Tine kitchens is ideally arranged. Our big kitchen case style "C" is included at no extra cost. A detail of this case is shown on the colored insert in this catalog. The work table is directly under the big twin window. It would be rather difficult to improve on this particular kitchen.

The entry which opens out on the rear porch provides a place for the ice box and other kitchen articles—it will be found most convenient. Like the front porch, the rear porch is essentially a part of the house proper.

The cellar stairs are well placed, leading down direct from the kitchen. The plan provides for a basement under the entire house and cellar sash and other material is furnished.

You may just as well concentrate your attention on this home if it suits your purpose—you will find improvements rather difficult as it is now complete. It is a compact, comfortable, and economical home to build and you will do well to consider it.

PAINT—Unless otherwise instructed, we will furnish Lemont stone paint for the body of this home, white for trim and brown shingle stain for the wall shingles of this home.

For Plumbing, Heating, Lighting for This Home, See Last Pages of Book

Gordon-Van Tine Home No. 605

Exceptionally Well Planned Suburban Home

For Prices on This Home, See First Page.

Read Pages 9 and 10 for Full Description of Materials.

WHEN you think of your new home, you think of comfortable rooms and good cheer on the inside. But you must give the appearance of the outside a thought also. In the above you find an unusually comfortable house that at the same time is especially well planned.

The combination of stucco and panels in the upper ; able end ·, the wide cornice with its attractive brackets, heavy barge boards and exposed rafters, together with the hooded and paneled Colonial entrance are all details that have been given the thought which they deserve.

But the really unusual features of this design are those that especially adapt themselves to making the interior more livable. The construction of the roof gives very good lines and permits of an exceptionally large main bed room—a room of full width and of full ceiling height, except for slightly rounded corners under the roof extension. This and the other two bed rooms all have plenty of closet space.

The hall, bath and linen closet have all been well and conveniently planned, as has the entire house.

The stair hall is so arranged that it is an economy in space, for, from the first landing, steps lead to the kitchen as well as to the living room. This and the landing part way up afford variety, while the windows on the second landing light both the stairway and hall. The coat closet on the first sanding is further evidence of the fact that this house is designed for comfort and convenience.

The living room, large in itself, has the added advantage of the wide openings both into the dining room and onto the sun porch. Across from the French doors of the latter opening is the fireplace with casement windows on either side. There is a large window toward the front making this indeed a pleasant room.

PAINT—Unless otherwise instructed we will furnish straw paint for the body and white trim for this house.

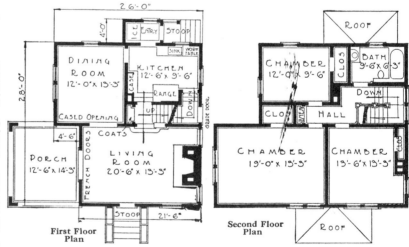

First Floor Plan

Second Floor Plan

It is the placing of the sun porch that has furthered the low broad effect of the house. Greater privacy is also afforded than if the porch were placed at the front of the house.

The square conveniently arranged dining room is well lighted by its large windows. Large double windows abound throughout the house, in fact there isn't a dark or poorly ventilated spot in this comfortable six room house. The broad wall space here in the dining room provides two good places for side board or buffet. The kitchen has our case "A" and a case special "B" which provide ample shelf room. And do not overlook the compact a d convenient arrangement of the entry.

In fact the entire house has been so well planned that it is worthy of the attention it has attracted, and the praise bestowed upon it by those who call it home.

Sectional sash for sun porch are additional and will be quoted on request.

For Plumbing, Heating, Lighting for This Home, See Last Pages of Book

Gordon-Van Tine Home No. 547

An Economical and Ever Popular Type

**For Prices on This Home, See First Page.
See Pages 9 and 10 for Description of Materials.**

First Floor Plan

Second Floor Plan

Gordon-Van Tine Co., Davenport, Iowa.   Algona, Iowa.
  Gentlemen: Some days ago I received a letter from Mr. H. B. Nelson requesting
me to have a picture taken of my house plan and also one picture from the interior.
I have complied with his request. The stairway is certainly as fine a feature as there
is in any part of the house and the finish is certainly fine. I did the work on the
case myself and most of the finishing.
  I must say I am more than pleased with my home. Everybody that has seen the
house expressed themselves more than pleased with the material and plans. You will
remember Mr. Bert Peck of Algona has purchased material for a barn of your company, shipped to Comfrey, Minn. Mr. Peck is a business man, in the hardware
business. I recommended your material to him and several others that will buy in
the spring.   Mr. Geo. Koch.

These Options Will Save You $93.70

  Deduct the above amount from the regular price on this
house if you are willing to buy it with the following changes
from regular specifications.
  6 to 2 Star A Star Red Cedar Shingles instead of 5 to 2 Clear;
plain square edge casings for doors and windows instead of
Craftsman design; all subflooring and kitchen case omitted.

THIS is an attractive but simple home with no unnecessary
  ornamentation, just the cozy home for which you have been
  looking. Its comfortable appearance and convenient
  arrangement have gained favor with many.

  The twin windows above the porch roof light one of the two
good sized upstairs bed rooms, both of which have full ceilings.
The other, having windows at the rear, is almost the counterpart
of the front room.   Do not fail to notice the splendid closet space.

  The bath room is so located as to be convenient to all bed rooms.
It is only a short distance from this to the downstairs bed room,
opening just off the foot of the stairs.   In every family there are
occasions when a bed room on the first floor is an especial convenience.

  The open stairway becomes almost a part of the living room.
It is of clear selected Slash Grain Douglas Fir as is all of the interior
finish.   Hence this stairway is an addition to the large, pleasant
family room, which, with the dining room, occupies the front of
the house.   These rooms are especially well planned for the placing
of furniture.   They look out upon a large front porch, one of the
attractive features of this home.

  The dining room is separated from the kitchen by a large pantry,
fully equipped. Without this equipment we would not consider
one of our homes complete. Our regular price includes the wall
case to the ceiling and the work cabinet complete with all doors,
draws, and bins, all material ready to put up—our "B" case.
The basement stairway descends from the pantry also.

  The kitchen is large, adequately lighted with two well placed
windows, and also by the glazed rear door. The location of the
sink has a two-fold advantage, since the dishes need never be taken
far from the cupboard, as the sink is near to this and the stove.
In building there is also great economy in this arrangement as the
location of the sink to the bath room makes an extra stack unnecessary.

  You will find this house exceptionally convenient throughout,
and one making comfort possible to a marked degree. The cost
to you is not comparable, as the Gordon-Van Tine Company offers
you its superior service and the advantage of its immense organization at a price far less than you find elsewhere.   You cannot afford
to disregard this fact when deciding upon your home.

  PAINT—Unless otherwise instructed, we will furnish light gray
paint for the body and white for the trim of this home.

For Plumbing, Heating, Lighting for This Home, See Last Pages of Book

Gordon-Van Tine Home No. 557

A Handsome Two-Story Bungalow

For Prices on This Home See First Page.

Read Pages 9 and 10 for Full Description of Materials.

IF a bungalow is a favorite with you, but you feel that you need the space afforded by the two-story house, this plan offers a happy solution. Our architects succeeded remarkably well in keeping the characteristics of the one and giving the added advantages of the other.

The substantial lines of the porch, the wide cornice, and the exposed rafter ends all unite to make this a distinctive home. The outside walls are covered with Clear Red Cedar shingles, another pleasing feature. These extend to the grade line, helping to further the low broad effect sought after in the bungalow. The hooded dormers add dignity to the exterior, and room and light to the house sized attic.

The wide porch along the whole front is roomy. The living room is large, light and airy and connected with the dining room by a wide cased opening, making the entire front of this home practically one large room, receiving light and air from every direction. A hall opens from the back of the living room.

The room opening off the left of this hall will make either a very cool and quiet ground floor bed room, not far from the bath at the head of the stairs, or a mighty fine den or library. The closet to the right of the stairway can be used with this room, or as a coat closet, near to the living room.

The kitchen, besides opening from the dining room, is also easy of access to the other rooms, because of its connection with the lower hall. The built-in kitchen case, design "D", must

First Floor Plan

Second Floor Plan

meet with your absolute approval, since its location is ideal. See the colored insert for illustration of this handsome and convenient case. In fact, the entire kitchen arrangement is such as will make work easy and pleasureable, and at the same time leave the room always orderly and attractive.

Not an unnecessary step will be taken in getting supplies from the basement or refrigerator, and the putting away of winter stores will not result in an untidy kitchen, for the grade door at the walk level prevents this. The basement extends under the entire house. It is well lighted, as we furnish four cellar sash, as well as stairs, girders and girder posts.

On the second floor are two large well lighted chambers, a bath and an attic. The attic gives splendid storage space, without the necessity of climbing a second flight of stairs. The bath is unusually large. The linen case which we supply is shown in the colored section.

All in all this is a plan for a home that is comfortable, economical and attractive. From those who have lived in it, we learn that the longer they have called it "home" the more they have to say in its favor.

PAINT—Unless otherwise instructed, we will furnish brown shingle stain for wall shingles and white trim.

For Plumbing, Heating, Lighting for this Home, See Last Pages of Book

Gordon-Van Tine Home No. 572

An Unusually Well Planned Bungalow

For Prices on This Home, See First Page.
Read Pages 9 and 10 for Full Description of Materials.

Floor Plan

FOLKS who have built this home and lived in it tell us that this bungalow is the most comfortable, satisfying home they ever had. It's a home that wears well, because it owes its beauty to good proportions and harmony of details, rather than any striving for effects or freakish styles. The porch has a brick rail—the material of which is bought locally. Porch floor is fir and steps cypress. The outside wall of the house are sided with clear Louisiana cypress or California redwood. If you paint the body a Lemont stone and use a light gray for the trim you will have one of the best looking homes in your community no matter where you live

The living and dining room claim your immediate attention. Big, wide, well-lighted rooms with a cased opening between, they impress you most favorably. The flower box set under the triple window in the front wall of the dining room is included. Notice how pleasant is the dining room with this big triple window and the two windows in the left wall. The living room is entered through a glazed door. In addition it has a window in the front wall and two windows in the side wall. To the right of the hall leading to the bath and chambers, is a coat closet, opening into the living

room. This will always be found a convenient feature. There is another closet at the right just as you pass into this hall. Also notice our linen closet in the bath room. The bath is commodious, a feature often overlooked.

In the rear are the two large chambers with windows in each outside wall. Notice particularly that these sleeping rooms are set apart from the other rooms. Also notice how easily the housewife can reach the bath room or chambers, through the kitchen door opening into the hall. This is an excellent provision.

The central location of the kitchen with its ideal arrangement can hardly be improved. Our kitchen case, style "C" which is included, will prove a valuable aid to the housewife in her culinary duties. Directly over the work table is a twin window, assuring ample light and air.

From the entry a glazed door opens into the kitchen. Opposite is a recess for the ice box. The rear door opening into the entry is also a glazed door and permits direct access to the cellar.

The entire arrangement is excellent. The full basement under this house is well-lighted by eight cellar sash.

To everyone there comes the sense of responsibility in provision for others. In no other way can it be better done than in making the home life ideal. With this thought in mind you will find this bungalow a valuable suggestion. Review it again, most critically and let your good judgment decide.

PAINT—Unless otherwise instructed, we will furnish Lemont stone paint for the body and light gray for the trim of this home.

For Plumbing, Heating, Lighting for This Home, See Last Pages of Book

Gordon-Van Tine Home No. 514

An Ideal 3-Bedroom Bungalow

For Prices on This Home, See First Page.
Read Pages 9 and 10 for Full Description of Materials.

AN attractive inviting modern home for you whether you live in town or country. A careful inspection will show its large number of admirable features both within and without. In appearance, it is as attractive as any other bungalow and in arrangement we have kept the needs of the farmer and his family well in mind.

The roof which extends some distance is supported by wide brackets. The shingled walls are divided by the belt course which takes the place of window caps. The roof, railing and pillars of the unusually large porch are all in good taste.

The triple window in the front gable lights the large, roomy attic over the entire house and provides excellent storage space as the entire attic is floored. Entrance to it is gained by means of a stairway ascending from the central hall. This attic is a convenience which will be appreciated.

The bed rooms and bath are removed from the living room by this hall also. They are connected in such a way as to give a better circulation of air and from them one can have access to the kitchen without going through the living room. The closet space has not been disregarded and the towel case over the bath tub takes care of many small articles.

The entrance directly from the front porch into the living room means that

there is no outer hall to heat or care for.

And notice the twin windows in the living room and in the dining room. This can well be used as a combination living and dining room, especially during the winter months, simply by equipping the opening with a pair of French doors' and so closing off the big living room.

The arrangement of the roomy kitchen is such as to save steps. Cooking here could never be very unpleasant. Notice how well the windows and doors are arranged, and what a complete equipment it has. Our kitchen case, design "C," is placed near to the window as well as near to the sink. The fact that the basement stairs descends from this room is a further convenience. Supplies are always close at hand and during the canning season the newly filled jars and glasses are easily put away.

The wash room connects directly with the back porch, the kitchen and the dining room. This is a special feature which will be distinctly appreciated by every farm housewife, for she will be saved the annoyance of having the outdoors help crowding through her kitchen, just as she is serving a meal.

The result of suggestions received from many country people during several years have been embodied in this plan; thus making the result an unusually practical country home, convenient within and attractive both within and without.

PAINT—Unless otherwise instructed will furnish brown stain for the wall shingles and white paint for the trim of this home.

Floor Plan

For Plumbing, Heating, Lighting for This Home, See Last Pages of Book

Gordon-Van Tine Home No. 549

Conservative 2-Story Stucco Home

This House Can be Furnished with Siding or Shingles on Outside Walls Instead of Stucco if Desired.   Write for Prices.

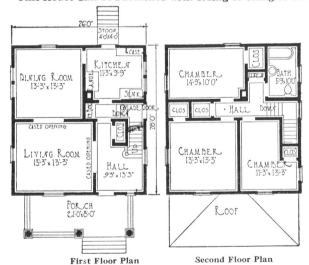

First Floor Plan   **Second Floor Plan**

I am very much pleased with my home, it being a distinctive from the ones they build in Brookland and is very much admired. Could have sold it a dozen times at an advantage, but prefer to live in it.
Very respectfully,
R. J. Flood,
1248 Monroe St., Brookland, D. C.

All the material for this house was furnished by you, on which there was a saving to me of at least $300, and I am well pleased with it.
If I ever do build again, I will sure buy the lumber of you.
Pete Drolson,
R. F. D. No. 2, Beldenville, Wis,

For Prices on This Home, See First Page.

Read Pages 9 and 10 for Full Description of Materials.

A CLEAR cut dignity of appearance impresses itself upon you during your first consideration of this home. The broad porch, big windows and front dormer have added much to the always satisfactory effect of the square hip roof. The walls are finished in stucco. The entire exterior, in fact, makes a distinct appeal.

The interior exemplifies comfort and cheer, at the same time emphasizes the fact that there is not an inch of waste space. The reception hall is large, and is light as well, because of the two windows and glazed door. The coat closet near the stairs and the door to the central entryway are both features of convenience. You will notice that this entry helps to shorten the trip on a chilly winter morning from the sleeping rooms to the furnace. It also offers an excellent place for the refrigerator. Do not overlook the outside door opening directly onto the basement stairs at the grade line. We supply these stairs, as well as the necessary basement sash.

There is no more popular or satisfactory arrangement of living and dining room than the one found here. The wide opening between the two rooms is a decorative feature as well as a pleasing arrangement.

The entrance to the kitchen at the side of the dining room means that the culinary secrets are not revealed to the entire house each time this door is opened. This kitchen offers you as much storage space as many a pantry and at the same time brings everything absolutely convenient to the house-wife's hand. This is due to our built-in kitchen case, design "B", see color pages for illustration.

The cost of installing the plumbing will be low here since the bath room is directly over the kitchen. A further saving will result from the location planned for the furnace, the compactness of the rooms and consequent possible arrangement of furnace pipes which always means economy in heating.

The three fine chambers and bath all open from the upstairs hall, as does the linen closet built-in at the end of the hall. This is perfectly convenient to all, and the bedding, linens and towels kept here will always be at hand when wanted. This is in reality an additional convenience, since each of the three well-lighted sleeping rooms has a nice closet of its own.

Your judgment has shown you that this entire house is an exponent of homelike comfort and true economy. If it is of the size to fit your needs you can find nothing to supply these at a price as satisfactory.

PAINT—Unless otherwise instructed, we will furnish white for the trim of this home. The walls are stucco.

For Plumbing, Heating, Lighting for This Home, See Last Pages of Book

Gordon-Van Tine Home No. 518

A Substantial Five-Bedroom Farm Home

For Prices on This Home, See First Page.
Read Pages 9 and 10 for Full De-
scription of Materials.

"ONE of the finest and most practical farm houses I have ever seen," is the verdict of hundreds of farmers regarding this splendid country house. But in fact it is as suitable for the city dweller as for the farmer.

The exterior has the appearance of massiveness, of architectural beauty, and of hospitality, showing plainly that its owner is a man in prosperous circumstances, looking for the best for his family and himself.

Notice the effect produced by the hip roof, broken by the dormer with the twin sash. The sturdy effect of the exterior is increased by the rugged front porch. The massive roof, with its lines unbroken by center pillars is supported at the corners by triple columns, resting on boxed-up piers. Even the open railing above the floor line adds to the general appearance of dignity.

The interior arrangement was planned with an eye to the practical. The big living room is connected with the dining room by a wide cased opening, so that the two rooms may be thrown into one.

At threshing time or Christmas time, you will find our kitchen well planned for the ease of the busy housewife. It is roomy without demanding extra steps while working. The kitchen case is our design "D", placed near to the sink and not far from the range.

An inner hallway also leads from the kitchen to the stairway, and to the down stairs bed room or den, which also opens from the living room. This back stairway is shut off from the living room by a two panel fir door.

To the rear of the kitchen is a cosy, enclosed entryway, which is connected with the rear porch. Many use this entryway for a wash room for the men folks.

The basement is reached either by way of the outside hatchway or by the cellar stairs descending from the kitchen. Cellar windows, which we provide, furnish plenty of light and ventilation for the entire basement.

The four upstairs bed rooms are all light and airy with a wealth of closet space. The linen closet at the end of the hall is like the one

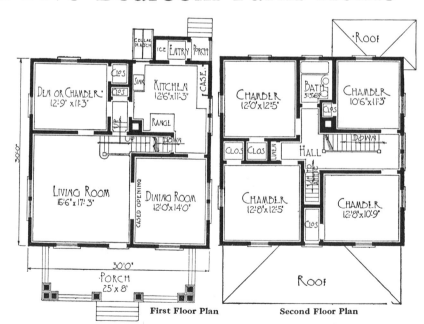

First Floor Plan   Second Floor Plan

shown on the center color pages and the drawers and shelves will be found a convenient place for bed linen and blankets.

Notice that the bath room fixtures and sink are so arranged as to utilize the same stack of pipes, thus economizing in installation costs. All piping will thus be placed on inside walls away from the cold. If a basement laundry is installed it should of course be placed directly below the kitchen. In this instance the outside basement stair will be an especially convenient feature.

The stairway between the front bed rooms leads to a great big attic 9 feet high at the ridge-board. It is floored making a fine storage place.

Eight rooms and bath, seven closets, a big attic, outside and inside basement stairs, a closed-in entryway or wash room, a fine looking exterior and a splendidly low price—here you have a house that will give you solid comfort and add many dollars to each acre of your farm.

PAINT—Unless otherwise instructed, we will furnish cream for body and white for trim.

For Plumbing, Heating, Lighting for This Home, See Last Pages of Book

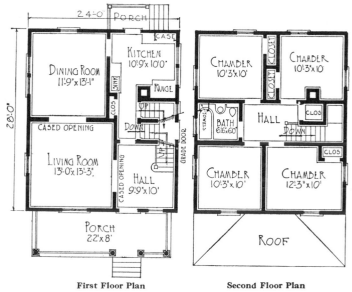

Gordon-Van Tine Home No. 551

Substantial Two-Story Home

For Prices on This Home, See First Page.
Read Pages 9 and 10 for Full Description of Materials.

First Floor Plan

Second Floor Plan

My house cost me $2,210 all told to build, plumbing, cistern and furnace included. I would not trade my house for any other house built at the same time in this town that cost $3,000.

I am well satisfied with my home and I had enough lumber left to build a sleeping porch on the back of the house.   *Very truly yours,*

Garwin, Ia.   *W. C. Mauck.*

Options That Will Save You $98.65

Deduct the above amount from the regular price on this house if you are willing to buy it with the following changes from regular specifications:

6 to 2 Star A Star Red Cedar Shingles instead of 5 to 2 Clear; plain square edge casings for doors and windows instead of Craftsman design; all subflooring and kitchen case omitted.

THERE is nothing that answers your purpose so well, if room is required, as the big, square house. In this plan we show you a splendid example of the type. For real economy of construction and material, as well as design, this house could well serve as a model.

The exterior is pleasing, consistently holding to straight lines. Monotony is strictly avoided in the fine balance obtained—the plan and illustration show you readily how well we have succeeded in giving this home an imposing appearance. The broad front porch with the big round columns, and the wide cornice, with the dormer, lend to the exterior the effect of greater breadth and height.

Study the floor plans—notice the big square rooms. Not an inch of waste floor space. The windows are perfectly proportioned permitting cross ventilation and floods of sunlight. Take particular notice of the combination stairway—open from the reception hall to the landing which is also reached from the kitchen hall. This is an exceptionally handy arrangement, giving you a front and rear stairway in one. The stairway landing is well-lighted by the twin window directly over it. Also notice the big closet off from the hall on the second floor—plenty of closet space here. Then there is the small, handy closet in the hall between the reception room and the kitchen.

There is a convenient outside cellar entrance through a grade door set in an open areaway two steps below grade. The basement is also reached from the inside by the stairway leading down from the kitchen hall.

Like all Gordon-Van Tine kitchens perfect arrangement is featured in this kitchen. Our big kitchen case, style "B", as shown on the color pages, is included. The kitchen will have plenty of light and air through the big twin windows and glazed door. The rear stoop is large enough for the ice box and other articles.

These features which recommend this home are plain to be seen —it is roomy, imposing and withal economical to build. It has everything you need. Consider it thoroughly.

PAINT—Unless otherwise instructed, we will furnish French gray for body and white for trim.

For Plumbing, Heating, Lighting for This Home, See Last Pages of Book

Gordon-Van Tine Home No. 526

An Ever Popular Home of Fine Proportions

HERE we have the conservative type of a house, large and well built. Its square lines are relieved by the room projection at the side and the two-window dormer to the front. The broad dignified porch gives further character, and is one of the features that makes this house always popular. The steps leading to the porch and the Monterey front door have been placed at the side, leaving space for a swing or other porch furniture.

When deciding upon your new home you naturally picture it, as it will appear to you after years of occupancy. This is when you realize that the plainer, more substantial type gives undoubted satisfaction and service. A square house admits of no waste space and bespeaks equal sized rooms and plenty of light.

Here the entrance brings one into a room-sized reception hall lighted by two windows and the glazed front door. The stairway really seems a part of the hall furnishing, but leaves ample room for other furniture besides. The living room, big and square, is made to seem even larger by the cased openings eading from the hall and to the dining room.

The dining room is worthy of careful attention, for it can be used as a cheery, roomy, living and dining room for the family desiring to put it to that use. And at no time would there be a question as to how it would be possible to seat the large family party.

The kitchen lighted by twin windows has our Gordon-Van Tine case and work table design "B", the latter well lighted, since it is placed under one of the windows. These cupboards supply the place for all stores, except the large supplies which will probably find their place in the fruit cellar. The basement affords enough space for fruit cellar, a laundry and furnace room, if you desire them.

The inner hall is the logical place for your refrigerator. The door to basement stairs opens just opposite the space for it. An outside entrance to the basement stair is provided by means of a door at the grade landing. A direct entrance from the outside is also planned

**For Prices on This Home See First Page.
Read Pages 9 and 10 for Full Description of Materials.**

STOOP

CASE

KITCHEN
11'3" x 9'10"

SINK

RANGE

DINING ROOM
14'3" x 13'3"

GRADE DOOR

DOWN

HALL ICE

28'0"

CASED OPENING

REC HALL
9'3" x 13'3"

CASED OPENING

LIVING ROOM
13'3" x 13'3"

PORCH
24'0" x 8'0"

24'0"

First Floor Plan

CHAMBER
8'6" x 9'9"

BATH
5'6" x 6'5"

CHAMBER
11'0" x 10'9"

CLOS

HALL

DOWN

LINEN

CLOS

CLOS

CHAMBER
11'0" x 13'3"

CHAMBER
11'6" x 13'5"

PORCH ROOF

Second Floor Floor

for the kitchen as is indicated by the stoop in the rear.

This upstairs hall is well ventilated and lighted by the window on the stair landing. The four large sleeping rooms also have most excellent ventilation and light with their windows in adjoining walls. Good closet space has

been provided here, and the bath has been carefully planned. A feature which will be particularly appreciated is the built-in linen closet in the hall.

PAINT—Unless otherwise instructed, we will furnish light gray paint for the body and white for trim.

For Plumbing, Heating, Lighting for This Home, See Last Pages of Book

Gordon-Van Tine Home No. 577

Particularly Attractive Two-Story Home

First Floor Plan

Second Floor Plan

PAINT—Unless otherwise instructed, we will furnish green stain for the wall shingles and white paint for the body and trim of this home.

WHAT THE WORKMEN SAID

Findlay, Ohio.

Gordon-Van Tine Co., Davenport, Iowa.

   Gentlemen: The workmen declared without hesitation that the material furnished in the construction of this bungalow was the best ever shipped into Findlay. This attractive and comfortable home must be seen to be appreciated.

Dr. W. H. Drake.

For Prices on This Home, See First Page.

Read Pages 9 and 10 for Full Description of Material.

THE popularity of a home is measured by its desirability. In this house you see a home that is justly popular, because it is roomy, as well as economical, although the size is modified to permit the greatest economy of material. Herein is full measure of home comfort.

This is a standard type of dwelling of which there are many variations. This design is developed to afford the maximum home-service at the minimum cost. The exterior is carefully planned. Sided walls to the belt line with shingles above is especially good treatment on a house of this size and type. The porch gable harmonizes with the main roof gable. The heavy timber brackets always are consistently used with a wide cornice.

The interior impresses one even more favorably—the large living room lighted on three sides, with the beautiful open stairway, gives the impression of comfort and beauty. The dining room is entered through a cased opening. If desirable to close one room from the other install a pair of the beautiful French doors shown on the center color pages.

The kitchen is planned just like all Gordon-Van Tine kitchens— everything is arranged to make the work a pleasure and most convenient. Our kitchen case, style "B," as shown on the color pages, is included. Note especially how readily accessible are all rooms to the kitchen. Entrance is made to the kitchen either from the grade door or the rear door. These doors are glazed.

The three bed rooms have windows in each outside wall, also good closet space. The bath leaves nothing to be desired. Our towel cabinet is provided for this room. The bed room doors are so arranged that the bath is but a step away.

Whether you are building a home to live in, or for investment, here is a house that will answer every requirement at a very low cost.

For Plumbing, Heating, Lighting for This Home, See Last Pages of Book

Gordon-Van Tine Home No. 504

A Very Pleasing 5-Room Bungalow

For Prices on This Home, See First Page.
Read Pages 9 and 10 for Full Description of Materials.

IT is especial attention to straight lines that places this bungalow so far out of the ordinary.

The panel strips and shingles used above the porch beam, the proportions of the porch itself, and the roof gables all illustrate this fact. The room extension in the dining room should not be overlooked either.

The living room and dining room can be considered together, for their wide cased opening makes practically one large room of the two. The large twin window in the dining room gives an ample supply of light and air.

The kitchen is a splendid work room. Our design "B" kitchen case has an ideal location both as to light and as to proximity to the stove and sink. The glazed door between kitchen and entry is another convenient feature.

The basement stairs descend from this rear entry. There is a well planned refrigerator space here also. The basement is intended to extend under the entire house. For it we supply the stairs and sash.

The fact that there is no room taken for an inner hall in this bungalow means that the bed rooms are larger than is frequently the case, and at the same time they are both accessible to the kitchen without its being necessary for one to pass through the living room and dining room.

The closets are ample, and the bath room convenient. For this is supplied a towel case like the one which we show on color pages.

When you consider all these features, and note the low price we are able to quote, you will understand why so very many people write such enthusiastic letters about this home of their own.

Floor Plan

Gordon-Van Tine Co.,   Bloomington, Ill.
   Gentlemen: Everyone that sees our home is sure ready to say a word of praise for it.
It sure makes a very attractive corner.
   The lumber was of the very best, and I am sure glad I purchased the material from Gordon-Van Tine Co.
                                         Yours very truly,
                                              Logan B. Perry.

PAINT—Unless otherwise instructed, we will furnish cream for body paint, white for trim, and brown stain for gable shingles.

For Plumbing, Heating, Lighting for This Home, See Last Pages of Book

Gordon-Van Tine Home No. 511

An Especially Pleasing Five-Room Bungalow

For Prices on This Home, See First Page.
Read Pages 9 and 10 for Full Description of Materials.

Options That Will Save You $98.15

Deduct the the above amount from the regular price on this house if you are willing to buy it with the following changes from regular specifications:
6 to 2 Star A Star Red Cedar Shingles instead of 5 to 2 Clear; plain square edge casings for doors and windows instead of Craftsman design; all subflooring and kitchen case omitted.

Floor Plan

Poughkeepsie, N. Y.

Gordon-Van Tine Co., Davenport, Iowa.

Gentlemen: In reply to your favor of the 3rd inst., in reference to the material I purchased from you, beg to state that so far I have no reason to regret that I entrusted my order for building material with your company. I can truly say that all of the material received from you, of whatever nature, was just as you recommended it to be. I have taken considerable pleasure in showing my house to several people who have called and inquired about it.

Assuring you of my kindly interest, I am,
Yours very truly, Moses K. Lee.

THE more you study this five-room house the more you will be impressed with its attractive exterior, its happy arrangement of rooms and its genuine economy.

The roof lines are excellent. Their broad sweep is emphasized by wide closed cornices.

The porch has been carefully designed. Here the main roof has been extended to cover it while the square columns resting on concrete piers give it an appearance of solidity and hospitality.

The cosy front hallway with its coat closet indicates the care that has been given to the planning of the interior. From the hall one gets a view of the unusually large living room with its three windows.

The dining room is connected with the living room by a cased opening. Sunlight streams through the twin windows and gives to it a warmth and hospitality.

A swinging door leads from the dining room to the carefully arranged kitchen. The day of the big kitchen is gone, and the thousands of steps formerly wasted by the housewife are no longer required in this modern kitchen with its excellent arrangement.

PAINT—Unless otherwise instructed we will furnish French gray paint for the body and lead for the trim of this home.

Our kitchen case, design A, is placed near to the window with the sink and range not far away. And there is no part of the kitchen that will not receive excellent light from the twin windows at the right.

The fact that the basement stairs descend from the entry way just off the kitchen bring the supplies of the fruit cupboard and the vegetable cellar near at hand. And at the same time the winter's supply can be stored away in the basement without being taken through the kitchen. Two doors, the outside one our glazed Monterey, keep out the chilly winter blasts.

From the dining room also one enters the hall which separates the bath and sleeping rooms from the rest of the house. Each room has its own closet. A special designed linen closet takes up the angle in the hall and is convenient to the bed rooms and bath. The bath room window has purposely been made shorter and the lower sash is glazed with moss glass.

Viewed from every angle this is a cottage that is sure to give you solid comfort while the unusually attractive price we quote indicates its economy.

For Plumbing, Heating, Lighting for This Home, See Last Pages of Book

Gordon-Van Tine Home No. 578

Impressive Home—A Space and Money Saver

For Prices on This Home, See First Page.
Read Pages 9 and 10 for Full Description of Materials.

FOR the size, here is indeed a massive appearing home. It is substantial and will reflect your good judgment in building it. Study the floor plans. You'll be impressed with the fine proportion and balance which is so evident throughout.

The gabled porch with boxed rails of siding and heavy columns harmonize with the dormer and general outline of the house. Above the belt the house is shingled up to the wide closed cornice. These features tend to give the house an appearance of greater size, still the balance is so perfect that no suggestion of over-size is at all evident.

A beautiful Monterey front door, glazed bevel plate leads into the reception hall. The hall is not just a hall—it is of room proportion. The open stairway enhances the beauty of this home—it is characteristically a Gordon-Van Tine stairway. The living and dining rooms are spacious and well lighted. The living room has a window in each outside wall —the dining room has a large twin window in the right wall and a single window in the rear wall directly opposite the front living room window.

The kitchen has been given careful thought. Notice the ease with which the housewife can reach the front hall and the dining room. Each step saved means economy in doing the work. The kitchen case is design "C", shown on the color pages. The grade door and rear door are glazed doors and allow exit or entrance either from the side or rear.

Upstairs are three big chambers and bath with ceiling height 8 feet in the clear. Plenty of windows in each wall assure good light and air. Don't overlook the handy linen case we furnish— every home should have one. Plans provide for a basement under entire house, which provision is of course very practical.

Build this house and you build for the future. The design will never be "out-of-date." It will look well in any surrounding. Here is beauty, comfort and economy

PAINT—Unless otherwise instructed we will furnish white paint for siding and trim, and moss green shingle stain for the wall shingles.

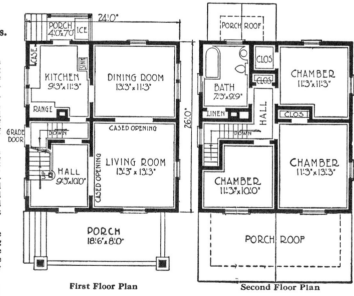

First Floor Plan   Second Floor Plan

For Plumbing, Heating, Lighting for This Home, See Last Pages of Book

Gordon-Van Tine Home No. 556

A Substantial Seven Room House

First Floor Plan   Second Floor Plan

For Prices on This Home, See First Page.

See Pages 9 and 10 for Full Description of Materials.

EVEN a hasty glance at the above photograph and the accompanying floor plan will bear evidence of the fact that there is an undoubted distinction to be found in this home. Whether you are planning to build your home in town or country this must make an especially strong appeal to you.

This home has been designed with square lines and the always popular hip roof. But any tendency toward plainness here is relieved by the dormer, the splendid large twin window to the front and the house width porch, with its well shaped pillars resting on concrete buttresses.

Since this house is both wider and longer than many, the rooms are all of ample size. The living room is made to seem especially roomy because of its separation from the hall only by a cased opening. The coat closet opening off of this hall is also a commendable arrangement.

The dining room cannot prove other than satisfactory in size. It affords ample space for all dining room furniture. This furniture especially can always be best placed in a square room.

The kitchen opens off the dining room, and access may likewise be gained to it, by means of the center hall, which connects with the reception hall and at the same time with the basement stairway and grade door. The kitchen itself is provided with our kitchen case design "B". An illustration is shown on the colored insert.

The location of the bath room just above the kitchen means the greatest saving to you when the plumbing is being installed. Near to the bath room is located the linen closet, a most convenient feature. This we furnish with the house—see the center colored pages.

Each of the three large well lighted chambers has an unusually large closet. This must win the heart of the one whose problem it will largely be to find a place for everything. For how much more easily everything can be kept in place, if the closets are adequate.

Furthermore, no room can be enjoyed without an abundance of air and light. This fact also has been kept well in mind when planning the second as well as the first floor.

Wise thought and consideration before building means no regret afterward. If you appreciate exceptional values this house has made a distinct appeal to you, for you must realize that our architects have given it the most careful study. You cannot do better than decide in its favor.

PAINT—Unless otherwise instructed, we will furnish clear gray paint for the body and light gray for the trim of this home.

For Plumbing, Heating, Lighting for This Home, See Last Pages of Book

Gordon-Van Tine Home No. 702

Space Saving Lines—More House for the Money

Options That Will Save You $85.61

Deduct the above amount from the regular price on
this house if you are willing to buy it with the following changes from regular specifications:
6 to 2 Star A Star Red Cedar Shingles instead of 5
to 2 Clear; plain square edge casings for doors and
windows instead of Craftsman design; all subflooring
and kitchen case omitted.

NOTHING is more satisfying than a home designed
along conservative and quiet lines. For people
with discriminating taste, the above house will have
a strong appeal.

The broad lines of the gable roof with its return cornices
mean simple and economical construction. The large
rooms with plenty of light and splendid arrangement for
convenience combine to make the interior of this home
unique. This would be a splendid home for either the
farm or city.

The twin windows in every room on the second floor are
unusual, but undoubtedly make a strong appeal. They
also insure adequate ventilation.

Note the compact way in which the architect has designed the stairway and has provided for easy access to
both the basement and second floor stairs from the kitchen.

The front door opens into the well proportioned living room
which has plenty of unbroken wall space for placing furniture. To the one side is the first floor chamber or a den
or sewing room if you so prefer, and to the rear the cheery
dining room. The small hall gives direct access to the
second floor and to the unusually well planned kitchen.

The position of the range in the kitchen will be handy at
all times and will receive direct light from the window.
The kitchen is also equipped with our handsome kitchen
case, design "B". See the illustration of this case in the
colored insert.

Examine again the cellar stairway on the first floor plan
and you will notice a small jog on the cellar landing. Here
we have provided for a shelf which will prove convenient
in numerous ways.

There is a large basement under the entire house with
ample space for heating plant, coal room, vegetable room and
the laundry, if desired. The cellar windows are furnished.

This house is furnished as you note Not Ready Cut
only.

PAINT—Unless otherwise instructed we will furnish
clear gray paint for the body and white for trim.

For Prices on this Home, See First Page.
Read Pages 9 and 10 for Full Description of Materials.

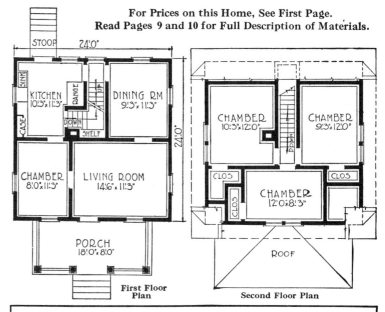

First Floor Plan

Second Floor Plan

For Plumbing, Heating, Lighting for This Home, See Last Pages of Book

Gordon-Van Tine Home No. 522

A Model Five Room Bungalow

For Prices on This Home, See First Page.

Read Pages 9 and 10 for Full Description of Materials.

AFTER building this house, Mrs. Rose Wright of Hooker, Oklahoma, wrote to us: "I am very thankful to Gordon-Van Tine Company for giving me the opportunity of getting such a beautifully arranged and splendidly built house."

The illustration gives only a faint idea of the attractiveness of this house. The roof is a simple gable, with nothing to break its lines except the heavy barge board and the exposed rafters of the cornice. The walls are covered with cypress siding to the belt course. Above this red cedar shingles are used, laid alternately 2 inches and 7 inches to the weather.

The front porch is excellently designed. The architects have given careful thought to size of the columns, to the sided rail, and to the shingled effect in the gable ends, so as to give a touch of originality to this charming house. This is further emphasized by the Colonial windows and the San Diego bevel plate front door.

The interior arrangement is especially satisfactory. The twin windows flood the living room and dining room with sunlight. The bed rooms also are well lighted and ventilated. This latter point is particularly important, especially when you wish to catch the stray breezes of a warm summer night.

Large closets are provided for each room, while off the hallway, a special linen closet is installed. This is similar to the one shown in the color pages, and is almost indispensable for the storage of bed linen. Chamber B is connected with the bath room by this small hallway.

From it a stairway leads to the attic. Here the height from the ridge board to the floor, which covers the entire space, is 7 feet. This assures plenty of storage space and in cases of "rough-and-tumble" emergency, a place for an extra cot or two.

Particular care has been given to the arrangement of the kitchen. Compactness has been the constant aim of the architect. Note the practical arrangement of the kitchen case, our "D" design. The wall case is placed along the right wall. Nothing could be more compact or more convenient for those who do the housework than this convenient kitchen case, located between the stove and sink, with the entrance to the basement not far away.

The basement stairway is well placed, for it can also easily be reached from the latticed rear porch. The cellar should be as large as the house. Our plans call for it this way, we provide the necessary windows for it, and all the space can easily be made use of, particularly if a furnace room, vegetable cellar and laundry are desired.

It seems to us that Mrs. Wright spoke truly, when she referred to her house as "beautifully arranged and splendidly built." You, too, will find it comfortable and roomy.

First Floor Plan

PAINT—Unless otherwise instructed, we will furnish Lemont stone paint for the body and white for the trim of this house.

For Plumbing, Heating, Lighting for This Home, See Last Pages of Book

Gordon-Van Tine Home No. 519

A Model Six-Room, One Floor Home

For Prices on This Home, See First Page.
Read Pages 9 and 10 for Full Description of Material.

Options That Will Save You $95.45

Deduct the above amount from the regular price on this house if you are willing to buy it with the following changes from regular specifications:

6 to 2 Star A Star Red Cedar Shingles instead of 5 to 2 Clear; plain square edge casings for doors and windows instead of Craftsman design; all subflooring and kitchen case omitted.

THIS is a practical home of ample size, equally well suited for a farm tenant house or for a town home.

The living room and dining room are both very cosy. They have been planned with the same care that is given to these rooms in a much more pretentious house.

The kitchen, because of its convenient arrangement, deserves particular mention. You will notice that our special case design B is used (see color pages), and is most advantageously placed near the windows.

Opposite to the living room there are three splendid bed rooms. Each has two windows and each has a closet of its own. Furniture space has been well planned in each.

You will note that we include basement stairs and sash, sufficient for a basement of house size. The placing of the basement stairs directly opposite the rear door affords the advantage of both an inside and an outside stairway.

PAINT—Unless otherwise instructed we will furnish Lemont
Stone paint for the body and white for the trim of this home.

"SOUR GRAPES"

Galena, Illinois.

Gordon-Van Tine Co., Davenport, Iowa.

Gentlemen: In regards to our house must say that we are well pleased with it and are more than satisfied with every piece of lumber that went into it. Am not at all surprised about what the lumber dealers in this town say about me, as I have heard some of their stories myself. It is certainly nothing more than a case of "sour grapes."

Yours very truly,
Mr. Ernest Lind.

SAVED ALTOGETHER $350.00

Des Moines, Iowa.

Gordon-Van Tine Co.

Gentlemen: I just want to say the Ready-Cut house I bought of you is the nicest home in Des Moines, Iowa, for the price I paid. We had no trouble at all in erecting same, every piece fits nicely and I saved in carpenter work $146.00. In all, I am sure I saved altogether over $350.00. I wouldn't buy anything else but a Ready-Cut home.

Yours very truly,
(Signed) F. L. Todd.

For Plumbing, Heating, Lighting for This Home, See Last Pages of Book

Gordon-Van Tine Home No. 548

A Universally Popular Cottage at Low Cost

For Prices on This Home, See First Page.   **Read Pages 9 and 10 for Full Description of Materials.**

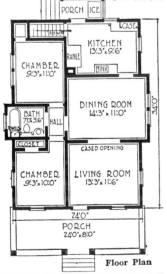

Floor Plan

Options That Will Save You $97.45

Deduct the above amount from the regular price on this house **if you are willing to buy it with** the following changes from regular specifications:

6 to 2 Star A Star Red Cedar Shingles instead of 5 to 2 Clear; plain square edge casings for doors and windows instead of Craftsman design; all subflooring and kitchen case omitted.

THE exterior of this home has a definite charm in its substantial lines and appearance. The porch is large and roomy with four square columns and boxed rails of siding. This style of porch is most practical because screens or sash can easily be placed in the openings, with the minimum of expense and effort. The main roof of the house extends over the porch, adding to the beauty of the outline. The small dormer is justified—it breaks up the otherwise plain roof expanse. It balances the open area of the porch and adds considerable value to the general contour. No perspective or illustration can really properly visualize this fine, modest home to you—you should see it to fully appreciate it.

The interior is a fine example of skillful planning. Notice particularly how the bed rooms and bath are kept apart from the living room. The chambers are both roomy—no trouble to set your pieces in these rooms. The front chamber has a big window in each outside wall. The bath has a short window, same design and style as the other windows, lower sash and glazed with moss glass, which is an example of the forethought of the architects.

To offset the space utilized in the floor plan for the hall, a projection in the left wall is made extending the full width of the bath room. This jog breaks up the straight wall-line, as does the dining room projection on the opposite side. The rear chamber has a twin window. Both bed rooms will

be light and airy, with ample closet space. The bath room has our towel case, a convenience always appreciated.

Very important are the living and dining rooms of any home. These rooms concern the entire household. Here, you have two fine, big rooms. Lots of space—plenty of light from the big twin window in the dining room and two windows of the living room, one in each outside wall. The front door is also glazed adding materially to the lighting. Between the dining room and kitchen is a swinging door with a double-acting floor hinge. This door always swinging shut keeps cooking odors in the kitchen and prevents a view into the kitchen, all of which, at times, is appreciated by the housewife.

The kitchen is a model in arrangement and planning. The Gordon-Van Tine kitchen case style "B", as illustrated in the colored section, is included in this kitchen at no extra cost. Two big windows and a glazed outside door admit plenty of light and sunshine. The time spent in this kitchen will be cheerful moments for the housewife.

The inside basement stairway leads down directly to the left of the rear outside door. The latticed rear porch is large enough for the ice box.

PAINT—Unless otherwise instructed, we will furnish straw paint for the body, and white trim for this home.

For Plumbing, Heating, Lighting for This Home, See Last Pages of Book

This area was damaged
on the original copy

Gordon-Van Tine Home No. 555

A Fine Looking Home at a Big Saving

For Prices on This Home, See First Page.   **Read Pages 9 and 10 for Full Description of Material.**

Options That Will Save You $89.80

Deduct the above amount from the regular price on this house if you are willing to buy it with the following changes from the regular specifications:

6 to 2 Star A Star Red Cedar Shingles instead of 5 to 2 Clear; plain square edge casings for doors and windows instead of Craftsman design; all subflooring and kitchen case omitted.

IN this home is another pleasing variation of the standard, ever-popular, square house. The popularity of a square house efficiently planned is deserved because of the wonderful opportunities it represents in Home Utility—not an inch of waste floor space.

The plain hip roof of the porch of this substantial home conforms to the lines of the main roof—all open cornice shows exposed rafters. Throughout this design you'll find a pleasing harmony of detail. Note the Colonial windows and doors. Also the solid boxed rail of the porch which makes it possible to enclose it with screens or sash at small cost, adding much to the comfort.

The outside walls are sided to the belt and shingled above; this is especially good treatment on the square house. In this construction monotony is avoided—the second story is given emphasis.

The unusually large living room extends clear across the house. At the front is a glazed door enclosing the entrance, to the right is a big twin window and up over the stair landing is a smaller window. With the exception of the buttressed stairway at the rear wall and the cased opening on the left these wall spaces are unbroken—plenty of room to place the larger pieces of furniture.

Opposite the cased opening, in the dining room is another big twin window, in the front wall looking out on the porch is another good-sized window.

These openings permit good air and light, both essentials in present-day living.

The kitchen is entered from the rear by the grade door. This room though small and compact is a model of convenience. The kitchen case is style "C", as shown on the colored insert in this book. The two windows, one in each outside wall are placed to best advantage. The housewife will enjoy her duties with every essential so convenient.

Upstairs the well-lighted hall connects the bath with three good chambers. Careful planning has given these rooms ample closet space and perfect light and ventilation. The rear chamber has a twin-window. The linen closet is another Gordon-Van Tine feature you will surely appreciate.

For a real serviceable house, you should consider this home. Think of it as an investment. Your dividends will be permanent and liberal.

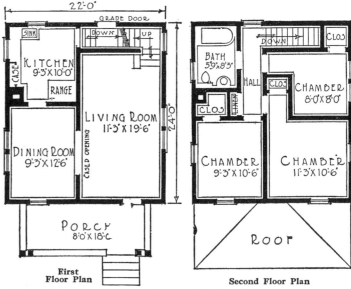

First Floor Plan

Second Floor Plan

PAINT—Unless otherwise instructed, we will furnish white paint for the body and trim, and brown shingle stain for the wall shingles of this home.

LIKE A PIECE OF CABINET WORK

Gordon-Van Tine Company, Davenport, Iowa. New Hampton, Iowa.

Gentlemen: My house is now finished and am occupying it; and I am well pleased with the same. The house is praised by everyone (who is not prejudiced). The Jap-A-Top shingles used have been a source of comment, because of their beauty and artistic effect, particularly where used in the gables. The workmanship on the house is of the best, so the completed structure is like a piece of cabinet-work. The different workmen praised the millwork, thinking it generally better than the millwork from Charles City, where most of the millwork for the houses in this town comes from. Very truly yours,
Harry H. Dane.

For Plumbing, Heating, Lighting for This Home, See Last Pages of Book

This area was damaged
on the original copy

Gordon-Van Tine Home No. 532

A Money Saving, Space Saving Home

For Prices on This Home See First Page.   Read Pages 9 and 10 for Full Description of Materials.

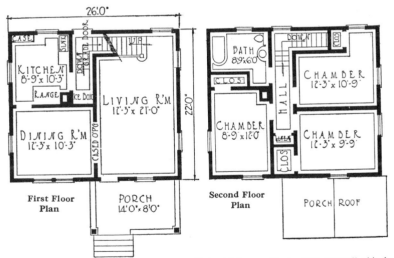

First Floor Plan

26:0"

KITCHEN 8'-9" x 10'-3"
RANGE   ICE BOX
DINING R'M 12'-3" x 10'-3"
LIVING R'M 12'-3" x 21'-0"
CASE
PORCH 14'0" x 8'0"
22'-0"

Second Floor Plan

BATH 8'9" x 6'0"
CLOS
HALL
CHAMBER 12'-3" x 10'-9"
CHAMBER 8'-9" x 12'0"
CHAMBER 12'-3" x 9'-9"
PORCH ROOF

PAINT—Unless otherwise instructed, we will furnish brown shingle stain for wall shingle cream paint for the body, and white for the trim of this home.

Options That Will Save You $85.00

Deduct the above amount from the regular price on this house if you are willing to buy it with the following changes from regular specifications: 6 to 2 Star A Star Red Cedar Shingles instead of 5 to 2 Clear; plain square edge casings for doors and windows instead of Craftsman design; all subflooring and kitchen case omitted.

THERE is always economy in building a square house. Simplicty gives real value for every cent invested, and assures one of a style of architecture good for many years. This house, designed for a suburban home, well illustrates this fact

The outside walls are sided to the belt course, having Red Cedar shingles above it. A cream paint for the siding with brown shingle stain and white trim, would be appropriate for this type of house.

The generous proportions of the porch with its boxed rail and shingled gable, the Monterey front door, and the exposed rafters beneath the wide cornices are all features that are especially good.

The great big living room entered directly from the porch and having an open stairway at the back, provides a wealth of space for even a large family. It is connected with the light airy dining room by means of a cased opening.

Two excellent features of the dining room are the location of the swinging door which hardly permits of a view of any part of the kitchen, and the splendid wall space, on the same side of the room, offering a place for a large piece of dining room furniture.

The kitchen, while small, is a step saver, owing to its convenient arrangement. There is space planned for a range, a sink, a table as well as our special kitchen case, design "B". The refrigerator will be most accessible in the entry near by. Just opposite the stairs descend to the grade door and the basement stairway. We supply these stairs as well as basement sash and frame.

Each of the bed rooms, as each of the rooms on the first floor, have light and air from two sides. A closet opens from every room while a linen closet, like the design shown in the color section, opens off the hall.

The bed rooms are, in fact, unusually uniform in size, and are so planned that the usual furniture can be placed in them, and still leave them uncrowded.

This home must appeal to you from the standpoint of convenience, of attractiveness and of economy You could not well want more.

For Plumbing, Heating, Lighting for This Home, See Last Pages of Book

This area was damaged on the original copy

Gordon-Van Tine Home No. 566

A Well Designed Home of Moderate Cost

For Prices on This Home, See First Page. Read Pages 9 and 10 for Full Description of Materials.

THE lines and proportions observed in the porch make this home especially attractive. The graceful columns resting on solid piers, the rail and the broad steps are among its noticeable features.

Upon entering the immense living room one will have a view of the pleasant dining room and the stairway, in Slash Grain Douglas Fir, which ascends directly from the living room. Only the first run is open. The staircase and the triple windows at the front are both attractive features of the room, which has unusual furniture space.

A convenient connection between the kitchen and the second floor has been provided for by means of the door in the rear living room wall. Just to your right is the stair leading to the grade door and basement.

Our kitchen cabinet stands against the kitchen wall made by this stair. It is design "B" and is shown in the colored section. The space for the case as well as that for the sink is well lighted by the twin windows. From the kitchen you can go directly onto the latticed rear porch, which offers a good place for your refrigerator.

The basement under the entire house can be made very convenient. We furnish five windows for the basement as well as all girder posts and girders.

The splendid sleeping rooms all having light and air from two sides are further examples of the careful attention which our architects have given to the planning of this house, and notice especially the splendid large closets for each room, as well as the towel case in the bath room. This is shown in our color section.

Bevel siding up to the belt and Red Cedar Shingles above, give a decidedly pleasing exterior to this home.

Imagine then for a moment that this house is already yours, built in just the spot that you have long coveted for your home. Find the right places in which to put your belongings and see what a homelike place it is. No matter where you build, such a house cannot be other than a source of pride to you.

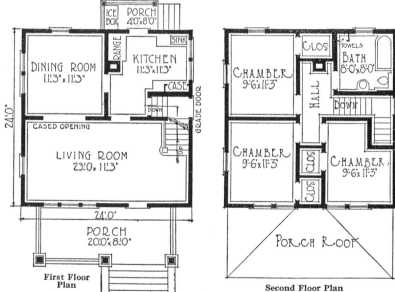

First Floor Plan

Second Floor Plan

PAINT—Unless otherwise instructed, we will furnish oxide red stain for wall shingles, cream paint for body and white trim.

Gordon-Van Tine Company, Davenport, Iowa.   Calhan, Colo.
Gentlemen: I take this opportunity to thank you for the way you have treated me and for the fine grade of material you sent. My carpenter said it was first class and better than the local dealers carry. Have not been able to complete my house as yet. Have it enclosed and have plenty of all kinds of material and am well pleased with it.
My home is located three and one-half miles south and west of Calhan, Colo., on the ocean to ocean highway. I will be glad to show anyone our home and tell them we got fine treatment from the Gordon-Van Tine Company.   Yours very truly,
Mr. J. M. Long, Calhan, Colo.

For Plumbing, Heating, Lighting for This Home, See Last Pages of Book

Gordon-Van Tine Home No. 710

A Home That Will Always Be Popular

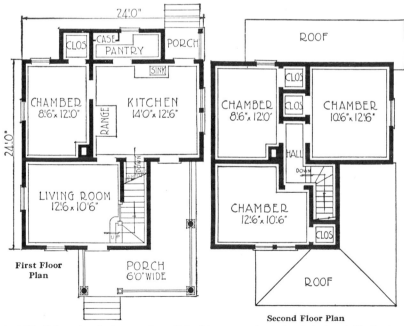

First Floor Plan

24'0"

CLOS | CASE PANTRY | PORCH
SINK
CHAMBER 8'6" x 12'0" | KITCHEN 14'0" x 12'6"
RANGE
24'0"
LIVING ROOM 12'6" x 10'6"
DOWN
UP
PORCH 6'0" WIDE

Second Floor Plan

ROOF
CLOS
CHAMBER 8'6" x 12'0" | CLOS | CHAMBER 10'6" x 12'6"
HALL
DOWN
CHAMBER 12'6" x 10'6"
CLOS
ROOF

PAINT—Unless otherwise instructed we will furnish maroon red paint for the body and white for trim.

For Prices on This Home, See First Page. Read Pages 9 and 10 for Full Description of Materials.

SIX rooms and a big pantry, for the price of a five-room cottage, is what you get here. Economy is the keynote of this design.

A practical house for a practical builder was planned by our architects to meet the demand for those who know values and are content with a more conservative plan. It is typically a farm house with big rooms, big kitchen, big porch and plenty of closets.

Outside it is finished in clear bevel siding up to the belt, with shingles in the gables. Note the big porch 6 feet wide, which extends from the side door clear around past the front door.

As one enters the living room from the porch, the Colonial stair with a square panel newel and handsome rail and baluster are immediately at your right. These add to the attractiveness of this large room, which is well lighted by the windows and glazed door. There is excellent space for furniture here. Note the economy secured by the placing of the chimney.

The down stairs bed room and big closet are sure to prove a convenient feature. While if the additional sleeping room is not needed, the room is cheery and light enough to be used for any purpose.

The porch is much appreciated. Part of this could be screened for use as a dining room in the summer time and it would make a most welcome retreat in the evening when the breeze springs up after sundown.

The kitchen provides space for the dining table in front of the large twin windows. In the pantry is our work table, design "B". This is shown in the colored section. It is so placed as to receive excellent light. This is a splendid place to work with all supplies and utensils nearby.

The basement stairs descend from the kitchen. We supply these and frames and sash for a basement under the entire house.

This comfortable farm house, roomy but not expensive, represents the planning of experienced architects and the low cost made possible y quantity production. Upstairs there are three bed rooms opening from the hall. The ceiling heights here are 8 feet. There is a slight slope at the side. These rooms are all well lighted, and by leaving the hall doors open excellent ventilation can be secured.

For Plumbing, Heating, Lighting for This Home, See Last Pages of Book

Gordon-Van Tine Home No. 701

A Practical and Popular 3-Bed Room Home

For Prices on This Home, See First Page.   Read Pages 9 and 10 for Full Description of Materials.

Options That Will Save You $86.90

Deduct the above amount from the regular price on this house if you are willing to buy it with the following changes from regular specifications:

6 to 2 Star A Star Red Cedar Shingles instead of 5 to 2 Clear; plain square edge casings for doors and windows instead of Craftsman design; all subflooring and kitchen case omitted.

A NEATLY designed six-room house that is comfortable and homelike and placed on the market at such a low price that it is within the reach of all.   No family can afford to rent long, when they can buy this splendid home for the small amount quoted. Straight simple lines predominate, meaning low construction costs and a saving in material. Every foot of space is used to the best advantage. It makes a desirable house for renting or selling as well as a cosy and comfortable home.

Many families desire a chamber on the first floor, and we have one here, with a large closet. This room can be used for a den or parlor, if preferred.   The living room is large and contains the open stairway which lands between walls on the second floor. Both dining room and living room are well-lighted.

The kitchen is remarkably handy—a large wall case with drawers and doors makes it unnecessary to go to the extra expense of building a pantry.   It is our case "B" shown on the color pages.   There is plenty of room for your table, your stove and your sink. Cellar stairs go down under the main stairs. The kitchen opens onto the back porch, which is of ample size.   The chimney is located in the center of the house so that it can be easily heated with stoves in a very economical manner if the owner so desired.

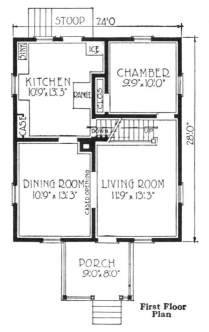

First Floor Plan

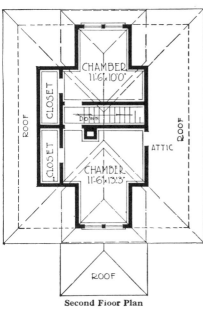

Second Floor Plan

Large dormers on the front and rear of this house give light and head room for two chambers on the second floor. These rooms are practically full height, having sloping ceilings for only about two feet at the corners, and the lowest point is seven feet from the floor. Here you have a good sized modern house—at-

tractive and comfortable, built strongly and warmly, and at the price quoted will save you many dollars.

PAINT—Unless otherwise instructed, we will furnish Lemont stone paint for body, and white for trim.

For Plumbing, Heating, Lighting for This Home, See Last Pages of Book

Gordon-Van Tine Home No. 520

Sunshine Bungalow—5 Rooms and Bath

For Prices on This Home See First Page. Read Pages 9 and 10 for Full Description of Materials.

First Floor Plan

GRADE DOOR

ICE ENTRY DOWN   CASE

CLOS   KITCHEN 13'-3" X 9'-0"   SINK

RANGE

CHAMBER 11'-3" X 10'-0"

DINING ROOM 11'-0" X 13'-3"

BATH 7'-3" 5'-6"

HALL   CASED OPENING

CLOS

LIVING ROOM 13'-3" X 14'-0"

CHAMBER 11'-3" X 10'-0"

26'-0"

36'-0"

PORCH 26'-0" X 7'-0"

PAINT—Unless otherwise instructed, we will furnish silver gray shingle stain for the wall shingles and white trim.

Options That Will Save You $99.60

Deduct the above amount from the regular price on this house if you are willing to buy it with the following changes from regular specifications.
6 to 2 Star A Star Red Cedar Shingles instead of 5 to 2 Clear; plain square edge casings for doors and windows instead of Craftsman design; all subflooring and kitchen case omitted.

TAKE a moment's time and notice some of the many commendable features in this little bungalow. In fact, consider it well, for this house merits your careful attention. You can be comfortable in it, proud of it, and realize money on it.

The bold strokes of the porch, with its effective combination of gable and pergola effectively frame the front of the house and bring out its proportions perfectly. The craftsman note is faithfully carried out in the open cornice and the shingled walls also.

The floor plan of the house provides for five good sized and well arranged rooms. Especially attractive are the living room and dining room, thrown well together by the wide cased opening. The five large Pasadena windows admit all the air and light wanted, while the outside doors make a thorough draft possible at any time.

Entirely shut off from the living rooms are the

two convenient bed rooms, connected with this part of the house only by the hall. From this the bath and linen closet open also. Turn to the color pages and see just what this is like. Perhaps the most important feature in connection with these rooms is the two splendid big closets.

Since there are almost 1100 meals to be prepared in this kitchen each year, our architects have given thought accordingly to its arrangement. Every bit of work here can be done near to the windows, with no unnecessary steps in any direction, and notice the kitchen case, design "B".

The iceman's hob-nailed boots need not affect the floor, for there is a most convenient place for your refrigerator in the entry leading to the grade door and the basement. The arrangement here is excellent. The basement should be as large as the house itself. We provide enough windows to furnish light and ventilation.

For Plumbing, Heating, Lighting for This Home, See Last Pages of Book

Gordon-Van Tine Home No. 530

Charming Bungalow with Compact Floor Plan

For Prices on This Home, See First Page.
Read Pages 9 and 10 for Full Description of Material.

THIS is a roomy bungalow with a perfect floor plan. Combined with this pleasing feature is a truly beautiful exterior. Your eye follows the broad sweep of the roof with the twin dormers. These dormers not only give the exterior perfect balance— a heightened effect is created, so desirable in the low, broad-roofed bungalow.

The brick foundation is extended under the porch showing a continuity of line, giving the house a more massive appearance. This particular style must have good breadth to properly balance—in this fine home every attention has been given to the necessary qualities which make the home perfect in detail and appearance and without sacrificing the ever-essential economy.

The porch roof is a continuation of the main roof—really a part of it. There are prospects of solid comfort in this broad veranda. And notice the beautiful front entrance with its glazed side lights and door. On either side of the front entrance is a twin window. You'll admit that the front view could hardly be improved.

The living room is big and cheery. The fireplace adds that touch of comfort and a quiet dignity that places this home in the better class.

For the fireplace, we furnish a massive mantel shelf, dome damper, ash trap and clean-out door. On either side of the fireplace is set a two-light window, well up in the wall, beneath are ample wall spaces for cases or other wall pieces. A beautiful room setting can be arranged around this side of the room.

Plenty of windows distinguish this home —each room, with the exception of the bath and kitchen, has cross-ventilation. In studying this plan you'll find every desirable feature amply provided—nothing is lacking to make this a practical, convenient and thoroughly comfortable home.

For the housewife, the kitchen is the center of the home. To save her steps notice how each room is easily reached direct from the kitchen. Our kitchen case style "B", as shown on the color pages is furnished with this home at no extra cost. For the bath, we include our towel cabinet. Notice how the bath is placed apart from the living room giving it the necessary privacy.

Across the entire house extends the attic which is floored, affording in addition to the basement a wealth of storage space. Even the attic is well-lighted by the two twin dormer sash and the single sash in each gable. The latticed rear porch has plenty of room for the ice box. The attic stairs lead up from the dining room.

PAINT—Unless otherwise instructed, we will furnish cream paint for body, white for trim, and oxide red for wall shingles for this home.

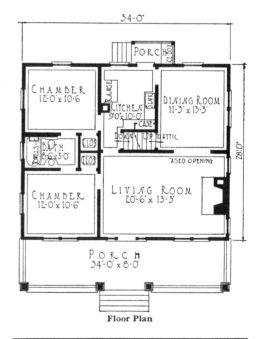

Floor Plan

For Plumbing, Heating, Lighting for This Home, See Last Pages of Book

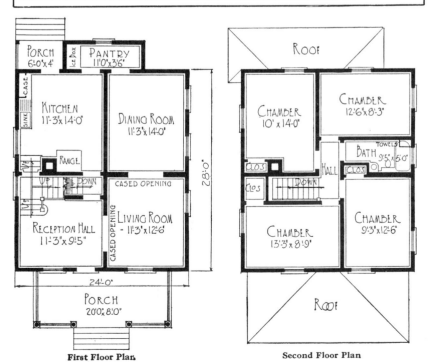

Gordon-Van Tine Home No. 568

A Square House With Big Comfortable Rooms

Options That Will Save You $91.50

Deduct the above amount from the regular price on this house if you are willing to buy it with the following changes from regular specifications:
6 to 2 Star A Star Red Cedar Shingles instead of 5 to 2 Clear; plain square edge casings for doors and windows instead of Craftsman design; all subflooring and kitchen case omitted.

For Prices on This Home, See First Page.

Read Pages 9 and 10 for Full Description of Materials.

COMFORT and economy are the all important features of this house. It is another of the square type where every inch of floor space is utilized for a good purpose.

Monotony in appearance has been avoided by the clever usage of a well proportioned dormer. The large front porch with grounded columns and wide cornice give an impression of massiveness and stability which is typical of the entire house.

The housewife will realize at once the great number of steps saved by having the stairway arranged so that the second floor may be reached both from kitchen and reception hall. The reception hall, with its handsome open stairway, and the living room as well as the dining room are connected by attractive and well designed cased openings.

The arrangement of the kitchen and pantry is unique. The pantry is convenient to both kitchen and dining room and is under the same roof as the convenient little rear porch. There is a handy space in the end nearest the kitchen for the ice box. Notice that it is well lighted by the window in the rear wall. Our kitchen case "A" placed just at the side of the sink gives an excellent working combination plentifully lighted by the large window and glazed rear door. In the corner of the kitchen next the range is the basement stairway. We supply basement frames and sash, as well as this stairway.

Maximum chamber space is available on the second floor as well as ample closet room. Each chamber has two windows affording floods of cheery sunshine and fresh air. The bath is conveniently located. Here we supply a towel case, like the one shown in the colored section.

For solid comfort and economy in a style of home as good in 20 years as it is today you will never regret a decision to buy this home.

PAINT—Unless otherwise instructed, we will furnish light gray paint for body of house and white for trim.

First Floor Plan

Second Floor Plan

For Plumbing, Heating, Lighting for This Home, See Last Pages of Book

Gordon-Van Tine Home No. 552

A Popular Home—Fine For a Narrow Lot

For Prices on This Home, See First Page.   **Read Pages 9 and 10 for Full Description of Materials.**

Options That Will Save You $81.80

Deduct the above amount from the regular price on this house if you are willing to buy it with the following changes from regular specifications:

6 to 2 Star A Star Red Cedar Shingles instead of 5 to 2 Clear; plain square edge casings for doors and windows instead of Craftsman design; all subflooring and kitchen case omitted.

THIS house because of its width is especially good for a narrow lot. And at the same time it is two full stories in height, has six big rooms, a bath, and plenty of closet space.

The same attention has been given to comfort and economy as in all Gordon-Van Tine homes. The exterior is simple and dignified. Common sense features of construction are evident everywhere.

The porch following the general design of the house relieves any possible monotony of line, and during the hot summer days and evenings the refreshing breezes which are sure to find their way there, will be more than welcome.

One enters the living room directly from the front porch A special attraction here is the handsome open stairway with rounded starting step, paneled fir newel and Colonial rail and baluster.

The living room and dining room are joined by a 6-foot cased opening. This means that they are in reality one big room, but with all the convenience of two.

A double acting swinging door leads from the dining room into the kitchen. Here windows and wall space are properly arranged with regard for the kitchen case, our design "B"—the sink and the range.

The basement stairway descends from the entry, which opens both from the kitchen and the front hall. Here there is an excellent space for the refrigerator, near to the grade door, through which the ice can be brought. The stairway turns at the grade door and continues to the basement.

In the second story the bath is located just over the kitchen an economy from the plumbers' viewpoint. A towel case like the one shown in the colored section is furnished for the bath room.

Besides the bath on the second floor there are three good sized bedrooms all with windows on adjoining walls, preventing the possibility of hot stuffy rooms during the summer time. There is good closet room in this house also.

Designed on conservative lines there are in reality a number of pleasing architectural features emphasized here.

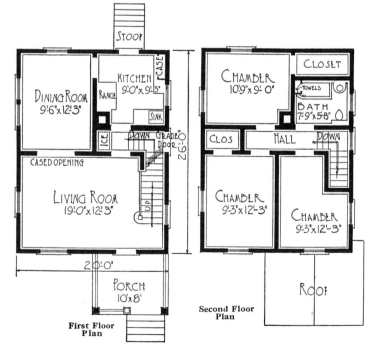

First Floor Plan

STOOP

KITCHEN 9'0" x 9'3"

DINING ROOM 9'6" x 12'3"

RANGE

SINK

ICE

DOWN GRADE DOOR

CASED OPENING

LIVING ROOM 19'0" x 12'3"

UP

20'-0"

PORCH 10'x8'

Second Floor Plan

CHAMBER 10'9" x 9'0"

CLOSET

TOWELS

BATH 7'9"x5'8"

CLOS

HALL

DOWN

CHAMBER 9'3" x 12'3"

CHAMBER 9'3" x 12'3"

ROOF

PAINT—Unless otherwise instruced, we will furnish Lemont stone for body paint and white for trim.

For Plumbing, Heating, Lighting for This Home, See Last Pages of Book

Gordon-Van Tine Home No. 544

Exceptionally Well-Arranged Bungalow

For Prices on This Home, See First Page.
Read Pages 9 and 10 for Full Description of Materials.

Floor Plan

I sent you by mail a photo of the house which I bought from you to enter in your contest.
If you and your judges think as much of it as we do, it will win first prize sure.
Very truly yours,
Camphill, Pa.   *J. W. Carlson.*

THE porch of the dining room will prove a very pleasant feature of this comfortable little bungalow—and an incentive to have one of those charming back-yards which the magazines like so well to picture.

It is also desirable as a breakfast porch or outdoor dining room. It is entered from the dining room through a pair of attractive French doors. The kitchen porch is hidden from view by the dividing partition.

Other features that add to the charm of the exterior are the broad porch across the entire front, the neat cornice effect produced by the large boards and exposed rafters, the divided windows, the neat dormer and the gable lines. This home is sided to the belt with shingles above, which is admittedly a desired effect.

The present vogue of compact, conveniently arranged interiors is emphasized in this plan. Every bit of space is utilized to the best possible advantage, permitting a decided saving of steps and time in the household duties.

There is cross ventilation possible in every living and sleeping room and an ideal porch accessible for any time of day. The dining room is made doubly pleasant by the French doors opening onto the enclosed porch at the rear. On the rear porch there is ample room for the ice box.

The living room easily reached from every part of the house, is large, light and airy. It has unusually good wall space for the practical placing of furniture. Between the living and dining rooms is a large cased opening. In throwing these rooms together there is obtained an appearance of spaciousness. The dining room is made very pleasant by the view in three directions.

The bath room is directly connected with each bed room. In the closet arrangement there is not taken an inch of space from the bed rooms. Our towel case is included in the bath room.

Overhead is a floored attic which covers the entire house. At the ridge the height is 7 ft. 8 in. Since it is well-lighted by windows in each gable and the two dormer sash in front it can be used for many purposes. Even the stairway leading to it has not wasted any space as it is placed over the basement stairway.

The kitchen is very neatly arranged. Most convenient is the big Gordon-Van Tine Kitchen case style "B" as shown on the color pages of this catalog. This is included without any extra cost.

If it is compactness you want, as well as good design and appearance, together with the always acceptable economy, then consider this home. It is unusually well planned and will realize your expectations 100 per cent.

PAINT—Unless otherwise instructed, we will furnish cream for body, white for trim, and brown stain for gable shingles.

For Plumbing, Heating, Lighting for This Home, See Last Pages of Book

Gordon-Van Tine Homes

Gordon-Van Tine Home No. 524

A Most Popular Five-Room Home

For Prices on This Home, See First Page.   Read Pages 9 and 10 for Full Description of Materials.

Options That Will Save You $91.35

Deduct the above amount from the regular price on this house if you are willing to buy it with the following changes from regular specifications:

6 to 2 Star A Star Red Cedar Shingles instead of 5 to 2 Clear; plain square edge casings for doors and windows instead of Craftsman design; all subflooring and kitchen case omitted

---

Floor Plan

A HOUSE that is popular must have proved good to live in and a practical investment at the same time. Those who know have found this house to be a combination of these two necessities.

They have found it attractive, comfortable and as an investment something that is hard to beat. It shows big returns and can always be cashed in for more than its original cost.

The plain lines of this five-room home are both practical and pleasing. The breaking of the roof line by the dormer gives a bit of variety, and the in-set porch, neatly railed, adds a touch of hominess and contributes much to comfort.

The interior surprises one with its space. The dining and living rooms form practically one large room, running from front to back. Plenty of windows, well placed, especially commend these rooms to you. They are almost equally comfortable, cheery and well arranged. Each is large with walls planned for furniture. The closet in the rear dining room wall is a convenient addition.

The ample bed rooms opening off of the living room and dining room each have two windows and

a big closet. Since this house has no inner hall, not only is every foot of space used but these rooms are much more airy, because of the fact that the windows in the opposite rooms make direct draft always possible.

The compactness will prove a distinct advantage when heating arrangements are being made, whether by stove or furnace, for a distinct economy of fuel will always be possible.

Here is a modern handy kitchen, and it can be made a pretty kitchen, too. It is light, conveniently arranged and of a size to require no unnecessary steps. The Gordon-Van Tine case, design "B" and the cellar, easily reached directly from the kitchen, offer places for all supplies near at hand. Our plans provide windows for the entire basement.

The more you study this house, the more you will be won to it. No matter whether you are looking for a home for your family on your 80-acre farm, or near to your work in town, or whether you want to find just the right house to build for your tenant, we want to urge you to consider this. It is ideally adapted for any of the above uses as well as pleasing to the eye.

PAINT — Unless otherwise instructed, we will furnish cream for body paint, and white for trim.

For Plumbing, Heating, Lighting for This Home, See Last Pages of Book

Gordon-Van Tine Home No. 513

Unusually Fine Arrangement in This Bungalow

For Prices See First Page.   **Read Pages 9 and 10 for Full Description of Materials Furnished for This Home.**

Floor Plan

Options That Will Save You $103.00

Deduct the above amount from the regular price on this house if you are willing to buy it with the following changes from regular specifications; 6 to 2 Star A Star Red Cedar Shingles instead of 5 to 2 Clear; plain square edge casings for doors and windows instead of Craftsman design; all subflooring and kitchen case omitted.

THIS is a practical bungalow that will appeal to those who wish to combine a good design with economy.

The exterior has low, broad comfortable lines of a true bungalow, which are emphasized by the wide eaves and the deep inset porch. The walls are covered with 6-inch Cypress siding, and a pleasing break is made in the left wall by the dining room extension. The large two-light windows are effectively grouped, while the broad frieze above them adds that touch of style that always distinguishes a well planned house.

The porch is large, but so designed that the minimum amount of material has been used. Our architects have made it an integral part of the house by projecting the main roof to cover it. The piers are of masonry giving the appearance of solidity and strength. The rear porch is enclosed with lattice.

The interior is excellently planned. The closet in the living room just behind the front door, offers a most convenient place for coats and umbrellas.

The living room is a large attractive room; the dining room still larger. When occasion demands it, the two can be practically thrown into one large one.

The dining room and kitchen are separated by a double action swinging door. The kitchen like the rest of the house is just right. Our kitchen case, design "B," is used here. Turn to the colored section and see how convenient it is.

You want also to note the convenient connection between the basement stair and the rear porch.

Just a word about the basement. We include cellar windows so as to provide a basement under the entire house. This is advisable. You can never have too much space, particularly if you are planning on having a furnace room, vegetable cellar and a laundry.

Housework is minimized in this plan. Every requirement of design has been most successfully met. The device of separating the sleeping rooms by the small hallway which connects them with the bath, has well recognized advantages.

The sleeping rooms have an ideal window arrangement. The projection to the front chamber will make an attractive sewing corner overlooking the front porch, and there will still be ample room for all bed room furniture left.

This entire house plan has something about it that is restful and satisfying.

PAINT—Unless otherwise instructed, we will furnish light gray paint for the body of the house, and white for trim.

For Plumbing, Heating, Lighting for This Home, See Last Pages of Book

Gordon-Van Tine Home No. 533

Well Arranged and Comfortable Cottage

For Prices on This Home, See First Page.
Read Pages 9 and 10 for Full Description of Materials.

Options That Will Save You $94.40

Deduct the above amount from the regular price on this house if you are willing to buy it with the following changes from regular specifications: 6 to 2 Star A Star Red Cedar Shingles instead of 5 to 2 Clear. Plain square edge casings for doors and windows instead of Craftsman design. All subflooring and kitchen case omitted.

A PRACTICAL home this; without frills or furbelows—a plan that gives the maximum in comfort at a minimum of expenditure. It is finely proportioned and very well planned indeed.

The front porch, which makes an especial summertime appeal, is unusually large, and the boxed rail makes it especially home-like.

Besides selecting a house which appears well, you naturally are looking for one with a comfortable interior arrangement. Here the dining room and living room are of practical size, well-lighted and ventilated, with a wide cased opening between, giving the always desired effect of space.

A closet for each bed room, a cabinet for the bath room and a case for the kitchen, all included as a part of the house itself, is a rule followed by our architects. Note how well this is carried out; while the arrangement of the rooms and bath around the central hall separates them from the living rooms, at the same time makes them most convenient to the bath.

The kitchen is never neglected in a Gordon-Van Tine home. Here the case is our design "B," like the one illustrated on the color pages.

The work table is placed where it receives the best light possible.

The basement steps are close at hand, and still very near to the outside door—a splendid combination. This, and the fact that the refrigerator can stand where the ice man need not come into your kitchen, oftentimes saves the housewife annoyance.

Floor Plan

PAINT—Unless otherwise specified, light yellow paint will be furnished for body of house and white paint for trim.

For Plumbing, Heating, Lighting for These Homes, See Last Pages of Book

Floor Plan

**For Prices on This Home
See First Page**

Gordon-Van Tine Home No. 583

Unequalled for Convenience at Twice the Price

Read Pages 9 and 10 for Full Description of Material

FRANKLY designed for the small family, this house can't be beaten for convenience and all around livability. Picture to yourself the joy of fitting your own key into this handsome front door and stepping into your own home.

The living room is plenty large to accommodate a dining table on special occasions—and for regular everyday use there is the handy dinette opening right off the kitchen. The convenience of this feature is hard to over-estimate. It cuts down the work so—why, you can set the table and serve the meal in half the time with half the steps—and as for cleaning up—it's all done before you start, no carrying dishes—just put them in the sink and wash them. See how conveniently this kitchen is arranged. Sink and the fine big built-in pantry case are right opposite each other. You can reach either by simply turning around—ice box right at hand, but in the cool entry—stove where you serve right from it to the table, and the path from front to back absolutely clear of all obstruction. Did you ever see a better, more easy-to-work-in kitchen?

Note the fine closet space, and the very convenient bath room arrangement which includes doors into each bedroom. This feature is unusual in a place of this size. This is a real home—combining all the convenience of a city apartment, with the comfort and joy of **your own** place, at a cost that is possible to all.

PAINT—Unless otherwise instructed we will furnish brown shingle stain for wall shingles and white paint for the trim of this home.

Gordon-Van Tine Home No. 576
For Prices on This Home, See First Page

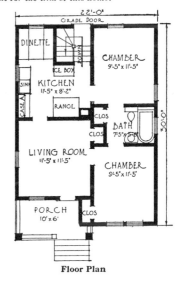

Floor Plan

Compact, Convenient Bungalow Home

Read Pages 9 and 10 for Full Description of Material

FOR the purchaser who wants to make every dollar buy a dollar's worth of usable, livable home, this plan will have a distinct appeal. Its very simplicity is its chief charm. The outside walls are sided up to the belt course and shingled above. Note the timber brackets supporting the eaves.

As you look at the plan, notice how every partition serves a double duty, how every bit of space is conserved, and how there are no "lost corners" of unusable space. Inspect the kitchen particularly closely. Notice the position of the sink under the window where light and air is plentiful—see how the icebox is placed where it is instantly accessible, yet close to the steps, it can be iced without muss or confusion. The big kitchen case with cupboard shelves reaching to the ceiling and drawers, bins, etc., underneath is just where it is handiest.

That wonderful modern convenience, the dinette, or Pullman dining nook, is included right in the kitchen, yet secluded, and is placed where it gets the best of light and air.

The range, between the two doors is so situated that it helps heat both living room and back bedroom.

Note the fine proportions of the rooms, the splendid ventilation, the wall space for furniture, the closets, etc. There isn't an inch, or a cent, wasted.

PAINT—Unless otherwise instructed we will furnish tan paint for the body, brown shingle stain for the wall shingles and white paint for the trim of this home.

For Plumbing, Heating, Lighting for These Homes, See Last Pages of Book

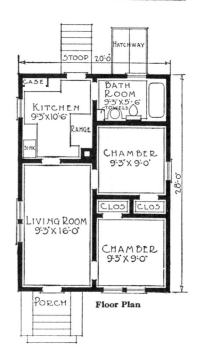

Gordon-Van Tine Home No. 510

A Distinctive 5-Room Cottage

In this design every inch of space has been utilized and the entire plan has been so well thought out, that the builder profits from the skill of the architects.

As an illustration of this consider the big living-dining room. See how well-lighted it is, and note what excellent furniture space it affords.

Both bed rooms open off this room. Their unusually large closets and unbroken wall space place them out of the ordinary.

Just back of the living-dining room is the kitchen—our usual model of convenience. Our kitchen case, design "B", is placed at one side of the window, while there is excellent room for the sink just opposite. The range has a large corner all to itself.

The bath opens off the kitchen. It is large, well arranged and has a towel case like the one shown in our colored section.

The basement is reached by an outside hatchway, located not far from the back stoop. Basement sash and hatchway door are supplied in the bill of material.

A more dignified small house would be hard to plan. Expert designing has indeed made this a model of economy and convenience.

PAINT—Unless otherwise instructed, we will furnish silver gray paint for body and lead for trim.

For Prices on This Home, See First Page.

Read Pages 9 and 10 Full Description for of Materials.

Floor Plan

Options That Will Save You $75.50

Deduct the above amount from the regular price on this house if you are willing to buy it with the following changes from regular specifications:

6 to 2 Star A Star Red Cedar Shingles instead of 5 to 2 Clear; plain square edge casings for doors and windows instead of Craftsman design; all subflooring and kitchen case omitted.

Floor Plan

For Prices on This Home, See First Page.

Read Pages 9 and 10 for Full Description of Materials

Options That Will Save You $92.25

Deduct the above amount from the regular price on this house if you are willing to buy it with the following changes from regular specifications:

6 to 2 Star A Star Red Cedar Shingles instead of 5 to 2 Clear; plain square edge casings for doors and windows instead of Craftsman design; all subflooring and kitchen case omitted.

Gordon-Van Tine Home No. 567

Attractive Home at a Bargain Price

A cosy cottage, in good taste, presents itself here. The simple hip roof protects the well designed front porch, and the broad frieze gives a distinctive touch to the wide cornice. The window arrangement is also especially good.

The living room, which is almost square in design, has good furniture space. If it is intended to use this as a living room-dining room, the end of the room nearer to the kitchen offers a splendid place for the dining table, and the location of the front bed room door is such that this room can be heated by the living room stove.

The kitchen, too, is of ample size with plenty of sunlight and air. The place for the range is very near to the rear bed room door. This means that in cold weather the stove will always keep both rooms comfortable.

The rear kitchen door and grade door here are one. This arrangement is always an economy of both material and space. And the fact that supplies can be brought from the basement to the kitchen, without its being necessary for one to step out of doors, is rarely true of so small a house. We supply the frames and sash for the basement.

PAINT—Unless otherwise specified, straw paint will be furnished for body and white paint for trim.

For Plumbing, Heating, Lighting for These Homes, See Last Pages of Book

Gordon-Van Tine Home No. 538

A Really Attractive 4-Room Cottage

For Prices on This Home, See First Page.
Read Pages 9 and 10 for Full Description of Materials.

There is good cheer in this little four-room cottage with its inviting porch, its well arranged windows and its generally good lines and proportions.

Both the front and back doors of this cottage are glazed, which makes the living room and kitchen unusually light and cheery, for all of the rooms already have windows facing in two directions assuring good light and ventilation at all times.

The big Gordon-Van Tine kitchen case, design "B", that has been provided makes it easily possible to keep kitchen utensils out of sight, and the maple topped work table next to the sink together with it, makes all the working space there that one might need. We believe that the cottage kitchen should be as conveniently arranged as the one in the larger house.

There has been no hall space taken from the bed rooms, but each connects directly with the bath. Here a towel case, such as is shown in the colored section is furnished. Each has a conveniently arranged closet, and good summer and winter spaces for the bed. There is no front bed room, and back bed room idea here. In size, light and general convenience they are almost identical.

The bath has been planned with the same space-saving idea as the rest of the house, and it can be just as complete as one that calls for a far greater expenditure.

PAINT—Unless otherwise specified, Lemont stone paint will be furnished for body of house and silver gray paint for trim.

Floor Plan

Second Grade Specifications
Save You $83.95

Deduct the above amount from the regular price on this house if you are willing to buy it with the following changes from regular specifications:

6 to 2 Star A Star Red Cedar Shingles instead of 5 to 2 Clear.

Plain square edge casings for doors and windows instead of Craftsman design.

All subflooring and kitchen case omitted.

Gordon-Van Tine Home No. 564

Attractive 4-Room Home—Low in Cost

Options that Will Save You $76.75
Deduct the above amount from the regular price on this house if you are willing to buy it with the following changes from regular specifications: 6 to 2 Star A Star Red Cedar Shingles instead of 5 to 2 Clear; plain square edge casings for doors and windows instead of Craftsman design; all subflooring and kitchen case omitted.

Here you find a simple convenient home, built most economically and with no great labor outlay.

The outside walls are covered with siding to the belt line, and clear Red Cedar shingles from there to the frieze board. We have left the cornice open, for it's much simpler to build, and the effect of the exposed rafters is more pleasing

The attractively shingled porch gable and the simple, but substantial pillars give a pleasing effect.

Within you will find every bit of space utilized to the best advantage. There are four comfortable rooms. Each has windows in two walls. A glance at the floor plan will show you that the entire house is light and airy, because of the splendid window arrangement.

For Prices on This Home See First Page.
Read Pages 9 and 10 for Full Description of Materials.

Notice the two splendid closets, for which we even furnish coat hooks. The one off the kitchen is an especial illustration of our theory that there is no reason why the simple home should be less convenient than the elaborate one.

The entire kitchen emphasizes this belief. It is completely equipped with our space-saving, labor lightening kitchen case, design "B", like the illustration on the colored plate of this book. These are exclusive Gordon-Van Tine features.

It is just such touches as these that make our houses distinctive and make Gordon-Van Tine home owners enthusiastic boosters.

The plans do not provide for any cellar under this house. The chimney was placed so that the stoves can be put in each room if desired—a very thoughtful arrangement.

PAINT—Unless otherwise specified, we will ship Lemont stone paint for body, and white for trim. Brown shingle stain for shingles.

For Plumbing, Heating, Lighting for These Homes, See Last Pages of Book

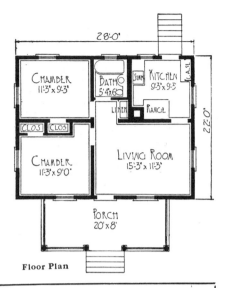

Floor Plan

Gordon-Van Tine Home No. 543

Neat Hip-Roof Cottage— Well Planned

For Prices on This Home, See First Page.
Read Pages 9 and 10 for Full Description of Materials.

A great deal of attention was given the interior of this cottage and you will find things you would not expect, either for the money or in a house of this size.

The bath room is conveniently placed, has plenty of light and ventilation. A Gordon-Van Tine linen case, as illustrated, provides ample space for the bed room and bath linen. Both chambers have good light, with lots of air and big closets. The living room is so situated that it is convenient to all the rooms of the house. The kitchen is equipped with a Gordon-Van Tine case "B", which is illustrated in this book.

There is no basement planned for this cottage, but one could be easily excavated, and the necessary frames and sash would cost very little extra.

A large porch is provided, all or part of which could be screened.

The exterior with its six-inch siding is neat and attractive, while the interior is a genuine surprise for anyone looking for real comfort and value in a four-room house.

Second Grade Specifications Save You $80.40

Deduct the above amount from the regular price on this house if you are willing to buy it with the following changes from regular specifications:

6 to 2 Star A Star Red Cedar Shingles instead of 5 to 2 Clear; plain square edge casings for doors and windows instead of Craftsman design; all subflooring and kitchen case omitted.

PAINT—Unless otherwise specified, we will ship lead paint for body and white paint for trim.

Two Floor Plans to Choose From

For Prices on This Home, See First Page.

Read Pages 9 and 10 for Full Description of Materials.

Options That Will Save You
$74.40 on 553-A
$73.10 on 553-B

Deduct the above amount from the regular price on this house if you are willing to buy it with the following changes from regular specifications:

6 to 2 Star A Star Red Cedar Shingles instead of 5 to 2 Clear; plain square edge casings for doors and windows instead of Craftsman design; all sub-flooring and kitchen case omitted.

Gordon-Van Tine Home Nos. 553A and 553B

A more attractive small cottage than this splendid little home, would be hard to conceive. The same high grade specifications apply on this home as on our higher-priced homes.

The outside walls are sided to the belt, above which is laid shingles. This, is decidedly a good treatment on a home of these dimensions, giving it the appearance of greater size.

The front entrance is charming with the glazed bungalow door with windows flanking each side.

In Plan A, the bed rooms are separated from the living rooms by a hall, which connects the bed rooms with the bath between. In both plans the bed rooms have windows in each outside wall. And twin windows in the living room and kitchen. These little homes are exceptionally well-lighted. They will be cheerful and comfortable—a cosy home for those who want a small cottage.

The kitchens have our Gordon-Van Tine kitchen case, style "B", as shown in the color pages, so placed that the work table will get plenty of light from the rear door, our Monterey design (glazed double strength), and the twin window to the left. The bath room has our towel case included.

PAINT—Unless otherwise specified, we will ship white paint for body, and white paint and green shingle stain for trim.

Floor Plan 553-A

Floor Plan 553-B

For Plumbing, Heating, Lighting for These Homes, See Last Pages of Book

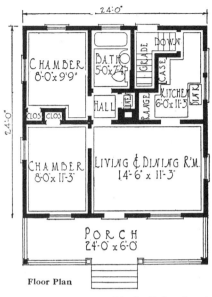

Gordon-Van Tine Home No. 560

Floor Plan

Two Bedroom Bungalow of New Arrangement

For Prices on This Home, See First Page.

Read Pages 9 and 10 for Description of Materials Furnished for This Home.

Options that Will Save You $78.75

Deduct the above amount from the regular price on this house if you are willing to buy it with the following changes from regular specifications:

6 to 2 Star A Star Red Cedar Shingles instead of 5 to 2 Clear; plain square edge casings for doors and windows instead of Craftsman design; all subflooring and kitchen case omitted.

PAINT—Unless otherwise instructed, we will furnish seal brown paint for body and white for trim.

Here is a distinctly individual little cottage with dignified and neat exterior that you cannot help liking. The porch 6 feet by 24 feet stands for comfort and beauty. The front steps are planned to be of concrete.

The living room and dining room are joined in a happy combination making one large room in place of two cramped ones, always a more desirable arrangement. The two windows and the Monterey front door assure cheery sunshine and on hot days, cool breezes.

To secure a well-lighted, compact and convenient kitchen is one secret in home building. Here you have an ideal kitchen which is not only pleasant for the housewife to work in; but because of its equipment of a splendid kitchen case, our design "A", with bins, drawers, shelves, etc., you are given a complete pantry in itself. The kitchen case is found illustrated in the colored insert.

The bath and rear chamber are reached by a center hall which contains a cleverly built-in linen closet of special design and generous size. Both bedrooms are pleasant rooms with plenty of light and ventilation.

Floor Plan

Options that Will Save You $72.40

Deduct the above amount from the regular price on this house if you are willing to buy it with the following changes from regular specifications:

6 to 2 Star A Star Red Cedar Shingles instead of 5 to 2 Clear; plain square edge casings for doors and windows instead of Craftsman design; all subflooring and kitchen case omitted.

Gordon-Van Tine Home No. 569

An Unusual Value In This Little Home

For Prices on This Home, See First Page.   Read Pages 9 and 10 for Full Description of Materials.

Here is a well-planned small home which is really an unusual value. Just the kind of home to build where a low building cost is necessary. It is entirely practical—especially desirable for tenant homes.

The gabled roof-porch breaks the otherwise straight front line of this design. The porch is not just "stuck on" but is decidedly a part of the house. Big square columns make the porch appear substantial and massive. Porch rail and square balusters complete the outline.

This house is sided with ½x6 siding. This effect makes the house look larger than it really is. The porch gable is shingled.

Through the glazed front door we enter a good-sized living room. This room can be made comfortable and pleasant because there is space enough for many convenient arrangements. From the living room you enter into either the front or rear chamber—both bed rooms large enough to prevent the necessity of "crowding in" your furniture. Large closets are provided for these chambers. Each chamber has two large windows—one in each outside wall which permits perfect ventilation.

The kitchen has two windows and a glazed door—always plenty of light. It is very convenient, the range placed close to the chimney insures a good draft—the sink is under the window in the right wall, and there's the big

Gordon-Van Tine kitchen case. You'll find the kitchen case a distinctive feature of the kitchen —and deservedly so from the housewife's viewpoint. This complete case is furnished with teis home at no extra cost. This is our design "A" as shown in the colored section—note the fine detail of arrangement.

As planned, no basement is provided for. At a small extra cost, we add cellar sash and frames, outside-hatchway and door, and the necessary posts and girders required in basement construction.

PAINT—Unless otherwise instructed we will furnish silver gray paint for the body and white paint for the trim.

Low Priced Ready Cut Cottages

For Prices See First Page.   Specifications Below.

These industrial cottages are without doubt the greatest value obtainable in a medium priced workman's home. They are substantial and of pleasing appearance without anything fancy to run up the cost.

The uniform high grade material used will be appreciated immediately when you read the specifications below. The fact that material is cut to fit results in savings in construction that makes them the cheapest buildings of their type when erected it is possible to purchase today.

Special discounts are offered on quantity orders and will be quoted on application.

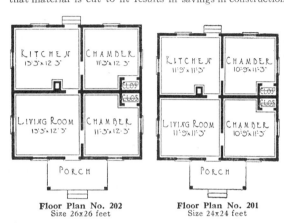

Floor Plan No. 202
Size 26x26 feet

Floor Plan No. 201
Size 24x24 feet

Gordon-Van Tine Cottages No. 201-202

Cottages 201-202

This is a simple but economical and roomy cottage. Note the good size of living room and kitchen and the light and air afforded by two windows in each room.

No. 202 is 26x26 while No. 201 is 24x24 feet.

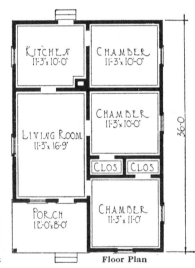

Gordon-Van Tine Cottage No. 203

Comfortable Five-Room Cottage

For Prices, See First Page.   Specifications on Page 110.

Three big bed rooms, living, dining room, and kitchen in this model cottage—a plan that gives you absolutely the most house for your money. It's a strong, sturdy home that will last for generations. You simply can't afford to go on paying rent when such a home is possible at such a price. And *you can build it yourself*. Absolutely all you need is a few tools and a few evenings' time, for all the materials are included in the bill, and they are all cut-to-fit—not by guesswork and a hand saw, but by scientific calculations and electrically driven machinery in the hands of experts.

The outside dimensions of this house are 24 feet wide by 36 feet deep. Ceilings are 8 feet high.

Floor Plan

Specifications of Material for Ready Cut Cottages Shown on Pages 110 and 111.

All timbers and dimension lumber No. 1 Yellow Pine.

SILLS—4x6 sills and girders, *cut-to-fit.*

JOISTS—2x8 floor joists, 2x4 ceiling joists, *cut-to-fit.*

STUDDING AND RAFTERS—2x4 for outside and inside walls and rafters, *cut-to-fit.* (Ceilings are 8 feet, 1 inch high.)

NOTE:—Owing to extreme simplicity of construction of these cottages, we have found it unnecessary to notch the wall plates as we do for Gordon-Van Tine Ready-cut houses. This, of course, results in a substantial saving in cost.

SIDING—1x6 Clear Yellow Pine Drop Siding, *cut-to-fit.*

ROOF BOARDS—Main roof covered with 1x6 No. 2 Yellow Pine boards, laid tight. Cornice and porch roofs covered with 1x4 No. 1 Yellow Pine Drop Siding. *Cut-to-fit.*

ROOFING—Jap-a-Top slate surfaced roll roofing—red or green. (State which color is wanted.)

FLOORS—1x4 (3¼-inch face), No. 1 Yellow Pine. *Cut-to-fit.*

WALLS—All inside walls and ceilings are lined with Gordon-Van Tine Blackhawk Wall Board.

DOORS—Glass front and rear doors. Inside doors five cross panel Fir or Yellow Pine, 1⅜-inch thick. All doors mortised for locks.

WINDOWS—Standard White Pine four-light windows as shown including White Pine frames, *Cut-to-fit* and bundled.

INTERIOR FINISH—All doors and windows are cased with square edge casings. Base square edge, necessary moulding, etc., all Clear Yellow Pine.

HARDWARE—Nails for the complete building, locks and hinges for doors, spring bolts for windows.

PAINT—Two coats of Quality paint for all outside walls and porch ceilings. Two coats Quality porch floor paint for all porch floors. One coat Mission stain for all interior woodwork. One coat of boiled linseed oil for interior floors. Gordon-Van Tine wall tint kalsomine, any color, with proper sizing, furnished for all inside wall and ceilings. Unless otherwise instructed we will furnish light gray for the outside walls of of this home and white for the trim, French gray wall paint for interior walls and cream for the ceilings.

CEILINGS—Blackhawk Wall Board is furnished for ceilings.

Plans and directions free.

These specifications apply only to houses illustrated on pages 110 and 111.

All joists, studding and rafters are spaced 2 feet on centers. Size of material is properly figured to provide ample strength for all parts of the building.

We do not furnish piers as native blocks are often available or masonry is preferred.

We include sufficient scaffold lumber for the easy erection of the building; also tar paper for covering the finish lumber.

Ready Cut Cottages for All Purposes

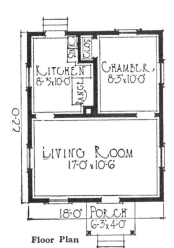

Floor Plan

KITCHEN 8-3x10-0 · CHAMBER 8-3x10-0 · LIVING ROOM 17-0 x 10-6 · PORCH 6-3x4-0 · 18-0

**For Prices
See
First Page
—
Specifications
on
Page 110**

Gordon-Van Tine Cottage No. 210

Comfortable Three-Room Cottage

For the man who has little money to invest, who wants to put up his house himself, this cottage is ideal. In its very simplicity of construction is the economy realized, and it can be made most attractive and cosy. We furnish everything complete at our price. All that is necessary is to nail it together—every piece is cut-to-fit. No experience needed to erect. It should prove interesting to quantity buyers.

**See
First
Page
for
Prices**

KITCHEN 10-0 x 7-0 · CHAMBER 8-6x10-3 · DINING ROOM 10-0 x 10-0 · CLOS · CLOS · CHAMBER 8-6x10-3 · LIVING ROOM 10-0 x 11-0 · PORCH 9-0x6-0 · 20-0 · 30-0

Floor Plan

Gordon-Van Tine Cottage No. 204

This five room cottage has the same floor plan which we have used in many of our finest bungalows. We have found it one of the most convenient and space-saving possible to contrive. The two chambers both have big closets and all the rooms are large.

And remember that you can do all the work yourself if you wish, or if you hire a carpenter he will only be a few days on the job when ordinarliy it would take him weeks. The outside dimensions of this house are 20 feet wide by 30 feet deep. Ceilings are 8 feet high.

Floor Plan

KITCHEN 13-3x9-0 · CLOS · CHAMBER 9-3x11-6 · DINING ROOM 13-3x11-0 · CHAMBER 9-3x11-0 · CLOS · CLOS · LIVING ROOM 13-3x14-0 · CHAMBER 9-3x11-6 · PORCH 18-0x6-0 · 24-0 · 36-0

Gordon-Van Tine Cottage No. 205

A big, roomy cottage—six rooms. Comfortable, practical and the most economical home one can build. If you must hold to a price then, here is your solution.

Big living and dining rooms well-lighted. Kitchen of good size—ample.

Three good-sized, airy bed rooms. Closets for each bed room. Outside dimensions 24x36. Ceilings 8 feet high. Plain in its simplicity, yet attractive because of its substantial proportions and high grade construction. A value absolutely unsurpassed.

Specifications on Above Buildings on Page 110. **Write for Special Price on Lots of 5 or More.**

Summer Cottages

Gordon-Van Tine Summer Cottage No. 301. For Prices See First Page

Our Most Popular Summer Cottage

It is indeed America's most popular summer cottage. In outside appearance it is a beauty—with wide sloping roof and broad lines, which invite and suggest comfort within. The main roof is extended over the screened porch—it is really an outside living room—note how large it is, 28x8 foot. From the illustration you get just a slight idea how the rear wall is extended making perfect head room for the three chambers.

Below is a picture showing the interior of the big living room. Doesn't it carry a conviction of solid comfort within doors on the chilly nights in

early or late seasons. We do not furnish fireplace material as it cannot be shipped to you at a saving. The dining room and kitchen are also good-sized rooms. For a small family, or two or three couples, this home is ample.

The stairs and balcony heighten the open effect of the living room—also notice the outside balcony reached from the stairway landing through a glazed door. We furnish screen wire for porch and windows, which are 6-light, 8x14 inches glass size, and screen doors for both entrances. The chambers are exceptionally well-lighted and airy—two windows in each room.

First Floor Plan

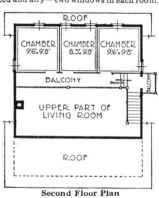

Second Floor Plan

Specifications of Material, Ready-Cut Summer Cottages
These Specifications apply only to those cottages shown on pages 112 to 115

All timbers and dimension lumber No. 1 Yellow Pine. All surfaced one side and one edge.
SILLS AND GIRDERS—4x6, cut-to-fit.
MAIN FLOOR JOIST—2x8, cut-to-fit.
PORCH FLOOR JOIST—2x6, cut-to-fit.
RAFTERS—2x4, cut-to-fit.
STUDDING—2x3, 8 feet high, cut-to-fit.
INSIDE DOOR POSTS AND PLATES—2x3, cut-to-fit.
PORCH POSTS AND BEAM—Cut-to-fit.
FLOORING—1x4 (3¼-inch face) No. 1 Yellow Pine, cut-to-fit.
PARTITIONS—1x4 No. 1 Yellow Pine beaded and matched (partitions are 8 feet high), cut-to-fit.
OUTSIDE WALLS—1x6 Clear Yellow Pine Drop Siding, cut-to-fit. Cottages Nos. 302, 303 and 304 have outside walls of 1x6 No. 2 matched sheathing, covered with Star A Star Red Cedar Shingles.
EXTERIOR FINISH—No. 1 Yellow Pine.

ROOF BOARDS—1x6 No. 2 Yellow Pine dressed and matched, cut-to-fit, laid tight.

ROOFING—Jap-a-Top slate surfaced roofing in a beautiful natural gray-green color.

All joists, outside studding, and rafters are spaced two feet on centers. Size of material is properly figured to provide ample strength for all parts of the building.
Summer cottages do not have ceilings. Partitions are 8 feet high, and do not extend up to roof in 1 story cottages.

OUTSIDE MOULDINGS—Screen moulding and quarter round Clear White Pine, Fir, or Yellow Pine.

DOORS—Outside glass doors, 2-6x6-6, 1⅜, mortised for locks. Inside doors 5X Panel Fir, or Yellow Pine, mortised for locks.

SASH—8"x14" glass size, divided 6 lights. Sash are hinged to swing in.

14 MESH GALVANIZED SCREEN WIRE— Has two more wires to the inch than the standard 12 mesh wire. For covering all porches and windows, complete with screen moulding. Also strong screen doors for front and back.
HARDWARE—Locks and hinges for all doors. Spring bolts for windows. Coat and hat hooks for closets. Nails complete as required for all parts of every house.
PAINT—Quality Brand Paint, two coats, for all outside woodwork. Floor paint for porch floors. Unless otherwise instructed we will furnish light gray paint for body, silver gray shingle stain for wall shingles when they are shown and white paint for trim.
We include sufficient scaffold lumber for the easy erection of the building; also tar paper for covering the finish lumber.
NOTE:—Owing to extreme simplicity of construction of these summer cottages, we have found it unnecessary to notch the wall plates as we do for Gordon-Van Tine Ready-Cut Homes. This of course results in substantial saving in cost.

Gordon-Van Tine Summer Cottage No. 302

A Most Comfortable Summer Home

See First Page for Prices on This Cottage

Cozy—comfortable—inviting is this summer home. It will be a jewel in any setting. The rustic appearance is enhanced in siding the walls with shingles. Every provision for comfort is made—plenty of room, light and air.

An ideal space for a fireplace is indicated on the floor plan. Material for this, however, is not furnished as it cannot be shipped at a saving.

The front chamber is exceptionally well pro-

vided with windows—the porch is screened—we furnish the screen wire for porch and all windows, which are 6-light, 8x14 in. glass size. Screen doors also furnished.

When you see how moderate is the cost for this substantial summer cottage, you will be even more favorably impressed. It is always worth while to investigate things of merit.

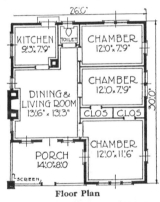

Floor Plan

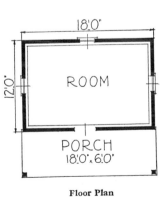

Floor Plan

Gordon-Van Tine Summer Cottage No. 306

For Prices, See First Page

Neat and Simple Summer Cottage

Although the simplest and cheapest of our ready-cut summer cottages, it is one of the most widely used. It's just the thing for a cabin up in the woods by your favorite trout stream, or a camp up the river, where you can spend the week-ends in summer, away from the heat and noise of the city.

The single room of the cottage is big—can be easily partitioned off by canvas curtains if desirable.

The porch is large—we furnish the screen wire, too—and being under the main roof is really an open living room.

For Specifications for Summer Cottages, See Page 112

Floor Plan No. 308

A Large Porch — Fine Interior

Prices on page 1

Specifications on page 112

Gordon-Van Tine Summer Cottage No. 308

The rear porch which may be used for either dining or sleeping is a real feature of this compact, yet comfortable, summer home. If you use this rear porch for sleeping the side porch affords an ideal outdoor dining space.

The living room, with its six windows and one outside door, will be cool and comfortable on hot days while the fireplace at one end will take the chill off on cool mornings and evenings.

The kitchen is amply large for storage of the quantity of supplies that must be carried away from town.

An unusually roomy summer house with just the necessary living quarters enclosed by walls—the balance porch—for which we furnish 14 mesh screen wire.

Gordon-Van Tine Summer Cottage No. 304

Floor Plan No. 304

A Cosy Home for the Summer

For Prices, See First Page

The quaint recessed porch, the shingled walls, the big living room with the fireplace, the excellent arrangement, all tend to make this a most desirable summer home. The sleeping rooms, located as far as possible from the kitchen and dining room make for greater privacy. We furnish screen wire for the porch and windows, and rear door. Let us tell you how easily you can build it. We do not furnish fireplace material.

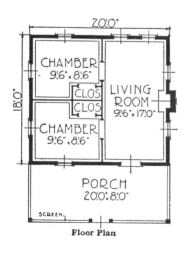

Floor Plan

Gordon-Van Tine Summer Cottage No. 307. For Prices, See First Page

A Dandy Cottage

Not too big—not too small—just the right size for a small party. A cosy, comfy, summer home. There's the big airy porch for the hot days and nights and the big cheery fireplace for the cold rainy days and chilly nights in early or late season. Material for the fireplace is not furnished as it cannot be shipped at a saving.

The main roof extends over the big screened-in porch, making it substantially a part of the cottage and assuring all the comfort of an open living room. Just drop us a line and we'll send it, all cut and ready to set up, direct to your favorite lake.

Specifications for Summer Cottages on Page 112

Floor Plan

An Ideal Summer Home

Prices on Page 1

Specifications on page 112

Have you yearned for the summer home where you could accommodate more of your friends over the week end? Here it is in a dandy, spacious home with a great screened porch along the entire width and part of the depth, for which we furnish screens, living room with a fireplace, two bedrooms and kitchen. Its arrangement is indeed ideal.

If you require a home for a medium large family, or want people to feel free to drop in over night without crowding, this is the home to buy.

Gordon-Van Tine Summer Cottage No. 309

Gordon-Van Tine Summer Cottage No. 303

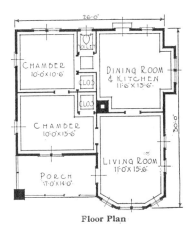

Floor Plan

Very Inviting Summer Home

For Prices See First Page. Specifications on Page 112

The four rooms are well arranged and the closet space unusual for such a cottage. Each room has windows in both outside walls. It will be a light, cheerful, airy place. All windows are 6-light—glass size 8x14 inches. The plan demands but the minimum of household work—your residence in this pleasant, attractive home will be enjoyed to the utmost. Porch is screened and screen wire is also furnished for all windows and rear door. If you are looking for the maximum value in summer homes build this beautiful cottage.

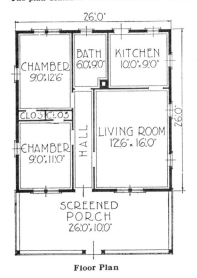

Floor Plan

Gordon-Van Tine Summer Cottage No. 305

An Excellent Summer Cottage

For Prices See First Page. Specifications on Page 112

You will certainly be attracted by this excellent design, if you intend to build a summer home. The excellent arrangement of the rooms which has provided for a bath room, and the attractive exterior prove a happy combination. It appears so substantial, and justly so because of its sound construction, that it is very likely to be considered as an economical solution to your desire. The big living porch, 26x10, is screened—windows there are plenty of them—are covered with 14-mesh screen wire. The kitchen has a screen door. Windows are 6-light, size 1'8"x3'11". Here's a lot of comfort, for a small price—in fact this is a decidedly popular summer cottage. It's popularity is well deserved.

Specifications for Above Summer Cottages on Page 112

Gordon-Van Tine Ready-Cut Garages

Every Bit of Lumber Cut-to-Fit
Build Them Yourself

See Page 1 for
Prices

Gordon-Van Tine Garage No. 101

These are the lowest-priced real garages in America. They are not tin-clad sheds nor woodsheds masquerading as garages, but real good-looking, honest-to-goodness garages with all material ready-cut and everything included, hardware, paint, roofing, nails, as well as the lumber all ready-cut.

You can put these garages up yourself without any trouble. The construction is extremely simple and you can therefore save the whole amount of the construction cost. Every stick of lumber is cut-to-fit—ready to set in place. Complete plans and instructions make mistakes impossible. Or if you employ a carpenter, you save from ⅓ to ½ the labor cost.

You will find them water-tight, durable houses for your car which will not detract from their surroundings and which will last you as long and serve you as well as any garage costing three or four times as much. Thousands of people have bought and built these garages all over the country and they have been entirely satisfied.

Specifications of Construction and Materials, for Garages Shown on This Page

SILLS, PLATES, RAFTERS AND FRAMING—2x4, No. 1 Yellow Pine with 2x6 ridge.

DOOR POSTS—4x4, No. 1 Yellow Pine.

HARDWARE—For doors on 101—strap hinges, foot and head bolts, and rim lock with two keys. For 110 a special hardware set including extra heavy tee hinges, chain bolt, foot bolt and handle or pull. For sash—hinges and fasteners. Nails for entire building.

PAINT—Two coats Quality Paint for outside walls and doors. Side Walls 8 feet high. Unless otherwise instructed we will furnish white paint.

SIDING—1x6, No. 1 Yellow Pine, dressed and match, set vertically.

ROOF—1x6, dressed and matched Yellow Pine—cut-to-fit, covered with 3-ply Asphalt Roofing of gray-green color.

DOORS—No. 101 (above)—1x6 Beaded Siding with stiles and rails for back—cut-to-fit but not nailed together, for opening 8 ft. x 8 ft. No. 110 (at left) has strong, good-looking factory built doors of design illustrated for opening, 8 ft. x 8 ft. Made of clear white pine or spruce 1⅜ inches thick.

SASH—Two sash for each garage, to open in. All material cut-to-fit. **PLANS** and blue prints are furnished free. Triple doors cannot be used on garages Numbers 101 and 110.

Sizes: 10 x 16 ft.   12 x 18 ft.   14 x 20 ft.

Prices on Page 1.

Important Note

No. 110 is identical to No. 101 except that we furnish strong, fine appearing factory built doors ready to hang for No. 110 shown at left.

Gordon-Van Tine Garage No. 110

Send for Special Garage Circular—All Designs Shown

Ready-Cut Garage No. 102—Double Garage This Design, No. 104

All Lumber Cut-to-Fit Put Them Up Yourself

Every bit of lumber which goes into these garages is ready-cut. Window frames are factory made and shipped ready to set into the wall. Doors are made complete in our own factories of clear white pine lumber and are shipped ready to hang. As finely made as the best house front door and cost much less than the usual nailed together door. They are 1¾ inches thick, mortise and tenon joints, and will always hang true and straight.

Because all material is sent in such shape, it is but the work of a few hours to build your garage instead of several days. Hundreds of our customers build these garages themselves at big savings and enjoy doing it too.

Note the specifications and see what excellent material we furnish. You get the finest hardware, heavy hinges and a cylinder lock set, two coats of quality paint and all plans and blue prints furnished free.

DOUBLE GARAGES are amply large for two cars, 104 being similar in design to 102; and 105 similar in design to 103. These double garages have two sets of double doors, two windows in each side and one in the end.

Specifications of Garages on This Page

SILLS—2x6, No. 1 Yellow Pine.

STUDDING AND RAFTERS—2x4, No. 1 Yellow Pine spaced 2 ft. on centers.

ROOF—1x6, No. 2 Yellow Pine dressed and matched sheathing, covered with Jap-a-Top shingle roll, slate surfaced roofing, in a beautiful gray-green color.

SIDING—1x6. Clear Yellow Pine Drop Siding.

DOORS—Clear White Pine Doors, each 4 ft. by 8 ft., 1¾ inches thick, with solid stiles and rails, and beaded panels below with glass panels above—very strongly built. Are ready to hang.

WINDOWS—Single garages have one window in each side and one end; double garages have two windows in each side and one in one end.

SASH—Size 2 ft. 7 in. by 2 ft. 5 in., divided six square lights. Hinged to swing in. Complete with all necessary hardware.

HARDWARE—Durable Japanned hardware for doors, including hinges; foot and head bolts, handle, and cylinder lock with small flat keys. Hinges and fasteners for sash. Nails for entire building.

PAINT—Two coats of Quality paint for outside walls and doors. Unless otherwise instructed will furnish white paint.

PLANS and blue prints are furnished free.

All material cut-to-fit.

Line Your Garage with Wallboard

For real winter comfort. A small heater will keep things from freezing and your car will start easily on coldest mornings.

Our Blackhawk Wallboard is made of three layers of highly compressed pure fibre, treated with a moisture proof sizing and two layers of asphalt cement, welded together to form a tough elastic board 3/16-inch thick. You can put it on yourself. Prices on page 1.

Garage No. 106. Double Garage this design, No. 107
Single Garage with Stucco Finish, No. 108; Double, No. 109

Ready-Cut Garage No. 103—Double Garage This Design, No. 105

For Sizes and Prices
See Page 1

Garages Nos. 106 and 107

Extra fine material furnished for garages of this design, including triple sliding doors with complete hardware, 5 to 2 Extra Clear Red Cedar shingles over 1x4 roof sheathing and clear bevel house siding (Cypress or Redwood). Material for lattice and gable brackets also furnished.

Other specifications similar to those given above on this page.

IMPORTANT NOTE—These garages are equipped with our Gordon Weathertight Triple Sliding Doors. These doors open by folding inside and require three feet of clear space to operate. Order your garage at least this much longer than your car. These doors are good looking, slide easily and are snug fitting. They are included in the price of Garages Nos. 106, 107, 108 and 109, quoted on page 1.

These triple doors are also furnished for any other garage on this page. See option on page 1.

STUCCO FINISH—We also furnish this style garage with Byrkitt Patent Sheathing in place of drop siding, so that outside walls may be stuccoed. Byrkitt Sheathing has special surface to which stucco firmly adheres. Single garage with stucco outside walls is known as 108; double garage, 109.

This Handy Side Door for Any Garage

(Except No. 101 and 110)

Especially convenient if your garage opens on to alley. Door is 5 cross panel fir, 1¾ inch thick, size 2-8x6-8 with frame, butts, lock set and night latch. Costs but little extra.

Price on page 1.

No. 1—A Gordon-Van Tine Furnace as it comes from the factory, assembled in your cellar and ready to erect.

No. 2—Note how easily the sections fit together.

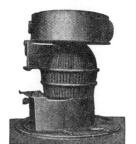

No. 3—The cast radiator in place. All main castings fit together without bolts or screws.

No. 4—Furnace complete. The holes are ready cut and the collars are ready set.

Gordon-Van Tine Heating System for Your Gordon-Van Tine Home

THE same efficient service and high quality of material that you get when you buy your home from this book is yours when you buy your complete heating system from the Gordon-Van Tine Company.

Whether you choose a warm air pipe furnace, a hot water plant, a steam system or a pipeless furnace, you will receive the benefit of our expert knowledge of heating systems. Our engineers have made a careful study of each of our many homes and have prepared the one perfect layout for each that insures the utmost economy of operation together with ideal heating results.

Every installation is guaranteed.

Van Tine Warm Air Pipe Furnace
Low Cost—Highly Efficient—Simple to Install—Easy to Operate. Special Furnace Plans for Your Home

The warm air pipe system of heating is, considering both first cost and operating expense, economical and efficient. We do not hesitate to recommend our Van Tine warm air systems for any of our homes. All the parts, warm and cold air pipes, registers, and the furnace itself, are easy to install. In operation the large water pan assures a plentiful supply of moist, healthful air.

The furnace heating plan for each Gordon-Van Tine home has been laid out by our expert heating engineers. In all of our layouts efficiency in heating is combined with a placing of registers that insures convenient furniture arrangement. The structure of the building is carefully studied, and the warm air pipes are arranged to conform with the framing to give the fewest possible number of curves and turns.

The furnace is all-cast, of heavy gray iron, with full height handsomely designed cast front. The ash pit is deep and wide and will hold a large quantity of ashes without danger of burning out the grates. The ash pit door is full width of the ash pit, has draft door for chain control, covered shaker holes and spring wire handle. The feed door is of ample size with a convenient housing for hot water coil. The cleanout door is large and furnishes easy access to the entire interior of the radiator.

The fire pot is made in two heavy corrugated cast sections. These will not crack from contraction and expansion as will a one-piece firepot. The radiator is of horse shoe type, and carries heat from the center of the firepot entirely around the furnace before reaching the smoke flue. The heat from fuel burned in the Van Tine goes into the house and not up the chimney.

Four extra heavy triangular revolving grates insure a clean fire at all times. Clinkers are cut up as the grates revolve.

Deeply grooved joints at edges where castings join insure a smoke-proof job.

The casing is extra heavy, with upper section double lined with sheet asbestos and tin.

Poker, shaker, handle, chains, chain plate, and pulleys are of course included to make the installation complete.

Furnace Casings Cut to Fit

Van Tine Furnace casings are ready to assemble, with collars placed for warm air pipes, and holes cut for smoke pipe and cold air ducts. The preparation of this material by us relieves you of the only difficult operation in installing your furnace.

We Furnish Everything Complete

Each room is provided with a japanned register of correct size. Oversize oak cold air faces, to return air to the furnace, are located to give greater efficiency in circulation. All wall stacks, register boxes, boots and angles are of double wall and air space construction, affording the highest type of fire-safe installation. All warm air pipes in the cellar are covered with asbestos paper—this means warm rooms and a cool cellar. Cold air pipe is of heavy galvanized iron.

Full and simple instructions, sent free with your order, enable you to install the entire system without difficulty.

Prices on Page 130—First Column

Van Tine Pipeless Furnace
Will Keep Your Home at 70°

FOR a small home when all things are considered, no system of heating can compare with the Van Tine Pipeless System, and especially is this true when the element of first cost is considered. This heating has stood the test of time and is today more popular than ever before.

The Van Tine one-register furnace is as easy to operate as a stove. No coal to carry upstairs, no ashes to carry down, just one fire in your cellar alongside your coal pile and one draft regulator in the living room. The Van Tine one-register heater can be installed by anyone in no longer time than it takes to set up a stove. It will heat every room in your house in even the coldest weather with less fuel than it would take to do it in any other way.

Perfect Circulation Assured

One large register is located in the floor at a central point in the house. This register is divided into two parts—the warm air in the center and the cold air around the sides. Volumes of fresh, warm air are heated and discharged through the warm air portion of this register and rises straight to the ceiling of the room in which the register is located. The ceiling then acts as a deflector, sending the heated air through open stairways and doorways to adjoining rooms. These afford a perfect course for the travel of the heated air to the second floor and other parts of the house and when the air reaches the second floor the same process of heat travel and deflection is repeated.

Thus rising and spreading naturally the heated air penetrates to even the most remote parts of the house displacing the cooler

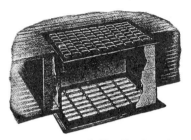

Ventilation Ceiling Register

For use in heating upstairs rooms. We advise using these ventilation registers in connection with our Pipeless furnaces where a quicker circulation is desired to the 2d floor rooms, especially bathroom. Comes complete with white enameled ceiling face and Black Japanned floor register; is adjustable connected with a spring and will fit any any size joist. Size of register 10 in. by 12 in.

air and forcing it downward until it is drawn back into the furnace through the cold air portion of the register. Here it is again heated and returned to repeat the same process of circulation. Warm air, therefore, is kept constantly circulating in a natural and easy manner making it possible to maintain a uniform temperature in every part of the house.

The construction of this furnace is of that same sturdy type as embodied in our pipe furnaces shown on opposite page.

The fire pot is corrugated, thus assuring you that you will always be free from the danger of a cracked pot.

And then the ash pit door is large; likewise the ash pit itself, so that you will not burn out the grates in allowing the ashes to accumulate for a day or two. As the ash pit is made extra high it also does way with all back-breaking labor. It is air-tight.

Base Is Air Tight

The ash pit door is fitted directly onto the face of the ash pit thus insuring a perfect joint. You, therefore, will have an air-tight base allowing you absolute control of the fire.

Special attention has been given to the ease with which it is possible for you to shake the ashes. Our grates are of the popular triangle type and they work with very little friction. Our grates are so constructed that clinkers, no matter how large are easily broken up and removed.

All parts of the grate, including the grate rests and grate rest support, can be easily removed through the ash pit door.

We have equipped our furnaces with a large vapor pan which will at all times provide an ample supply of moisture in the warm air discharged from the furnace. Warm air without moisture is like the dry, stifling wind of the desert, whereas warm air laden with moisture has the effect of a tropical sea breeze.

Radiators on the Van Tine one-register furnace are easily cleaned, thus allowing you to get the maximum heat from your coal at all times. The Gordon-Van Tine Company has sold many hundreds of these furnaces. They are working in all parts of the country and we will guarantee their satisfaction or refund your money.

Cold air returns are provided in some pipeless furnaces by cutting one or more openings in the bottom of the casing through which damp and often smelly cellar air is drawn. Where cellar conditions are not the best, such a system may prove a menace to the health of the entire family. The Van Tine draws air from the rooms of the house only.

In the last column on page 130, pipeless furnaces are priced for those Gordon-Van Tine homes in which our heating engineers may conscientiously recommend this form of heat.

These prices include furnace of a size to heat the home comfortably in any sort of weather, complete with register and 4 feet of smoke pipe and one ell.

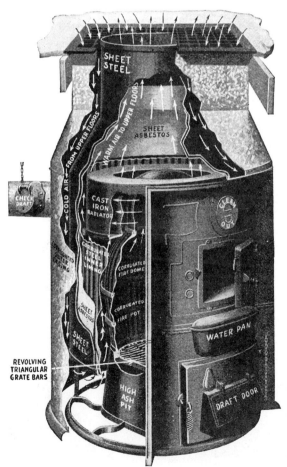

SHEET STEEL

WARM AIR TO UPPER FLOORS

SHEET ASBESTOS

COLD AIR FROM UPPER FLOORS

CHECK DRAFT

CAST IRON RADIATOR

CLEAN OUT

CORRUGATED FIRE DOME

SHEET ASBESTOS

CORRUGATED FIRE POT

SHEET STEEL

WATER PAN

REVOLVING TRIANGULAR GRATE BARS

HIGH ASH PIT

DRAFT DOOR

Van Tine Pipeless Furnace

Prices on Page 130, Fourth Column

Hot Water Heating Plants

HOT WATER HEAT is economical of coal, always dependable and easy to control. Many prefer it because of its comparative cleanliness, also. Hot water holds heat long after the fire has died down keeping the house warm and comfortable clear through the night. Radiators are placed near windows or along outside walls. This warms any cold air which enters the home thus maintaining an even temperature.

Our heating experts have prepared heating plans for all of our homes, carefully figured the necessary radiation for each room and accurately computed all pipe sizes. The results of their work are given in detailed instructions for installing furnished with every order.

Gordon-Van Tine hot water boilers are designed to extract a maximum of heat from the fuel fed to them. The water is divided into small parts, so

that it is **quickly** heated. A water jacket surrounding the outside walls of the fire pot insures the absorption of all of the heat instead of allowing it to escape into the cellar. The corrugated surface of the fire pot still further adds to the efficiency of the boiler and insures against the danger of cracking from expansion and contraction.

A high ash pit allowing a large accumulation of ashes without danger of burning out, and heavy, well proportioned grates made of iron specially selected to withstand hard use are important features.

All piping is of high grade welded steel with heavy cast iron fittings. Radiators are made of new iron, are heavy in construction, and are especially designed to permit cleaning between sections. All radiators are of ample size for best heating conditions, and always of a design to fit the space allotted.

Each radiator is equipped with a nickel plated quick-opening valve, with polished hardwood handle, and with a patented air vent, also nickel plated.

The prices shown on page 130, third column, are for systems designed to heat each room to a temperature of 70 degrees when the outside temperature is 10 degrees below zero. For colder climates larger plants are furnished at slightly increased cost. If you live in a warmer climate we will quote you a price which is substantially less than the printed prices. We design your plant for conditions in your locality from Government temperature records.

Each plant a complete boiler of proper size, asbestos cement for covering the boiler, all the necessary piping and fittings to connect each radiator with the boiler, hangers for pipe, black paint for basement pipes, radiators with all necessary valves and fittings, bronze for radiators, expansion tank, hot water thermometer, and altitude gauge — everything that is needed for a complete installation. We guarantee the system absolutely, when installed according to our plans.

PRICES ON PAGE 130—THIRD COLUMN

Note the solid substantial appearance of our boilers. Note that there are only five main parts. Easy to erect.

This shows the ash pit of our boiler. Note how simple the grate action is and the leverage given the grate shaker. The grates of our boilers are composed of only six moving parts.

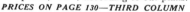
Complete Steam Heating Plants
Our engineers have designed steam plants for all of our houses in the same painstaking manner as described for our hot water systems. If you prefer a steam heating system we will supply you with the same high grade materials and service. Write for details. PRICES ON PAGE 130. COLUMN 3. PLANS FREE.

Gordon-Van Tine Disappearing Stairway
Strong — Easy to Operate — Out of Sight When Not In Use

The attic in practically any home in this book where stairway is not shown in plan can be made into a handy storage space by installing the Gordon-Van Tine Disappearing Stairway. This is a particularly desirable addition to the small home where every foot of room is valuable and where extra storage is always welcome.

It is just as substantial and practical as a built-in stairway, yet when not in use folds up into the ceiling completely out of sight and out of the way. It is usually placed in the hall ceiling but can be placed in any room.

Simple and Positive in Operation

When closed nothing is visible from below but a neat panel (furnished in pine, birch or oak to match your woodwork), with a chain hanging down from it. When this chain is pulled the panel comes down easily and the stairs slide slowly into position. An ingenious system of pulleys and counter-balances (see illustration) keep it from rushing down when opened. To close it simply raise and give slight push. Goes up easily as it slides on rollers and is perfectly counterbalanced in any position.

There is no danger of it falling accidentally — it will not come down unless pulled down. It is neat in appearance and made amply strong to carry weight of trunks, etc. Opening in ceiling is 2 feet 8 inches wide by 6 feet 2 inches long.

Ideal for use in bungalows and cottages. Gives large extra storage space at small cost.

Stair horses and upper side of panel are primed with a dark stain. Lower side of panel is in natural wood, not finished, so you can finish it to match other woodwork.

Shipped complete, ready to install. Complete drawings and instructions for installation sent with stairway.

Priced on Page 132

PANEL VIEWED FROM BELOW

System of pulleys and rollers make it easy and thoroughly safe to operate.

Fully Extended Ready for Use

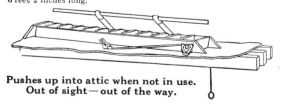

**Pushes up into attic when not in use.
Out of sight — out of the way.**

Plumbing Complete for Every Home

OUR Sanitary Engineers have carefully considered every Gordon-Van Tine home, and have laid out a piping and plumbing plan for it which is letter perfect. This service alone would cost at least $100.00 if you bought it for your house alone, but Gordon-Van Tine's great volume enables us to give this service with no expense to you. It is included with the order, like our architectural service.

Plumbing Planned by Experts

Plumbing is so important to health that you cannot afford to take chances. No matter how well intentioned a man might be, if he were not a doctor you would not let him prescribe for your children if they were sick, and no matter how well intentioned a plumbing mechanic may be, you should not let him lay out your plumbing plans. Get trained, professional advice and service every time.

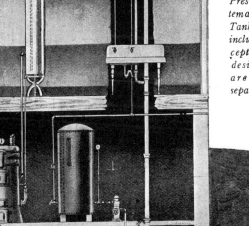

Illustration shows typical installation of Washington Set—showing also Pressure System No. 6A720 and Septic Tanks. Pressure System and Septic Tanks are not included except where desired and are priced separately.

Standard weight galvanized steel piping is used throughout for water supply pipes. Sizes are carefully calculated to secure an even water pressure throughout the house at all times. Piping is so designed as to drain the whole system from one point, making it easy in case you wish to close the house up in winter at any time.

Shut-off is provided for entire system. Hot water piping arranged so that even pressure and quick delivery of hot water are obtained.

Complete Directions for Installing

Complete plans and instructions furnished which will enable you to install the system without difficulty. Bills of materials are guaranteed complete. If there are any shortages or extras, we guarantee to furnish them or pay for them providing our plans and instructions are carefully followed.

A wide range of fixtures are shown on the following pages. Make your choice from the designs shown and see page 129 for prices complete for any house in our Plan Book for which plumbing is furnished. For customers living on the farm, we show complete pressure systems in a separate circular. (See Note at bottom of page.) These used in connection with our plumbing installation make it possible to buy direct from us a complete system to meet any requirements. Systems are illustrated and prices shown so that you can easily decide on combination you desire.

Sewage Disposal Systems

The cut also shows the Gordon-Van Tine Natural Way Sewage Disposal System. The most efficient system known to science today. Made of reinforced concrete, practical, saves you money and time and absolutely protects your family from sickness.

Chemical action, first in one tank, then in the other, reduces all sewage waste into a harmless odorless liquid, which is discharged from the second tank, and is easily disposed of.

GORDON Natural Way Sewage Disposal consists of two concrete tanks, made of best grade Portland cement. Tanks are cylindrical in shape, being molded in one piece and are thoroughly reinforced with special steel reinforcing. Covers are cast separate, also being reinforced. There are no metal fittings or parts of any kind, in our tanks, thus eliminating corrosive and electrolytic action. This feature is of great importance.

All tanks are thoroughly waterproofed inside and out, and if not used beyond rated capacity, need be cleaned only once in four or five years:

Two Tank Sewage Disposal System

Catalog Number	Capacity Persons	1st Tank	2nd Tank	Shipping Weight
6A9453	5	24 x 52	24 x 36	1550
6A9454	8	30 x 52	24 x 36	1850

If vitrified tile fittings are wanted with tanks add $5.00.

Prices on All Sizes on Page 129

Western shipments made from Davenport. Eastern shipments from North Carolina.

Pressure Water Supply Systems (cylindrical tank in basement in above illustration) are described, illustrated and priced very low in a separate circular. These are used where there is no city pressure and may be operated by hand, gas engine or electricity. *If interested send for this Free Circular.*

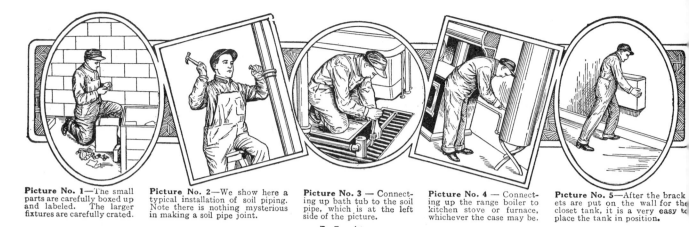

Picture No. 1—The small parts are carefully boxed up and labeled. The larger fixtures are carefully crated.

Picture No. 2—We show here a typical installation of soil piping. Note there is nothing mysterious in making a soil pipe joint.

Picture No. 3—Connecting up bath tub to the soil pipe, which is at the left side of the picture.

Picture No. 4—Connecting up the range boiler to kitchen stove or furnace, whichever the case may be.

Picture No. 5—After the brackets are put on the wall for the closet tank, it is a very easy to place the tank in position.

Madison

Bath tub on base, 5 feet long, 30 inches wide, 17 inches deep and 22½ inches high. Inside finished in glazed white enamel. Nickel plated compression double bath cock with hot and cold indexed china handles. Secret waste with indexed china knob.

Solid porcelain syphon wash-down bowl. Tank is all white enameled porcelain. Birch mahogany seat and cover. Height of closet 17½ inches, width of cover 22½ inches, ⅜-inch nickel plated supply pipe from tank to floor.

Porcelain enameled one piece square apron design lavatory. Size of top slab 18x24 inches, bowl 11x15 inches and back 12 inches high. Equipped with nickel plated compression faucets with china index tops. 1¼ inch nickel plated P trap and supply pipes to wall.

Porcelain enameled sink cast in one piece 46 inches long. Size of sink 20x28 inches, size of drain board 20x20 inches. Glazed white porcelain enameled with roll rim and grooved drain board. Nickel plated Fuller bibbs. 1½ inch nickel plated P trap, strainer and tail piece. Can be furnished either right or left hand drain boards.

Range boiler illustrated and described on opposite page.

Weight complete set 855 pounds.

Washington

Porcelain enameled one piece lavatory, supported on a porcelain enameled pedestal. Square pattern with top measuring 20 in. deep and 24 in. wide, basin size 12x15 in. All finished in glazed white porcelain enamel. Nickel plated Ideal lifting knob with china handle. Two nickel plated compression faucets, with porcelain cross index handles, marked "hot" and "cold" 1¼ in. "P" trap and supply pipes to wall. All trimmings finest grade.

Porcelain syphon jet closet bowl, with an all porcelain tank. White enameled wood finished seat and cover. Height of closet from floor 17½ inches, width over cover 20 inches, ⅜-inch nickel plated supply pipe from tank to floor.

Porcelain enameled bath tub for tiling in at back and one end. Cast in one piece. Enameled inside and out. Fitted with nickel plated compression nozzle, supply stop and waste. Porcelain cross index handle, secret waste with porcelain index knob. Length 5 ft., height 17 in., width 30 in.

Porcelain enameled one piece sink, length over all 45½ in. Size of sink 20x24 inches, size of drain board 20x24 inches, height of back 12 inches. Legs are adjustable. Grooved drain board.

Nickel plated Fuller bibbs. Nickel plated strainer, P trap and tail piece.
Range boiler illustrated and described on opposite page.
Tub and sink furnished either right or left hand.
All trimmings for Washington set are of heaviest brass, highly nickel plated. Weight of complete set 1255 pounds.

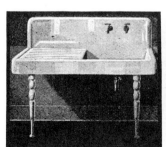

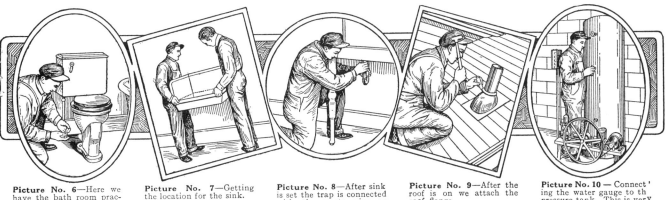

Picture No. 6—Here we have the bath room practically completed. This customer is connecting up the water supply pipe to the tank.

Picture No. 7—Getting the location for the sink.

Picture No. 8—After sink is set the trap is connected with the waste pipe as shown above.

Picture No. 9—After the roof is on we attach the roof flange.

Picture No. 10—Connect' ing the water gauge to th pressure tank. This is very simple.

Jefferson

Porcelain enameled bath tub, 5 feet long, 30 inches wide and 17 inches deep. Is 22½ inches high with a 3 inch roll rim. Equipped with nickel plated supply and waste pipes. Double bath cock, stopper and chains.

All porcelain syphon wash-down bowl. Tank is all white enameled porcelain. Finest quality wood seat and cover. Height of closet from floor 17½ inches. Width over cover 20 inches. ⅜-inch nickel plated supply pipe from tank to floor.

Porcelain enameled lavatory cast in one piece. Top measures 17x19 inches, back 6½ inches high and bowl 11x14 inches. Equipped with nickel plated low down compression faucets with china index handles. Two ⅜-inch supply pipes to wall, nickel plated P trap.

Porcelain enameled one piece 20x24 inch roll rim sink with back 12 inches high. Separate 20x24 inch interchangeable grooved drain board with concealed bracket, can be used right or left. Nicked plated Fuller faucets, 1½ inch nickel plated P trap, strainer and tail piece.

Range boiler illustrated and described below.

Weight complete set 815 pounds.

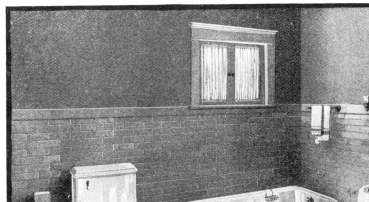

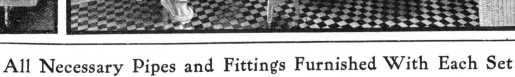

All Necessary Pipes and Fittings Furnished With Each Set

Priced on Page 129

In addition to the fixtures, prices on page 129 include all necessary waste pipe, soil pipe, water supply pipe and fittings for a complete installation. Enough soil and water pipe is furnished to extend four feet outside the basement wall. All soil pipe and fittings are standard grade and are provided with cleanouts at proper joints. The necessary lead and oakum for making joints is furnished. Water supply pipe is of galvanized welded steel and is proportioned in sizes to equalize pressure at all fixtures. Necessary elbows, tees and unions for water supply piping are galvanized malleable iron.

Besides the fixtures shown a heavy cellar floor drain, stop and waste cock for house supply and hot and cold water faucet for basement are included.

Where plan shows two baths, or one extra toilet, lavatory or any extra fixtures, the fixtures in the design of our Jefferson set are furnished together with all necessary pipes.

Our complete plans and detailed illustrated instructions, which are included with every order, make it a simple matter to install these plumbing systems for any of our homes. Every plan is laid out in a way that insures a perfectly satisfactory system. We guarantee the quality of every fixture and we guarantee to furnish sufficient material to complete the job according to plans.

All Plumbing Sets Shipped from Factory in Chicago

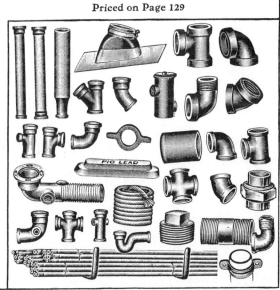

30 gallon standard weight galvanized range boiler with riveted seams. Guaranteed working pressure of 85 pounds. Furnished with all plumbing sets.

"Ambassador"

Hall
GA817

Dining Room
6A813

Living Room
6A811

"Traymore"

Hall
GA827

Living Room
GA821

Dining Room
GA823

"Marlboro"

Hall
GA837

Living Room
GA831

Dining Room
GA833

Electric Fixture Sets

Latest Designs—Finest Material
Prices on Page 131

AMBASSADOR

Porch, Bath, Kitchen and Bedroom included in this set shown below.

An exceptional value is offered in our "Ambassador" set. The general high quality of these fixtures makes them a decided bargain at our price.

The finish on all fixtures in this set except bath and porch is Flemish brass or brush brass and black. Canopies, pans and chains are solid brass except porch fixture which is cast iron.

No. 6A811—Living Room. Length over all 34 inches. Pan 14 inches in diameter. Key socket with white satin finished glass shades of Oakleaf design.

No. 6A817—Hall. Ceiling band 5 inches in diameter. Satin finish glass shade 7 inches bottom diameter. Length over all 7 inches. Keyless porcelain socket.

No. 6A813—Dining Room. Length over all 36 inches. Round 5 inch ceiling canopy. Pan 14 inches in diameter. White satin finished glass shades of Oakleaf design. Key sockets.

TRAYMORE

Porch, Bath, Kitchen and Bedroom included in this set shown below.

This set embodies the correct principles of semi-indirect lighting, with extremely fine appearing design.

The finish on all fixtures in this set except bath and porch is Flemish brass or brush brass and black. Canopies and chains are solid brass except porch which is cast iron.

No. 6A821—Living Room. Length over all 34 inches. Diameter of bowl 15½ inches. 5 inch canopy. Bowl is white satin finish glass with Lotus Leaf border and key socket in bowl.

No. 6A827—Hall. Semi-indirect ceiling fixture. Length over all 11 inches. Diameter band at ceiling 5 inches. Solid brass holder. 8-inch white satin finish, acorn ball glass shade of Lotus Leaf design. Porcelain keyless socket.

No. 6A823—Dining Room. Length over all 36 inches. Diameter of bowl 15½ inches. Solid brass canopy and chains. Bowl is white satin finish glass with Lotus Leaf border and one key socket inside. Three drop lights with key sockets and shades to match bowl.

MARLBORO

Porch, Bath, Kitchen and Bedroom shown below.

The "Marlboro" makes a distinctive appeal through its combined beauty and simplicity of design. You will be delighted with every piece in this set.

The finish on all fixtures in this set except bath and porch is Flemish brass or brush brass and black. Canopies, pans and chains are solid brass except porch which is cast iron.

No. 6A831—Living Room. Length to bottom of glassware 34 inches. Pan 16 inches diameter. Top canopy 6 inches diameter. Key sockets. Apple Blossom design glass shades in brown tint furnished.

No. 6A837—Hall. Length to bottom of acorn 11 inches. Porcelain keyless socket. Brass ceiling band 5 inches diameter. Acorn glass shade 8 inches deep, 6 inches diameter, finished in brown tint.

No. 6A833—Dining Room. Length to bottom of glassware 36 inches, spread 16 inches. Diameter top canopy 6 inches. Key sockets. Apple Blossom design glass shades and 12 inch bowl in brown tint.

Fixtures Shown Below Furnished with all Sets on This Page

Bath Room—Extends 7 inches when used as a bracket. Shade of frosted glass 6 inches in diameter. Key socket. Finished in highly polished nickel plate.

Porch—Length to bottom of ball 7½ inches. Cast iron ceiling band in dead black finish. Weatherproof keyless socket. Ball 6 inches in diameter frosted inside.

Kitchen—Canopy 5 inches in diameter. Length over all 6 inches. Keyless porcelain socket. Milk white glass shade 7 inches bottom diameter.

Bedroom—Length over all 34 inches. 5-inch ceiling canopy. White satin finished glass shade. Key socket. By removing all but two links of chain fixture may be suspended from wall similar to bath fixture. NOTE: Shade to match principal pieces of set will be furnished.

All sets shipped from factory completely wired with crowfeet, ready to install. No lamps or bulbs included.

Porch-Bath-Bedroom and Kitchen Fixtures for Sets on this Page

Kitchen
GA801

Bath
GA805

Shade in bedroom fixtures will be furnished to match set ordered from this page.

Kitchen and bath fixtures similar to these are furnished for "Chalfonte" and "Moraine" sets on opposite page.

Porch
GA803

Bed Room

For Every Home _{IN THIS BOOK}
Low Wholesale Prices on Page 131
CHALFONTE

Each piece in the "Chalfonte" set is exceedingly attractive. Canopies, chains and all metal parts solid brass except porch fixture.

6A841—Living Room. Made of solid brass in satin silver finish. Length over all 34 inches, spread 15 inches, body 10 inches diameter, heavy bent brass tube arms. Keyless standard base sockets—white fibre candles.

6A847—Hall. Length to bottom of acorn glass shade 18 inches, made of solid brass finished in brown tone with Etruscan gold shading. Top canopy 5 inches diameter. Acorn globe 8 inches deep, tinted in brown.

6A849—Porch. Made of cast metal in dead black finish. Extends 11½ inches over all. Heavy, square wall canopy, 5½ inches square. Width of lantern 6½ inches. Length 9 inches. Cut-out beaded cast metal sides. Pebbled crystal glass panels. Weatherproof, porcelain keyless sockets.

6A843—Dining Room. Length over all 36 inches. Spread 20 inches, band 16 inches diameter, in brown tone with Etruscan gold shading. Key sockets. 12-inch cut glass crystal white bowl. Glass shades may be attached. 1 light in bowl, 5 lights around.

6A845—Bedroom. Length over all 34 inches, spread 14 inches. Made of solid brass finished in brown tone with Etruscan gold shading. Top canopy 5 inches. Dimension of pan 14 inches long, 7 inches wide. Key sockets. Frosted white floral design glass shades.

Bath and kitchen fixtures shown and described on opposite page.

MORAINE

The "Moraine" is without doubt a most artistic set. Canopies, chains and all metal parts are solid brass except porch fixture.

6A851—Living Room. Has satin silver finish. Length over all 34 inches, spread 20 inches. Heavy bent brass tube arms. Keyless standard base sockets. White fibre candles. Diameter of canopy at top 5 inches.

6A857—Hall. Finished in satin silver. Length over all 24 inches, diameter 10 inches. Keyless sockets, white fibre candles, covered with clear glass cylinder.

6A859—Porch. Has a hexagon ceiling cap, 13 inches across corners with extended hexagon ornamental paneled body with closed bottom. Length to bottom of fixture 8 inches. Made of cast iron in dead black finish. Keyless socket for one electric light.

6A853—Dining Room. Finished in brown tone with Etruscan gold shading. Length over all 36 inches, spread 16 inches. Key sockets. Glass shades attached.

6A855—Bedroom. Made of solid brass in brown tone with Etruscan gold shading. Length over all 34 inches, spread 12 inches. Key sockets. Diameter of canopy at top 5 inches. White satin finished shades, Oakleaf design.

Bath and kitchen fixtures shown and described on opposite page.

Extra Fixtures—Shown Below

For walls in the living and dining room, halls, den, sewing room and bedroom. Do not have to be bought as a set. You can order one fixture only or as many of any one fixture as you desire. All metal parts of these fixtures made of solid brass—finished as described. Frosted bulbs not included.

6A883—Wall plate 6 inches long, 4 inches wide, finished in brown tone with Etruscan gold shading. Small switch conveniently located in plate. Standard base keyless sockets. White fibre candles. Fixture extends 6 inches, spread 9 inches.

6A884—Same as 6A883, only Butler's satin silver finish.

6A881—Wall plate 6 inches long, 4 inches wide, finished in brown tone with Etruscan gold shading. Small switch conveniently located in plate. Standard base socket. White fibre candles. Extends 6 inches.

6A882—Same as 6A881, only Butler's silver satin finish.

6A873—Extends 7 inches, canopy 4½ inches diameter. Key socket. White satin finished glass shade. White enamel finish.

6A874—Same as 6A873, only polished nickel.

6A871—Polished Nickel Adjustable Bracket. Very convenient when installed beside bath room mirror, bed or library table. Swings in complete circle at stem and is adjustable at shade and stem. Fitted with key socket and parabola shade. Extends 22 inches.

6A885—One Light Electric Wall Bracket. Wall plate 6 inches long, 4 inches wide. Finished in brown tone with Etruscan gold shading. Key socket. Fixture extends 6 inches.

6A886—Same as 6A885, only Butler's satin silver finish.

6A887—Two Light Electric Wall Bracket. Wall plate 6 inches long, 4 inches wide. Fixture extends 6 inches, spread 9 inches. Finished in brown tone with Etruscan gold shading. Key sockets.

6A888—Same as 6A887, only Butler's satin silver finish.

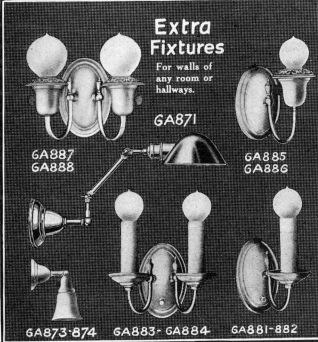

Extra Fixtures
For walls of any room or hallways.

GA871

GA887
GA888

GA885
GA886

GA873-874   GA883- GA884   GA881-882

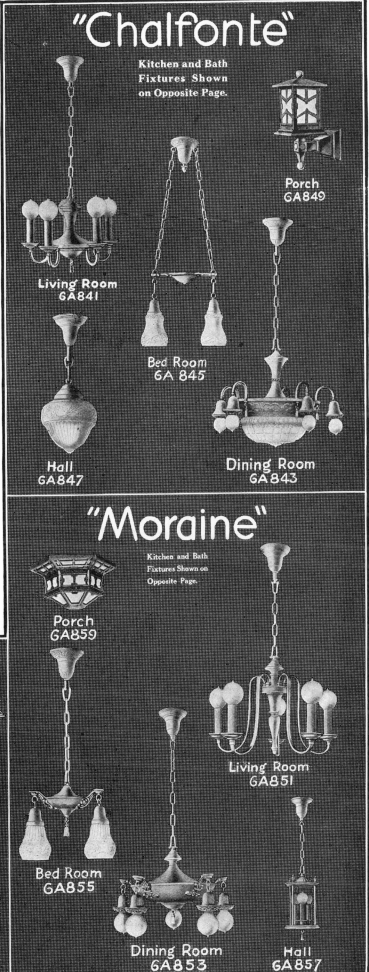

"Chalfonte"
Kitchen and Bath Fixtures Shown on Opposite Page.

Porch
GA849

Living Room
6A841

Bed Room
6A845

Hall
GA847

Dining Room
GA843

"Moraine"
Kitchen and Bath Fixtures Shown on Opposite Page.

Porch
GA859

Living Room
GA851

Bed Room
GA855

Dining Room
GA853

Hall
GA857

Side and Rear Porches

So many people have expressed a desire for a side or rear porch which could be added to their home that we have designed those shown on this page, combining and including all the good ideas brought out, yet keeping the cost down to the lowest possible figure.

One of these porches serves admirably as a place for the refrigerator, the storage of cleaning equipment and the many other articles which are needed daily but which do not belong in the kitchen. In the country it provides a place for the men to wash up before meals when the kitchen is a busy place. In town, it makes it unnecessary for the grocery boy, meat boy, and milkman to come into the house, which will be especially appreciated on rainy days.

If your kitchen is a south exposure you may have a vivid recollection of the stifling heat of the kitchen last summer. A porch will keep out almost all of that heat and make your kitchen a cool and comfortable place to work in.

These porches may be added to any of the homes shown in this

Porch X

book or may be purchased separately. The amount of comfort and space added to your home together with the greatly improved appearance they give to your home make their cost an excellent investment and an expenditure you will never regret.

Porch Y

SPECIFICATIONS

These porches have the same high grade material in tnem as our homes and are covered by the general specifications on pages 9 to 11. Our heavy Jap-a-Top slate surfaced roofing is furnished for the roof. The columns are 5"x5" box columns for which lumber is furnished in convenient lengths. The size of each porch is 6x10 feet. *Prices are given on page 132.*

A Hood for Rear or Grade Entrances

To the right is shown a hood for use over rear or grade entrances where there is no porch. The design is most artistic and it has a very definite purpose. It will add far more in appearance to your home than the actual cost.

This hood consists of two brackets of neat design with a beam across the brackets and rafters, roof sheathing and shingles above. The roof sheathing will be of dressed and matched ceiling to present a good appearance from below.

The roof is covered with our 5 to 2 Red Cedar shingles, but where our Jap-a-Top slate surfaced shingles are substituted for the house with which this hood is to go Jap-a-Top shingles are also furnished for the hood.

This hood may be added to any home shown in this book or will be sold separately. Price will be found on page 132.

Hood Z

White Pine Screens for Gordon-Van Tine Homes

Prices Complete for Every Home in This Book on Page 132

Gordon-Van Tine screen windows and doors are built to last—of the finest kiln dried White Pine 1⅛ inches thick. Each joint is mortised and tenoned and securely fastened with a steel pin. Such screens *do not warp, pull apart* or *loosen up* but remain firm and tight for many years after the average screen has to be thrown away.

Screened with 14 Mesh Galvanized Wire

14 mesh screen contains 14 wires to the inch—whereas the ordinary screen wire contains but 12. This fine mesh keeps out the smaller flies, bugs and mosquitoes which always work through the average screen.

Galvanized wire has a coating of spelter applied by electrolysis—not dipping—giving the wire a rust-resisting coating that increases the life of the screen by many years.

Complete Hardware Included

We furnish a pair of our interchangeable screen and storm sash hangers and two hooks and eyes for each window. For the front door we furnish a mortise latch and hinges with strong, adjustable spiral springs. For the back door and grade door we include our screen door set consisting

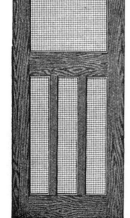

Mortise and Tenon

Used at every joint on our screens and storm sash. Makes a strong, durable frame.

of our 16 inch spring, two 3-inch hinges, door grip, hook and eye and necessary screws.

Our screens come to you unpainted. We are willing to have you *see* the quality of material we put into them. They can then be painted a color that harmonizes with your home. We furnish sufficient paint of the same color as you have selected for the trim of your house.

Prices on screens for all 2 light windows, movable sash, basement windows and all outside doors for every home shown in this book will be found on page 132.

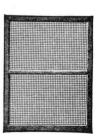

Prices Complete for Every Home in This Book on First Page

In various places fire ordinances, etc., require a fire-resisting roof. If you live in a city where such ordinance is in effect, you will want our Jap-a-Top Slate Surfaced Asphalt Shingles. They are guaranteed for fifteen years and are the regulation fire-resisting asphalt shingle approved by underwriters. You are offered your choice of two colors—either a dull rich red or a moss green. This color is not painted on but is imparted to the shingles by the slate itself, consequently is everlasting. These shingles are made of felt thoroughly saturated with asphalt and rolled out under pressure. The chipped slate is pressed in by heavy hydraulic rollers while the shingle is still hot and is firmly imbedded in the asphalt, making a practically everlasting shingle which we guarantee absolutely for fifteen years.

Shingles are furnished to lay 4 inches to the weather. We furnish nails in sufficient quantity to lay them. These shingles require a practically solid surface beneath them and consequently when they are ordered we supply enough 1x6 roof sheathing to cover the roof leaving but a fraction of an inch air space between the roof boards.

Even if you do not live in a city where the fire ordinance compels the use of these shingles, your taste may dictate their substitution for the regulation Red Cedar shingles.

In the sixth price column on page 132, we show the additional sum necessary to secure Jap-a-Top Slate Surfaced Asphalt Shingles, and the tight roof sheathing necessary to lay them on all Gordon-Van Tine Homes. When 5 to 2 clear Red Cedar Shingles are used, roof sheathing is laid about two inches apart to insure longest life.

5x2 Extra Clear Red Cedar Shingle and open Sheathing as furnished in regular specifications.

Jap-a-Top Slate Surfaced Asphalt Shingles and tight Sheathing.

Storm Sash and Doors for Gordon-Van Tine Homes

Prices Complete for Every Home in This Book on Page 132

Gordon-Van Tine storm sash and doors are solidly built of the best White Pine with mortise and tenon joints tightly fastened with a steel pin. They are 1⅛ inches thick, well glazed with plenty of metal points and pure linseed oil putty. Sash up to and including 24x28 are glazed single strength; larger sash are glazed double strength.

All sash receive a priming coat before being glazed which insures firm adherance of the putty and protects the surface of the wood.

Storm doors are strong and well made. Glass is of ample size to admit sufficient light and minimum of cold. Doors are 1⅛ inches thick, good looking and durable.

Complete Hardware Included

A pair of our interchangeable screen and storm sash hangers and one adjuster for holding sash open and closed furnished for every sash, hinges and Japanned wrought steel thumb latch for doors.

The price quoted for storm sash and doors on page 132 for any home illustrated and described in this book includes sash for all two-light windows, movable sash and outside doors except those in attic and basement.

Order your storm sash and doors when you order your home and get your carpenter to hang them when the house is finished instead of paying him extra when he does it as a special job later.

Complete List of Prices on Page 132

Oak Flooring and Woodwork Downstairs
For Gordon-Van Tine Homes

OUR regular specifications shown on pages 9 and 10 call for Fir woodwork, doors, etc., throughout the house, and Yellow Pine flooring. This makes an exceedingly rich-looking interior and is a fine finish which has given uniform satisfaction. Some of our customers, however, prefer to have Oak finish in their homes, and no one can deny their good taste in doing so for there is no wood finer than Oak for interior floors and finish.

We have therefore quoted an optional price on each house on page 132, for the addition of Oak floors and finish in the principal rooms down-stairs.

Beautiful Oak Flooring

This price is the necessary sum in addition to the price shown on each house for substituting these Oak floors and finish for the regular specifications.

This illustrates the beautiful grain of oak trim

Prices On Page 132

These prices include Oak flooring and woodwork—including doors —in the principal down-stairs rooms; the hall, living and dining rooms, and the den, library, and vestibule, etc., whatever combination of principal room is shown on the particular floor plan. In two-story homes, where the stairs go up from the front hall or living room, the stair balusters, treads, rails and risers are all of Oak.

All Oak woodwork is our Craftsman design, illustrated at the left. All doors are two-panel design—the same design as our regular Fir doors shown on the center color pages, but made of Oak. Front doors and vestibule doors where shown, and all French doors where shown, are finished in Oak, where Oak finish is specified.

The Oak flooring is our famous clear, plain sawed, red Oak flooring 13/16 in. thick by 2¼ in. face, tongue and grooved and end matched. You will find the use of Oak flooring and finish a particularly good investment in your Gordon-Van Tine home.

Genuine Brenlin Shades
For All Gordon-Van Tine Homes

THESE are the original Brenlin shades which you have seen advertised far and wide The cloth for these shades is cambric so densely woven that it requires no filling of any sort. You may crease it and it will stand up and show no cracks, nor pin holes for there is no foreign substance to crack and fall out. Brenlin shades are nothing more nor less than heavy tightly woven cloth with the proper color painted on. They will stand any ordinary wear without a sign of a break and the colors are fast and will not fade. Even in their soft delicate tints (they come in all colors), the sun will not dim their beauty nor will water spot them.

To our knowledge these things cannot be said of any shade but the Genuine Brenlin—the brand which we have been so fortunate in securing for you at factory prices.

Plain Shade

Buying Brenlin shades is true economy for it means that you buy once and for all the time and that your windows both from without and within will always look well. They are supple, not stiff, yet they always hang straight and smooth.

Through a fortunate connection direct with the manufacturer we are able to furnish these shades for Gordon-Van Tine Homes at practically jobber's discount prices. The prices quoted on page 132 are for shades for all windows and all doors with the exceptions enumerated at bottom of page 132.

All shades are shipped mounted on rollers ready to hang, hemmed around stick at bottom— the usual straight, horizontal finish.

Should you desire shades with tasseled bottoms in scallops or straight we can furnish them. Write for prices.

Shades are furnished in the following colors. (Be sure and specify color in your order.)

White, Ivory, French Gray, Mauve, Wistaria (a dark green), Stone Gray, Havana (tobacco brown), and Sage Green (a deep blue green). They can also be had in duplex. Each side a different color, as for instance, inside Sage, outside White. We can furnish these duplex shades in any combination of the above colors. In ordering duplex colors be sure to state which color you wish to appear inside and which color you wish to appear inside and which outside.

Note—If you want to inspect the various colors before ordering send to us for sample book of Brenlin Shade Cloth. This shows samples of the various colors and will be sent you at once.

Scalloped Shade

Prices Shown on Page 132 Are for Plain Shades

Prices on Plumbing for Gordon-Van Tine Homes

Each Price includes the Fixture Set Named, which are described on Pages 122 and 123
All piping, fittings, roughing-in, etc., as described on Page 123

House No.	Jefferson	Madison	Washington	House No.	Jefferson	Madison	Washington	House No.	Jefferson	Madison	Washington
501	$214.00	$239.50	$331.20	537-B	$210.60	$236.10	$327.80	579-A	$221.90	$247.40	$339.10
502	227.20	252.70	344.40	538	219.30	244.80	336.50	579-B	221.90	247.40	339.10
*503	261.50	287.00	378.70	539	212.70	238.20	329.90	583	222.50	248.00	339.70
504	219.40	244.90	336.60	540	212.80	238.30	330.00	584	229.20	254.70	346.40
505	209.50	235.00	326.70	541	229.10	254.60	346.30	585	228.60	254.10	345.80
506	217.40	242.90	324.60	543	204.50	230.00	321.70	586	222.80	248.30	340.00
507	232.10	257.60	349.30	544	223.60	249.10	340.80	587	224.70	250.20	341.90
508	214.10	239.60	331.30	*545	263.90	289.40	381.10	588	228.70	254.20	345.90
509	239.70	265.20	356.90	546	232.00	257.50	349.20	589	229.20	254.70	346.40
510	219.80	245.30	337.00	547	219.20	244.70	336.40	*590	236.40	261.90	353.60
511	210.40	235.90	327.60	548	225.10	250.60	342.30	*593	234.50	260.00	351.70
512	226.00	251.50	343.20	549	210.60	236.10	327.80	*594	253.40	278.90	370.60
513	226.10	251.60	343.30	550	225.90	251.40	343.10	*595	249.50	275.00	366.70
514	224.60	250.10	341.80	551	212.40	237.90	329.60	*596	260.70	286.20	377.90
515	221.00	246.50	338.20	552	218.60	244.10	335.80	597	220.20	245.70	337.40
516	221.20	246.70	338.40	553-A	190.10	215.60	307.30	598	204.80	230.30	322.00
517	223.40	248.90	340.60	553-B	43.00	Sink	only	599	217.70	243.20	334.90
517-B	223.40	248.90	340.60	554	223.20	248.70	340.40	†600	325.40	350.90	442.60
518	218.90	244.40	336.10	555	213.90	239.40	331.10	601	216.70	242.20	333.90
519	42.50	Sink	only	556	216.10	241.60	333.30	‡602	343.40	368.90	460.60
520	227.10	252.60	344.30	557	212.40	237.90	329.60	603	240.20	265.70	357.40
521	236.20	261.70	353.40	560	219.50	245.00	336.70	604	238.20	263.70	355.40
522	217.80	243.30	335.00	561	227.10	252.60	344.30	605	214.70	240.20	331.90
523	236.10	261.60	353.30	562	214.80	240.30	332.00	607	240.50	266.00	357.70
524	43.60	Sink	only	563	214.00	239.50	331.20	608	207.10	232.60	324.30
526	212.90	238.40	330.10	564	39.20	Sink	only	609	216.50	242.00	333.70
*527	261.30	286.80	378.50	566	207.30	232.80	324.50	610	235.50	261.00	352.70
528	237.40	262.90	354.60	567	220.20	245.70	337.40	611	218.90	244.40	336.10
529	218.50	244.00	335.70	568	230.10	255.60	347.30	612	219.30	244.80	336.50
530	225.90	251.40	343.10	569	39.90	Sink	only	613	218.60	244.10	335.80
531	216.40	241.90	333.60	572	211.00	236.50	328.20	614	208.00	233.50	325.20
532	215.70	241.20	332.90	573	224.90	250.40	342.10	615-A	226.10	251.60	343.30
533	227.80	253.30	345.00	574	216.80	242.30	334.00	615-B	226.10	251.60	343.30
534	229.10	254.60	346.30	576	221.70	247.20	338.90	701	43.20	Sink	only
535	216.90	242.40	334.10	577	208.20	233.70	325.40	702	43.10	Sink	only
536	215.10	240.60	332.30	578	213.00	238.50	330.20	710	43.40	Sink	only
537	210.60	236.10	327.80								

*Includes extra wall lavatory. Extra lavatory is Jefferson design.
†Includes extra toilet and wall lavatory as shown in plan. Extra lavatory and toilet are Jefferson design.
‡Includes two complete bath room sets as shown in plan. Jefferson set is furnished in maid's bath.

Two-Tank Sewage Disposal System

Described on Page 121

Catalog Customer	Capacity Persons	1st Tank	2nd Tank	Shipping Weight	Price
6A9453	5	24 x 52	24 x 36	1550	$19.50
6A9454	8	30 x 52	24 x 36	1850	$22.40

If vitrified tile fittings are wanted with tanks add $5.00.

St. L.—1923-7E

Prices on Heating Equipment for Gordon-Van Tine Homes

The following prices include all parts as described on pages 118, 119 and 120 under each system and are guaranteed to cover a complete outfit of the highest quality

Home No.	Warm Air Pipe Furnace	Steam	Hot Water	Pipeless Furnace	Home No.	Warm Air Pipe Furnace	Steam	Hot Water	Pipeless Furnace
501	$220.70	$430.20	$524.70	$ 96.40	555	$196.10	$372.10	$437.90	$ 96.40
502	157.60	342.20	397.80	80.80	556	206.00	415.00	508.30	96.40
503	266.70	568.40	688.10	....	557	180.70	367.90	433.80	96.40
504	146.90	333.70	362.60	80.80	560	128.90	270.20	308.50	80.80
505	220.90	435.90	506.20	....	562	213.10	410.70	471.30	96.40
506	214.60	430.10	530.70	111.20	563	250.20	566.50	669.30	....
507	209.70	405.30	462.70	96.40	564	....	....	....	80.80
508	193.80	413.60	475.20	96.40	566	200.40	406.30	467.30	96.40
509	194.80	370.10	....	96.40	567	146.70	282.50	330.60	80.80
510	132.90	....	....	80.80	568	229.50	460.40	547.60	96.40
511	166.30	346.40	410.40	96.40	569	....	....	....	80.80
512	185.10	406.60	435.60	96.40	572	177.20	372.10	442.30	....
513	164.70	330.90	355.20	80.80	573	166.40	331.80	369.70	80.80
514	166.00	374.60	431.70	96.40	574	270.00	553.70	649.30	....
515	157.00	343.30	404.10	80.80	576	125.90	279.00	312.50	80.80
516	164.60	334.90	363.40	80.80	577	197.60	376.00	454.80	96.40
517	166.80	366.30	419.70	96.40	578	212.70	407.40	471.30	96.40
517-B	202.80	426.90	501.40	96.40	579-A	151.70	292.00	347.80	80.80
518	276.00	505.80	579.40	....	579-B	151.70	287.60	339.00	80.80
519	161.70	335.00	363.40	80.80	583	133.80	278.90	326.00	80.80
520	158.30	339.10	370.90	96.40	584	201.30	419.10	468.30	96.40
521	212.90	452.60	521.90	111.20	585	204.40	419.10	508.30	96.40
522	179.60	343.30	394.10	96.40	586	171.80	330.70	369.60	80.80
523	194.30	410.70	463.50	96.40	587	177.00	367.60	437.90	96.40
524	150.40	295.30	342.70	80.80	588	153.50	354.60	418.20	80.80
526	246.60	459.30	552.00	96.40	589	185.30	410.60	499.70	....
527	281.20	538.90	640.40	....	590	311.20	686.50	775.50	....
528	233.50	496.40	567.60	111.20	593	235.50	458.30	551.70	....
529	193.70	463.30	552.00	96.40	594	192.40	406.40	471.30	96.40
530	167.10	389.90	429.60	96.40	595	191.20	376.20	450.70	96.40
531	183.80	376.00	454.80	....	596	162.50	326.50	365.20	80.80
532	187.70	406.50	467.60	96.40	597	163.30	350.30	420.00	96.40
533	163.70	296.20	347.80	80.80	598	138.00	283.20	335.40	80.80
534	232.90	431.90	526.30	96.40	599	252.50	511.20	588.50	....
535	272.30	606.50	765.10	....	600	228.90	585.10	677.30	....
536	262.20	533.70	669.20	....	601	280.50	601.70	689.90	....
537	161.90	350.30	407.60	80.80	602	323.90	688.80	814.80	....
537-B	190.50	424.80	510.90	96.40	603	234.60	490.10	575.80	96.40
538	139.00	....	....	80.80	604	322.00	619.70	718.40	....
539	189.60	402.20	454.90	96.40	605	236.40	449.20	536.90	....
540	202.00	427.60	524.80	96.40	607	245.40	490.10	580.40	....
541	175.10	387.50	423.70	96.40	608	193.90	423.40	524.60	....
543	120.30	....	....	80.80	609	263.80	638.00	722.50	....
544	175.50	350.30	410.90	80.80	610	255.50	543.90	665.10	....
545	280.00	601.60	702.10	....	611	207.60	378.90	467.50	96.40
546	199.40	444.90	540.90	....	612	201.00	387.00	479.50	....
547	174.60	363.30	422.40	80.80	613	215.80	449.20	540.40	....
548	146.00	327.60	365.30	80.80	614	251.90	538.00	618.50	....
549	217.70	427.60	524.70	96.40	615-A	238.40	449.20	540.40	....
550	172.80	354.60	423.70	80.80	615-B	228.20	387.00	479.50	....
551	220.90	449.30	520.50	96.40	701	159.80	350.30	415.50	80.80
552	179.70	372.00	438.20	96.40	702	166.70	372.00	437.90	96.40
553-A	......	....	....	80.80	710	163.90	335.10	361.30	80.80
553-B	......	....	....	80.80					
554	150.80	330.70	374.60	96.40					

Ceiling Register for Pipeless, $4.30

St. L.—1923-7E

Prices on Electric Fixtures for all Gordon-Van Tine Homes

Fixtures illustrated and described on pages 124 and 125

Home No.	Ambassador	Traymore	Marlboro	Chalfonte	Moraine	Home No.	Ambassador	Traymore	Marlboro	Chalfonte	Moraine
501	$30.80	$35.00	$57.90	$98.40	$135.70	555	$ 29.00	$ 32.00	$ 54.70	$ 91.40	$128.40
502	21.40	24.80	38.90	67.60	91.70	556	24.50	28.80	43.80	76.50	120.90
503	36.50	40.70	56.80	112.10	159.10	557	23.20	26.50	40.80	73.30	97.80
504	19.90	22.50	35.90	64.40	68.60	560	14.40	15.00	24.40	45.60	75.20
*505	34.80	39.10	54.00	78.80	125.80	562	27.40	31.70	48.00	83.30	128.20
506	32.30	35.70	50.70	102.20	128.80	563	34.00	38.20	53.80	101.70	147.80
507	28.60	32.00	46.80	90.70	116.40	564	17.50	19.90	33.30	61.80	65.90
508	24.60	28.70	43.80	76.50	120.90	566	28.90	32.00	54.70	91.40	128.40
509	26.40	30.60	45.80	82.20	127.10	567	12.80	12.40	21.20	46.00	51.80
*510	21.00	20.50	29.40	41.30	54.50	568	26.40	30.60	45.80	82.20	127.10
511	24.60	28.80	43.80	76.50	120.90	569	11.70	11.30	20.00	44.80	50.60
512	25.00	28.40	42.80	79.10	104.00	572	21.40	24.80	38.90	67.60	91.60
513	23.30	26.50	40.80	73.30	97.80	573	23.20	26.50	40.80	73.30	97.80
514	24.20	27.60	41.90	74.40	98.80	574	36.90	41.70	64.70	113.00	171.10
515	20.00	22.50	35.90	64.40	68.50	576	14.10	13.80	22.60	47.30	53.00
516	21.40	24.80	38.90	67.60	91.60	577	30.80	33.80	56.70	97.30	134.60
517	25.00	28.38	42.80	79.10	104.00	578	24.50	28.80	43.80	76.50	120.90
517-B	33.70	37.90	53.70	105.30	151.90	579-A	21.00	23.60	37.00	65.50	69.50
518	38.10	41.10	64.50	120.40	159.30	579-B	20.00	22.50	35.90	64.40	68.40
519	20.30	22.90	36.40	68.70	73.30	583	14.10	13.80	22.60	47.30	53.00
520	21.40	24.80	38.80	67.60	91.60	584	32.90	35.90	58.80	99.40	135.60
521	30.00	34.20	49.80	93.80	139.50	585	27.10	30.50	44.90	81.20	106.20
522	21.40	24.80	38.80	67.60	91.60	586	21.40	24.80	38.90	67.60	91.60
*523	32.90	36.30	50.70	79.10	106.50	587	23.20	26.50	40.80	73.30	97.80
524	18.60	21.10	34.50	62.90	67.10	588	23.20	26.50	40.80	73.30	97.80
526	28.20	32.50	47.80	88.00	133.40	589	26.10	29.40	43.90	80.10	105.10
527	31.10	35.30	50.80	94.80	140.60	590	39.40	43.60	59.80	118.90	166.30
528	27.40	31.70	46.90	83.30	128.20	593	32.60	35.90	50.80	98.50	124.60
*529	34.30	38.50	53.70	82.20	129.60	594	30.40	34.60	49.80	90.10	135.40
530	20.00	22.50	35.90	64.40	68.50	595	24.20	27.60	41.90	74.40	98.90
531	28.20	32.50	47.80	88.00	133.30	596	22.10	24.70	38.00	66.50	70.60
532	28.90	32.00	54.70	91.40	128.40	597	16.30	16.80	26.40	51.30	81.30
533	21.40	24.80	38.80	67.60	91.60	598	15.50	16.10	25.50	46.50	76.10
534	39.70	42.80	65.70	98.30	137.10	*599	46.30	50.20	73.90	114.90	181.60
535	36.90	41.70	64.70	113.00	171.10	*600	49.40	54.10	79.00	123.30	204.30
536	36.90	41.70	64.70	113.00	171.10	*601	40.90	45.80	71.10	126.40	191.60
537	22.80	27.00	41.80	70.60	114.70	*602	55.60	60.00	93.10	143.30	236.60
537-B	27.70	32.80	48.80	85.40	150.20	*603	41.20	45.00	68.70	101.50	160.20
538	13.10	12.80	21.50	41.30	52.10	*604	50.20	54.10	78.60	130.30	192.20
*539	32.50	36.80	51.70	76.50	123.40	*605	40.50	43.60	66.60	103.00	143.20
540	25.00	28.40	42.80	79.10	104.00	*607	42.60	47.30	71.60	104.50	184.40
541	23.20	26.50	40.80	73.30	97.80	608	35.10	38.10	61.20	105.50	143.22
543	13.10	12.80	21.50	41.30	52.10	*609	43.00	46.90	70.60	107.10	167.30
544	21.10	23.70	37.10	65.60	69.70	610	37.60	41.80	57.80	113.20	160.20
545	39.10	42.50	57.90	116.80	124.50	611	30.80	33.80	56.70	97.30	134.60
546	23.20	26.50	40.80	73.30	97.80	612	24.20	27.60	41.90	74.40	98.90
547	24.20	27.60	41.90	74.40	98.90	613	28.90	32.00	54.70	91.40	128.40
548	21.40	24.80	38.80	67.60	91.60	614	32.70	37.20	52.80	100.70	146.90
549	26.40	30.60	45.80	82.20	127.10	615-A	27.40	31.70	46.90	83.30	128.20
550	20.00	22.50	35.90	64.40	68.50	615-B	25.00	28.40	42.80	79.10	104.00
551	26.40	30.60	45.80	82.20	127.10						
552	29.00	32.00	54.70	91.40	128.40	701	22.20	24.80	38.40	74.50	79.60
*553-A	22.30	22.90	32.40	45.60	77.60	702	24.00	26.50	40.40	80.30	85.70
*553-B	19.60	19.30	28.00	44.80	53.00	705	27.40	31.70	46.90	83.30	128.20
554	24.20	27.60	41.90	74.40	98.90	710	17.70	18.30	28.10	55.70	87.10

Electric Fixture Options—Fixtures Shown on Page 133

6A871	Fixture each	$4.12	6A881	Fixture each	$2.72	6A884	Fixture each	$4.37	6A887	Fixture each	$3.96
6A873	" "	1.90	6A882	" "	2.97	6A885	" "	2.31	6A888	" "	4.37
6A874	" "	1·48	6A883	" "	3.96	6A886	" "	2.56			

*For front porch fixtures on homes starred (*) we will furnish artistic wall bracket No. 6A849 shown and described on page 125. Fixture No. 6A801 is furnished over all dinettes.

St. L.—1923-7E

Gordon-Van Tine Homes

Page 132

Prices on Following Options and Additions to Homes Shown in this Book:

Storm Sash and Doors (p.127) | Electric Wiring (bottom this page) | Oak Flooring and Woodwork(p.128)
Screen Windows and Doors (p.126) | Brenlin Window Shades (p.128) | Jap-A-Top Asphalt Shingles(p.127)

House No.	Storm Sash	Screens with Galvanized Wire	Electric Wiring	Brenlin Window Shades Complete	Oak Flooring and Woodwork See Page 128	Jap-a-Top Asphalt Shingles See Page 127	House No.	Storm Sash	Screens with Galvanized Wire	Electric Wiring	Brenlin Window Shades Complete	Oak Flooring and Woodwork See Page 128	Jap-a-Top Asphalt Shingles See Page 127
501	$103.02	$79.85	$39.30	$31.20	$154.80	$36.80	555	$74.52	$61.29	$38.50	$24.80	$116.50	$31.95
502	65.78	53.60	31.00	20.70	98.90	45.85	556	84.18	68.41	37.60	26.30	162.40	35.45
503	124.57	93.01	51.50	41.80	181.10	56.95	557	78.11	60.51	35.50	24.40	149.50	39.60
504	59.71	53.48	31.80	18.30	84.80	36.80	560	51.02	44.76	28.80	15.00	61.70	29.20
505	115.52	91.46	41.90	33.50	169.70	41.00	562	86.11	69.41	39.70	28.00	160.60	32.65
506	96.34	73.35	46.00	31.20	93.70	44.45	563	157.86	121.44	53.10	39.50	220.55	59.75
507	88.51	66.28	41.90	28.80	115.60	54.20	564	46.15	35.93	18.60	13.60	95.40	29.85
508	80.34	64.27	40.40	26.50	132.70	33.35	566	73.00	71.35	36.30	29.50	111.10	31.95
509	77.35	60.75	40.70	29.20	106.10	44.30	567	49.01	40.31	24.90	15.10	53.60	38.20
510	43.92	41.70	24.90	12.50	64.90	25.70	568	82.75	63.70	42.70	27.30	157.50	37.50
511	62.24	52.53	35.20	19.60	117.60	41.00	569	47.15	33.07	18.70	13.80	62.20	25.70
512	79.63	69.77	37.40	25.50	110.90	56.25	572	75.66	62.92	31.00	23.70	113.90	51.40
513	58.96	48.94	31.80	17.50	68.50	38.90	573	64.44	49.19	34.10	22.10	99.70	36.10
514	83.15	69.96	37.50	31.90	103.50	50.00	574	126.54	94.41	45.70	39.70	211.00	34.80
515	65.76	53.32	28.80	20.70	102.60	33.35	576	48.67	43.83	28.80	16.40	45.10	28.10
516	59.71	50.74	30.90	18.30	84.90	40.30	577	80.57	66.21	37.10	25.20	146.30	33.35
517	84.66	78.10	34.90	33.20	104.10	54.20	578	82.82	66.80	37.70	26.40	146.50	36.15
517-B	105.80	78.10	42.30	34.40	105.00	54.20	579-A	54.60	45.52	31.10	19.40	84.40	28.40
518	103.93	81.49	45.00	36.40	152.20	47.25	579-B	55.92	46.01	28.80	19.40	84.40	25.70
519	63.23	52.78	28.80	19.20	88.30	38.90	583	48.98	40.31	27.10	16.60	53.70	25.45
520	68.41	58.50	33.70	21.30	97.35	39.60	584	95.38	77.30	39.10	29.70	171.80	68.10
521	77.48	70.22	43.70	28.80	108.60	58.35	585	93.38	74.70	42.00	34.30	146.60	41.70
522	65.20	58.08	33.30	20.40	100.80	47.25	586	64.46	57.91	31.10	19.50	84.20	35.40
523	96.19	70.89	38.40	27.40	131.20	34.75	587	73.30	56.17	31.80	20.40	104.90	41.70
524	60.56	50.46	24.90	18.30	106.50	37.50	588	69.48	60.07	31.90	24.80	90.80	38.20
526	95.86	73.17	40.60	31.90	166.00	38.90	589	85.15	70.27	36.10	28.50	133.20	59.75
527	122.17	96.91	47.70	41.40	153.90	57.65	590	153.77	115.12	53.90	49.50	113.60	66.00
528	108.38	84.44	44.10	35.20	185.50	47.95	593	123.91	90.87	44.40	39.80	134.80	54.20
529	111.76	78.56	41.20	33.20	179.80	25.70	594	101.35	84.05	43.60	36.10	96.30	51.40
530	69.91	65.32	31.20	24.50	125.20	47.20	595	84.97	73.66	36.90	27.10	104.90	54.20
531	86.46	66.96	43.60	31.00	148.90	45.85	596	76.90	62.06	33.10	23.40	104.00	43.05
532	80.76	62.30	40.70	27.20	128.60	29.20	597	69.67	60.00	31.10	21.10	56.60	38.90
533	58.68	47.93	31.00	17.90	.78.30	36.10	598	53.84	47.42	31.00	19.60	58.30	28.25
534	125.86	93.56	41.40	34.50	174.00	42.40	599	143.15	115.68	36.00	41.30	210.00	31.40
535	158.10	131.91	48.30	56.30	200.40	47.95	600	151.48	120.09	53.40	43.00	249.70	44.40
536	143.24	111.98	46.40	51.50	189.40	47.25	601	147.26	128.87	52.60	45.60	237.60	35.40
537	81.96	67.31	38.40	27.80	126.30	52.10	602	244.52	167.67	55.50	59.50	359.80	67.40
537-B	83.58	67.31	45.00	27.80	117.20	52.10	603	120.30	99.16	42.70	41.90	189.10	31.95
538	50.27	39.91	25.00	15.10	52.00	29.85	604	180.70	142.75	56.20	52.20	249.30	55.55
539	91.74	67.57	37.60	25.50	151.80	29.20	605	126.92	96.40	41.60	36.90	166.80	48.60
540	86.75	69.40	40.60	30.20	163.60	26.40	607	124.94	94.61	45.70	42.50	282.90	40.30
541	68.86	59.21	35.90	22.80	91.70	47.05	608	138.05	115.09	40.70	39.14	126.40	45.15
543	48.98	35.58	23.50	15.10	74.10	28.50	609	120.37	93.32	45.70	45.10	232.20	45.15
544	90.66	69.27	31.00	26.30	119.10	46.55	610	156.24	109.16	50.40	49.30	118.00	50.00
545	130.50	102.12	53.90	46.90	163.20	64.60	611	114.84	80.37	34.80	39.30	148.50	65.50
546	117.13	90.60	35.30	36.20	117.90	50.95	612	120.18	84.02	35.30	40.95	165.00	80.00
547	73.06	55.39	37.60	22.80	129.30	40.30	613	140.94	97.93	35.30	47.55	146.50	61.25
548	60.56	50.46	30.90	18.30	91.00	40.30	614	145.92	102.71	48.30	49.20	197.20	50.65
549	85.96	67.34	38.40	28.00	169.10	36.80	615-A	109.86	76.72	39.80	37.65	138.00	50.00
550	68.10	58.71	28.90	23.30	115.80	38.20	615-B	149.70	106.36	35.50	50.85	138.00	56.25
551	87.29	70.29	43.10	29.50	152.42	35.45	701	60.31	49.10	33.40	18.70	119.70	34.75
552	81.82	66.44	36.30	25.40	131.30	26.40	702	74.62	58.71	35.50	23.90	88.00	34.75
553-A	48.38	35.20	23.00	14.80	50.20	22.95	705	103.75	76.71		34.10	152.50	45.15
553-B	45.84	33.28	19.30	13.50	56.30	22.25	710	68.87	53.65	35.40	19.80	65.30	34.70
554	63.11	55.26	35.30	19.60	141.10	41.70							

Prices on Side and Rear Porches

	Page 126 Ready Cut	Not Ready Cut
Porch X	$79.00	$75.73
Porch Y	90.00	87.00
Hood Z	16.00	16.00

Price of Disappearing Stairway
Page 120

Complete with Yellow Pine panel......................$74.50

Specifications of Electric Wiring

The prices on electric wiring include No. 14 rubber covered wire, porcelain tubes, knobs, **safety entrance switch, conduit entrance service** with No. 10 rubber covered wire, **steel service box** for branch blocks and fuse plugs, flush switches, solder, paste and tape, all in sufficient quantities to install a complete and first class system of knob and tube wiring, using **a flush switch in every room,** with outlet on front porch and in case of a two-story house, three way switches connecting upper and lower hall. Price includes two lights in basement controlled by a snap switch at top of basement steps. Where there is an attic, attic light included. In all chambers containing over 140 square feet, two outlets are figured. In houses where living room extends entire breadth of house, two outlets figured. No lights are figured in clothes closets.

(Base plugs can be furnished at **$1.20** each, complete.)

St. L.—1923-7E

Specifications of Brenlin Shades

The prices on Brenlin Window Shades cover complete shades for each one of our houses. The prices include single color shades for all outside doors, including the grade door and for all windows and sash thruout the first and second stories. No shades are furnished in the attic unless the attic has double hung windows, in which event all double hung windows and all single sash in the attic are equipped with shades. Each shade is mounted on genuine Hartshorn Roller complete with stick, silk crocheted pull and fixture, cut to exact size, ready for hanging. If these window shades are wanted in duplex add 10% to the prices given above. Scalloped shades quoted on request.

Prices on Gordon-Van Tine Homes

You can buy your Gordon-Van Tine Home either Ready-Cut or not Ready-Cut at prices shown below. For the very small difference between these two figures you get a home all Ready-Cut as described on pages 4 to 9.

This extremely low charge for ready cutting is made possible only by our large manufacturing facilities and big volume of sales, and is overwhelming proof of Gordon-Van Tine savings.

However, for those who cannot take advantage of the Ready-Cut savings, we show below prices Not Ready-Cut as described on page 8.

Keep in mind that these low prices are for complete homes, including not only lumber and millwork, but all hardware, paint, nails and tinwork as well as many convenience items not found in the ordinary house. Read the complete specifications on pages 9 and 10.

Order right from this book. Use the enclosed order blank, or write us for additional information and delivered prices on the home of your choice, freight paid to your station.

Home No.	Page No.	Price Ready-Cut	Price Not Ready-Cut	Home No.	Page No.	Price Ready-Cut	Price Not Ready-Cut
501	61	$2263.00	$2174.00	564	107	$1066.00	$1021.00
502	57	1749.00	1674.00	566	94	1918.00	1846.00
503	26	3046.00	2925.00	567	106	1423.00	1363.00
504	84	1579.00	1513.00	568	99	2155.00	2069.00
505	39	2281.00	2192.00	569	109	954.00	915.00
506	15	2356.00	2249.00	572	77	1975.00	1893.00
507	50	2651.00	2546.00	573	60	1479.00	1418.00
508	56	1951.00	1875.00	574	25	2860.00	2767.00
509	48	2092.00	2011.00	576	105	1283.00	1234.00
510	106	1056.00	1014.00	577	83	1958.00	1883.00
511	85	1594.00	1525.00	578	86	1933.00	1853.00
512	44	2243.00	2151.00	579-A	70	1323.00	1272.00
513	103	1560.00	1494.00	579-B	70	1201.00	1154.00
514	78	2167.00	2079.00	583	105	1196.00	1150.00
515	68	1472.00	1411.00	584	34	2586.00	2479.00
516	63	1643.00	1572.00	585	71	2286.00	2205.00
517	29	2295.00	2199.00	586	69	1653.00	1586.00
517-B	29	2652.00	2547.00	587	51	1926.00	1850.00
518	80	2807.00	2694.00	588	31	1684.00	1615.00
519	90	1547.00	1482.00	589	49	2455.00	2353.00
520	97	1607.00	1500.00	590	21	3678.00	3542.00
521	14	2738.00	2624.00	593	40	2874.00	2760.00
522	89	1936.00	1853.00	594	47	2652.00	2550.00
523	59	1693.00	1625.00	595	54	2388.00	2289.00
524	102	1437.00	1378.00	596	23	1833.00	1762.00
526	82	2181.00	2093.00	597	55	1626.00	1563.00
527	45	2972.00	2850.00	598	41	1375.00	1333.00
528	66	2593.00	2492.00	599	46	2704.00	2613.00
529	20	2220.00	2145.00	600	38	3363.00	3239.00
530	98	2022.00	1940.00	601	43	3383.00	3262.00
531	30	2261.00	2176.00	602	33	3919.00	3780.00
532	93	1717.00	1650.00	603	42	2087.00	2012.00
533	104	1510.00	1446.00	604	36	4087.00	3936.00
534	67	2512.00	2418.00	605	74	2756.00	2659.00
535	12	2863.00	2762.00	607	32	2687.00	2598.00
536	22	2649.00	2556.00	608	13	2950.00	2842.00
537	35	2189.00	2095.00	609	18	2925.00	2825.00
537-B	35	2556.00	2453.00	610	27	2889.00	2774.00
538	107	1284.00	1233.00	611	64	2390.00	2289.00
539	62	1825.00	1757.00	612	19	2788.00	2676.00
540	65	1998.00	1921.00	613	24	2467.00	2371.00
541	73	1978.00	1897.00	614	16	3119.00	3007.00
543	108	1178.00	1130.00	*615-A	28	2114.00	2037.00
544	101	1976.00	1892.00	*615-B	28	2356.00	2271.00
545	17	3397.00	3262.00				
546	53	2212.00	2123.00				
547	75	1853.00	1778.00				
548	91	1680.00	1610.00				
549	79	1930.00	1853.00				
550	72	1676.00	1608.00				
551	81	2183.00	2098.00				
552	100	1686.00	1623.00				
553-A	108	1017.00	977.00				
553-B	108	932.00	894.00				
554	58	1600.00	1531.00				
555	92	1722.00	1656.00				
556	87	2117.00	2033.00				
557	76	2145.00	2056.00				
560	109	1274.00	1224.00				
562	52	1976.00	1899.00				
563	37	3643.00	3503.00				

*Note—615-A does not include rear extension. 615-B is the plan complete as shown.

The following homes can be furnished Not Ready-Cut only:

Home No.	Page No.	Price Not Ready-Cut Only
701	96	$1501.00
702	88	1628.00
710	95	1674.00

Prices on Cottages, Summer Cottages and Garages, furnished Ready-Cut only

Ready-Cut Cottages

Plan No.	Page No.	Ready-Cut Price
201	110	$676.00
202	110	742.00
203	110	866.00
204	111	719.00
205	111	963.00
210	111	538.00

Ready-Cut Summer Cottages

301	112	$948.00
302	113	725.00
303	115	720.00
304	114	687.00
305	115	746.00
306	113	256.00
307	114	471.00
308	114	732.00
309	115	726.00

Ready-Cut Garages

Garage No.	Page No.	Size	Price	Add for Wall board Lining
101	116	10x16	$90.00	......
101	116	12x18	103.00	......
101	116	14x20	120.00	......
102	117	10x16	161.00	$27.80
102	117	12x18	182.00	35.40
102	117	12x20	194.00	37.40
102	117	14x20	204.00	41.30
103	117	10x16	162.00	28.20
103	117	12x18	185.00	35.80
103	117	12x20	193.00	37.80
103	117	14x20	209.00	41.80
*104	117	20x20	285.00	51.90
*105	117	20x20	294.00	51.90
106	117	12x18	208.00	35.80
106	117	12x20	220.00	37.80
106	117	14x20	233.00	41.80
*107	117	20x20	333.00	51.90
108	117	12x18	183.00	35.80
108	117	12 20	191.00	37.80
108	117	14x20	205.00	41.80
*109	117	20x20	294.00	51.90
110	116	10x16	105.00	......
110	116	12x18	119.00	......
110	116	14x20	135.00	......

*For Two Cars.

GARAGE OPTIONS
(See page 117)

1—For adding Side Door to any size of garages 102, 103, 104 and 105 ....$10.15 extra.

2—For Triple Folding Door and complete hardware instead of regular door on garages 102 and 103 ....$8.50 extra.

3—For two sets of Triple Folding Doors and complete hardware instead of two sets of regular doors on garages 104 and 105 ....$17.00 extra.

NOTE—Any house shown in this book with siding can be changed to stucco, and any house shown with stucco can be changed to siding. Write for prices.

Circular of Attractive Duplex or Two-Family Homes Sent on Request

Homes Guaranteed for Twenty Years!

You are protected for a generation. Order right from this book. It contains complete information, prices, specifications, plans and descriptions. Thousands have bought from it.

THIS book of GORDON-VAN TINE HOMES is the latest of many such volumes. It represents the experience of fifty-five years in the building material business. The statements made in it are *FACTS*—proven by time and tested by actual building in every part of the country. The homes shown in it HAVE BEEN BUILT. They are not simply fanciful *pictures, ideas* which may or may not prove practical, but actual accomplished facts. We have no theories to advance, no hobbies to ride; we have been in this business too long to operate on any but a fact basis.

This book is the work of GORDON-VAN TINE COMPANY from the first page to the last. Gordon-Van Tine architects drew the original plans. Gordon-Van Tine experts laid out the houses, passed judgment on the arrangement of every room, the position of every door and window, every kitchen case, linen closet and plumbing fixture. Gordon-Van Tine construction experts have tested every feature and specified the size and grade of every piece of material entering into the house, and Gordon-Van Tine Company at their great plants at Davenport, Iowa, St. Louis, Missouri, Chehalis, Washington, and Hattiesburg, Mississippi, *carry in stock* the carefully selected and graded material *to build these houses complete according to the specifications shown elsewhere in this book.*

Guaranteed Prices—No Extras or Unsatisfactory Materials

This may mean but little to the uninitiated. Those who have been in the building business, however, realize that it marks a new era in home building. No longer is it necessary for you to build with your eyes shut—to start with an *estimated price*, a guess at the cost of the material which will be needed to build the house—and when you are through find that additional material which had been left out of the original estimate ran the actual cost up from 15 to 50 per cent. Gordon-Van Tine have so systematized and specialized planning and construction of houses that the prices quoted in this book are guaranteed absolutely to build a house according to the plans shown and the specifications given. We bind ourselves to make good any defect or shortage in material. You take no chances—you know what your investment will be, *before you spend a cent.*

Prices Based on Costs at the Mill

But there is another thing, of just as great importance to you and your pocketbook. This price which is guaranteed to build the house you want without question, is not based on the retail cost of lumber at a small local lumber yard. It is based on the *cost* of the *lumber at the lumber mill and millwork at the millwork factory.* Gordon-Van Tine Company sell direct. At their great mills and assembling yards they carry the largest

stock of material of any independent lumber company in the country. Much of these stocks they manufacture. All of it is produced at rock bottom prices and sold to you at the producers cost plus one small profit. When you buy of Gordon-Van Tine you cut out at one stroke these middlemen's profits which add nothing to the value of the material, and which give you nothing in service, but often run the cost up 50 per cent and higher. When you deal with Gordon-Van Tine, you deal with one firm whose integrity is unquestioned, whose resources of over $1,000,-000.00 are behind every contract they make. When you buy a home in the ordinary way you deal through the architect, the local lumber dealer, the hardware dealer, paint dealer, the plumber, and heating man and goodness knows how many others, dickering and bargaining and making separate contracts with each and paying each a separate profit, or allowing some agent to bind you to contracts with them. And who is shrewd enough buyer to be sure he is getting full value from each, in either case? For those items which we do not furnish, such as cement, sand, brick, plaster, etc., because excessive freight rates make it to your advantage to buy them locally, we furnish complete and detailed lists of quantities so you know just what to buy. We also furnish blank form for any kind of a contract you may wish to draw up with your carpenter or contractor. Gordon-Van Tine service smooths every step of the way for you.

You Save Yourself From All Worry

You can, from this book of practically perfect plans, select just the house you want at the price you want to pay and by using the convenient order blank at the right save yourself all the worry and trouble of planning and figuring with many dealers and the consequent disappointment of having so many extras to pay for, as well as running the chance of getting an impractically planned house. Our Guarantee of Absolute Satisfaction or Your Money Back protects you absolutely. Do as thousands have already done, save money, time, trouble and insure yourself against loss—order your home right from this book.

"Save time, trouble and insure yourself against loss Order your Home, Right from this Book."

Every Home Guaranteed for 20 Years

This Guarantee signed by the President of the Gordon-Van Tine Co. is absolute insurance that your Gordon-Van Tine home will be staunch and strong for years to come. This Guarantee, all framed and ready to hang on the wall, goes with every Gordon-Van Tine home sold.

Gordon-Van Tine Twenty Year Guarantee

HATTIESBURG, MISS.   **Davenport, Iowa.**   CHEHALIS, WASH.

This Certifies that _John Doe_ is the purchaser of **GORDON-VAN TINE HOME NO.** _536_

This house is hereby guaranteed for a period of twenty years from date, provided that the plans and instructions furnished by Gordon-Van Tine Company are strictly adhered to in the construction of said house.

If at any time within the period of this guarantee the purchaser shall present this certificate and shall show that the house is defective due to poor material or to structural weakness, and not due to ordinary usage or action of the elements, and that the aforesaid plans and instructions were adhered to in the construction of said house, then Gordon-Van Tine Company agrees to replace such defective material.

In Witness Whereof, the said Gordon-Van Tine Company has caused this certificate to be signed by its President and its corporate seal hereunto affixed, this _fourth_ day of _June_ 19 23.

E. C. Roberts
President

GORDON-VAN-TINE COMPANY · CORPORATE SEAL · DAVENPORT, IOWA

Order Blank and Guaranty

GORDON-VAN TINE COMPANY.

Please ship me Home No................for which you agree to furnish all necessary material as follows:

Lumber, Millwork, Hardware, Tinwork, Painting Material and Convenience Features........$...................

I also desire the following changes or additions to the stock specifications:

Plumbing complete, as priced for this plan on page 129 ....$.................

Heating complete...........................as priced on page 130 ....$.................
      (Kind of System)

Oak Flooring, Doors and Woodwork as priced on page 132 ....$.................

Jap-a-Top Asphalt Shingles as priced on page 132 ....$.................

Electric Wiring for Entire House and fixture set priced on page 132...........$.................

....$.................

    Total...$.................

Less 2% for cash in full with order.................................$.................

    Net Total ....$.................

See other side of Order Blank for terms.

WE GUARANTEE SATISFACTION OR MONEY BACK

For the prices quoted on each building in this book, we guarantee to furnish all the lumber, lath, shingles, finishing lumber, doors, windows, frames, interior floors and finish, nails, tinwork, finish hardware, complete painting materials and built-in conveniences necessary to build it according to the picture, the plan shown, and the specifications given.

We guarantee that there will be no extras.

Should there be any shortages or unsatisfactory materials we agree to make them good,

We guarantee all material to be equal to, or better than the grades specified.

In six words—WE GUARANTEE SATISFACTION OR MONEY BACK.

All guarantees shall be considered warranties when made a part of the contract of sale.

E.L. Roberts

President

YOU ARE FULLY PROTECTED

In my opinion, the above guarantees, or any part of them, when made the subject of a bargain between your firm and a prospective purchaser, are legal and binding upon the Gordon-Van Tine Company and would be so construed in any Court.

Further, in my opinion, a reference in your order blanks to the effect that all catalog guarantees are made warranties therein, as a part of the bargain, is effective in making your catalog guarantees a part of each contract of sale.

C. M. Waterman

Former Judge, State Supreme Court of Iowa.

Please fill in the spaces below, so that we can make immediate shipment without further instructions.

Name ....

Shipping Point ....Post Office..

State ....Street or Rural Route................................

Is there any railway agent at your station?..(If there is no agent include extra money for freight, as shipments to closed stations must be prepaid.)

Color of paint wanted—Body..Trim...
Unless otherwise instructed, we will ship paint of colors given in description of house.

OUR LIBERAL TERMS

Your Choice of These Three Methods of Payment.

1. **Cash with Order.** 2% discount is allowed for cash in full with order.

2. **Part Deposit.** If for any reason you are not in position to send cash in full with order, but will have the money available when material is delivered, send us one-fifth of the total amount when you place your order; pay the balance when you receive the goods. Five days are allowed after material reaches your freight station for inspection. (No discount allowed under terms No. 2.)

3. **Statement of Deposit.** Send us $100 as an evidence of sincerity and good faith and deposit the balance with your banker in accordance with the terms of the statement of deposit below. Have him fill this out and sign it, and we will ship you the material subject to your instruction. (No discount allowed under terms No. 3.)

Statement of Deposit

We hereby acknowledge receipt of $...deposited by

Mr. ....for the credit of Gordon-Van Tine Co , Davenport, Iowa, to be remitted to them for material described above. Payment shall be made within five days after arrival of each shipment with the explicit understanding that the Gordon-Van Tine Co. **will make good** any shortage or unsatisfactory material (if there should be such) in accordance with their **Guarantee of Satisfaction or Money Back.**

....
Name of Bank (or Building and Loan Asso.)

Date ....

....
Signature of Pres. or Cashier

Town .... State................ ....

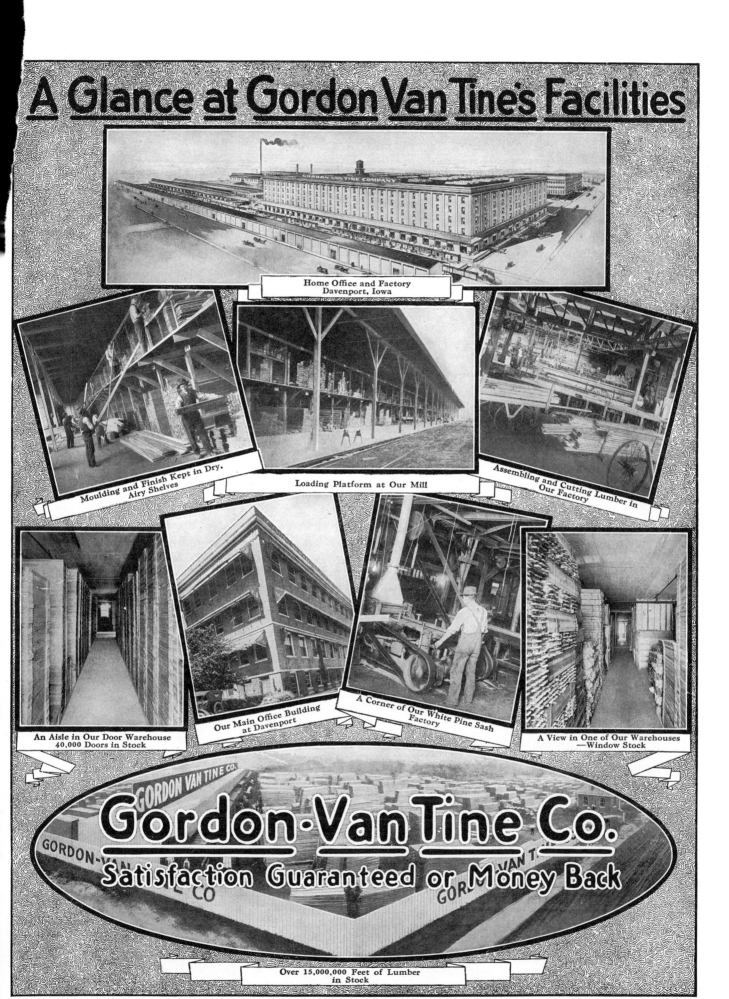

A Glance at Gordon Van Tine's Facilities

Home Office and Factory
Davenport, Iowa

Moulding and Finish Kept in Dry, Airy Shelves

Loading Platform at Our Mill

Assembling and Cutting Lumber in Our Factory

An Aisle in Our Door Warehouse 40,000 Doors in Stock

Our Main Office Building at Davenport

A Corner of Our White Pine Sash Factory

A View in One of Our Warehouses —Window Stock

Gordon·Van Tine Co.
Satisfaction Guaranteed or Money Back

Over 15,000,000 Feet of Lumber in Stock

Gordon VanTine Homes

Gordon-Van Tine Co.
Davenport, Iowa
U . S . A